YOU ARE NOT STUPID

Computers and Technology Simplified

Written by:
Jack C. Stanley and Erik D. Gross,
Co-Founders of The Tech Academy

IMPORTANT NOTE

We are very interested in your feedback regarding this book. Writing online reviews is helpful but we also have an email address that you can send suggestions, errors, wins, or whatever communication you have to: dictionary@learncodinganywhere.com.

This email address is available for all sorts of communication, including:

- Additional topics you'd like us to cover,

- Chapters or data that you had trouble understanding,

- What your favorite chapters were,

- More images you'd like to added, etc.

Feel free to email us about this book!

-The authors

TABLE OF CONTENTS

TABLE OF CONTENTS

TABLE OF CONTENTS

TABLE OF CONTENTS

TABLE OF CONTENTS

TABLE OF CONTENTS

TABLE OF CONTENTS

INTRODUCTION

"If you can't explain it simply, you don't understand it well enough."
-Albert Einstein (German scientist, 1879-1955)

In 2014, we (Jack Stanley and Erik Gross) founded a school called The Tech Academy. Our purpose was to bridge the gap between general society and technology and to make computers understandable and usable for all. We felt this was needed due to the prevalence of computers in nearly every aspect of modern life.

To that end, we created "boot camps" (intensive training programs in technology) that prepare students for working in technical positions. While our services have since expanded beyond just delivering boot camps, our purpose has remained the same.

A couple of years ago, we wrote the *Computer and Technology Basics Dictionary* that defined technical terms in a way that the average person could understand. Though our classes, dictionaries and other books assist people in understanding technology, we realized it would be beneficial if we utilized our combined knowledge and experience to write a book that accomplished The Tech Academy's purpose.

We are proud to say that you have that book here. You will remove the mysteries associated with tech and computers by simply reading this cover to cover. This book is useful to children and adults alike.

You may find parts of this book easy or simple. It was intentionally written that way. We erred on the side of simplicity. In fact, we attempted to write this at a "Young Adult" reading level. If anyone ever complained, "This book is too easy and basic," we'd take that as a compliment!

If you are already a tech expert, this book isn't for you. You've already successfully "climbed the mountain" – this book is an elevator for those still at the base.

Why would we write a book like this when there are already so many out there? Well, before we wrote this, we read several existing "introduction to technology" and "computers for beginners" type books and found the following issues:

1. Most were too advanced for beginners.

2. They utilized many technical terms without defining them.

3. They assumed prior tech knowledge on the part of the reader.

4. Inside definitions and explanations, other technical terms and concepts most readers don't understand were included without clarifications or descriptions, thereby making the material incomprehensible for the average person.

There just wasn't a resource that you could give to a normal person that would bring them up to speed with computers and technology.

The problem with most technology education (and educational materials in general) is that data is relayed as though the student already understands the subject. Meaning, to really grasp the content in existing technology educational resources, you must already be familiar with the basic terms associated with the subject and understand the fundamentals beforehand. If you don't believe this, go ahead and read some "basic" computer books or Google the definitions of tech terms. Unless you're a nerd already, you will most likely become lost because they're strewn with undefined terms and unexplained concepts!

There is a *strong* demand for technology professionals, and the main reason we don't have more is because of how hard it has been to learn the subject. Students are immediately hit with nearly 1,000 terms and concepts they don't understand – it's quite a barrier.

People have a tendency to tease that which they don't understand. Why do you think that nerds were bullied so much in the past?

The problem is compounded by the fact that some technically trained people have had a tendency to flaunt their knowledge by talking down to others through use of esoteric terminology. There's almost been a trend in the computer industry to "prove" how smart you are by spitting out terms only geeks know. Just watch any television show with a character who is a hacker or computer professional and listen to the words they throw out.

There's nothing wrong with competence or using what one knows. But speaking in English to someone who speaks only Japanese and expecting them to understand you, is rude. As the saying goes, "Arrogance is knowledge minus wisdom."

The Tech Academy breaks the subjects down to you – we don't break you down to the subject.

This book was written with no assumptions of past knowledge on the part of the reader. Meaning, we wrote this as though you have no tech background or education. In it, we will cover all the major components of computers and thoroughly explain popular technologies. We will also provide you with a timeline and history so you can see how we arrived where we are today.

The history we provide throughout the chapters will "bounce around" somewhat – meaning, this book doesn't start with the first computer development and sequentially move forward in time.

The book is sequenced in a logical order of concepts. Meaning, we start with the first piece of required knowledge, then the second, and so on, while covering important historical developments throughout. Towards the end of the book, we provide a historical recap that lays out major inventions in sequence so you can see it all with a deeper understanding.

We attempted to limit each chapter to the coverage of only one key concept. Considering there are so many interconnected parts to a computer, this was difficult. And while we would love to dive right into how computers display videos and how the internet works (both subjects are covered in this book), we must start with the most basic concepts and build from there.

We estimate that the average person has heard hundreds of technology terms in their life that they cannot properly define – 90-95% of those words will be defined in this book.

There are two points we'd like to ask you to keep in mind while reading this book:

1. *This book is meant to be educational, not entertaining.* We've done our best to keep it interesting but computers and technology can be quite dry.

2. You might feel confused at points in this book. The source of this confusion is years of society barraging you with undefined words and subjects. The solution is to persist and continue on through the book because the confusion will subside and in its place will be confidence, clarity and comprehension. We know this because we wrote the book so that it's virtually impossible to go past a word or concept you don't understand due to the fact that we explain them all along the

way! Therefore, we recommend pushing through and finishing the book in its entirety – when you get to the end, you'll be glad you did.

It is our wish that this book will be widely used. From schools to companies to your home, we hope this book travels far and wide because we feel that everyone deserves this information.

This book does *not* go over how to use a computer, devices, the internet, etc. There are plenty of existing tutorials and manuals that cover how to utilize technology. Instead, this book prepares you to study these training materials on your own. We intend to lay the foundation of knowledge and required vocabulary for you to study tech.

No other book like this exists. There is nothing that covers every common technology term and concept in a way the average person can understand. This is a manual for surviving amidst technology on modern-day Earth.

Technology has evolved quickly and proper measures have not been taken to catch people up, until now.

Jack C. Stanley & Erik D. Gross
Co-Founders of The Tech Academy

CHAPTER 1:
TECHNOLOGY

"Technology is anything that wasn't around when you were born."
-Alan Kay (American computer scientist, 1940-)

We place our lives in the hands of technology every day.

"Technology" is the application of knowledge with the purpose of solving problems or making life easier. The word comes from Greek *techne,* meaning "skill with art." Computers (machines that store and deal with information) are technology. Modern cars, phones, airplanes, televisions, refrigerators, ovens – virtually all of the machines we use in our day-to-day life – have computers in them.

Have you done any of the following in the past 24 hours:

- Driven in a car?

- Used a crosswalk or traffic light?

- Ridden in a modern elevator?

- Flown in an airplane?

If so, you've trusted technology with your life. These machines are controlled to one degree or another by computers. Those computers were created by people. An error in the manufacture (building; creation) or control of those computers can factually put your life in danger.

Therefore, wouldn't it be useful to understand this beast? As the saying goes, "Knowledge is power." In this case, a more appropriate phrase is, "Knowledge is safety."

It isn't necessary to know how something works to use it but it certainly doesn't hurt.

Technology can be frustrating. Some examples of this are: You hear a commercial that says, "Buy the XRC 2000-S today" and you have no idea what that means; you finally figure out how to use your new phone and then a newer version comes out; you try to get your computer to perform a basic function but it refuses to comply; etc. Simply put, the better you understand technology, the less frustrating it is.

Computers are such a major aspect of technology that the two words ("computers" and "tech") are sometimes used interchangeably. For example: due to the fact that virtually all modern technical machines contain computers, most "tech news" is really "computer news."

Technology constantly changes and advances, faster than virtually any other subject. Brick has been used as a building material for thousands of years and the way masonry walls are built hasn't changed much during that time. The operation of keys and locks have relied on the same basic principles for thousands of years. Yet computers seem to be replaced by newer versions all the time.

SUMMARY:

Computers, and all the technology related to them, are a part of almost every aspect of modern life. If you understand computers, you can operate better in life. A knowledge of the foundation and fundamentals of technology and computers makes it easier to keep up with future developments.

So, as we covered, cars, phones and computers are tech. What else do they have in common?

CHAPTER 2:
MACHINES

"When man wanted to make a machine that would walk he created the wheel, which does not resemble a leg."
-Guillaume Apollinaire (French artist, 1880-1918)

Machines are devices (equipment with a purpose; tools) made by humans to get work done. They are usually made out of durable materials like wood, plastic and metal. Normally they have some parts that move and some parts that don't; sometimes they have no moving parts at all. They receive some kind of energy that they use to do their work. One of the things that makes people different from animals is their ability to create complex machines.

Usually people create machines because there is some work they want to do that the machine could help them with. The help the machine provides could be to get the work done faster, to do the work with less chance of errors, or to do the work nearly continuously, without the need to stop for food or sleep. There are other reasons people make machines, but it usually comes down to getting more work done in a given amount of time with fewer errors.

As time goes on, machines often get improved or changed to make them more effective or to respond to changes in the area of society where they are used.

Cars, planes, telephones and ovens are all machines.

A computer is just another machine – it's a device made by people to get work done.

Computers were created to do a simple thing: they take in data (information), change the data in some way, and send out data. That's all.

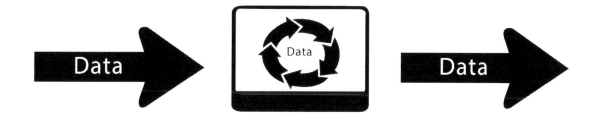

Some of the actions they perform are tasks that a person could do by hand. The difference is, computers can do them much faster than people, and (if they are set up properly) they can do them without making errors. This makes them very valuable tools.

There are certain truths regarding computers:

1. They are only machines. They are not people and are not alive.

2. They were created by people and can only act if a person tells them to. Even then, they can only perform actions that a person thought of ahead of time and built into them.

Computers do not have a soul. They cannot think. Everything ever done by a computer was predetermined by humans. Even so-called "artificial intelligence" (computer systems that are able to perform actions that require human intelligence, like being able to recognize sounds and images), or computers that can "learn," only have these abilities because we designed them that way.

As machines, some of the characteristics of computers include the following:

- They handle data. Data is information – such as words, symbols (something written that represents an amount, idea or word), pictures, etc.

- They obey instructions (commands entered into them that perform certain tasks).

- They automate (perform actions without human interaction) tasks that would either take too long for a person to do or be too boring. Keep in mind that these automatic actions were designed by a person.

- They process data. "Process" means to handle something through use of an established (and usually routine) set of procedures. When a computer displays the word "processing," it is saying, "Hold on while I perform some pre-established procedures." Processing refers to "taking actions with data." Searching through words to locate typos would be an example of "processing data." When data is being processed by a computer, you sometimes see a "progress bar" (a symbol that shows how far along something is) like this:

Processing...

Or you may see this symbol when data is being processed:

This circular symbol is called a "throbber" due to the fact that they originally expanded and contracted in size – i.e. the symbol "throbbed."

The purpose of computers is to take in data, process it and send it out. You will encounter this concept throughout this book.

When computers perform actions, it is referred to as "executing" or "running." For example: you can run a search on the internet by clicking the search button, or you could execute an instruction by pressing enter on your keyboard.

It is important to understand that machines are not life forms. Even though they can perform seemingly miraculous operations, the true source of their products is humankind.

In some television shows and movies, one sees machines taking over the world. The only ways that could happen are:

1. We designed them that way.

2. We failed to include adequate restrictions and safeguards (protections) in their design.

We are responsible for everything machines (including computers) do.

SUMMARY:

When you get down to basics, a computer is just a machine that takes in data, processes it, and passes it on. Even with the almost unbelievable complexity of

modern computers, at the end of the day, they can only do those things that a human has built them to do.

Computers are the most advanced machines that mankind has created. They are found everywhere, have nearly unlimited applicability and they all come down to: numbers. So, what do numbers have to do with all of this?

CHAPTER 3:
NUMBERS

"Numbers constitute the only universal language."
-Nathanael West (American writer, 1903-1940)

Talking about numbers isn't exactly the most exciting topic, but understanding how they relate to computers is necessary in order to grasp technology. So, please bear with us on this chapter.

It all starts with the idea of a number system. A number system is a method for naming and representing quantities (amounts). It is how you count and perform math with numbers.

The number system we are used to is the "decimal system." The word "decimal" means "based on the number ten." It comes from the Latin word *decimus*, meaning "tenth."

Using the decimal number system, you count like this: 1, 2, 3, 4, 5, 6, 7, 8, 9, 10, 11, etc. This is the number system you've been using since a very young age. But there are others. Computers don't operate on the decimal number system – more on that soon.

Number systems let you display quantities, count and perform math using digits.

"Digits" are symbols that represent a quantity. The symbol "3" is a digit and represents the quantity three. By combining the digits (symbols) "2" and "4" into 24, the quantity twenty-four can be represented. The quantity of eight cubes can be written as the digit 8, like this image shows:

(Quantity)   (Digit)

The "place" is the position of a digit in a written number – the position affects the value (amount) of the digit used. The decimal number system has places like "ones place," "tens place," "hundreds place," etc.

Here is a picture showing places:

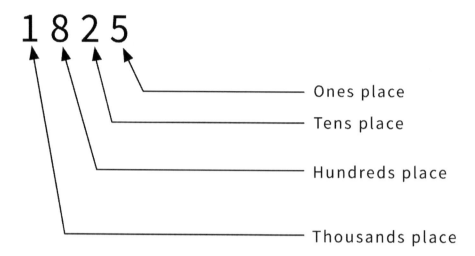

Written out another way with the number 1,329:

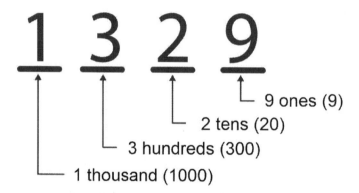

1329 : one thousand, three hundred and twenty-nine

1329 = (1 x 1000) + (3 x 100) + (2 x 10) + (9 x 1)

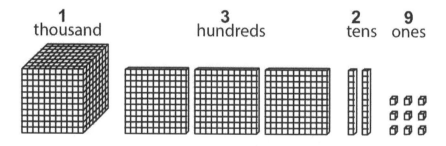

Now, the "base" of a number system is the total amount of unique digits (symbols) used in that system.

Because the decimal number system uses ten unique digits (0, 1, 2, 3, 4, 5, 6, 7, 8 and 9), it has a base of ten. It is called a "base ten number system."

Each number system has its own base. For example: There's a language in Papua New Guinea (a place on an island north of Australia) that uses a base 15 number system! A base 15 number system uses 15 symbols to count: 0, 1, 2, 3, 4, 5, 6, 7, 8, 9, A, B, C, D and E. Here it is converted to decimal (base ten – the number systems used in most of the world):

Base 15	Base 10 (decimal)
0	0
1	1
2	2
3	3
4	4
5	5
6	6
7	7
8	8
9	9
A	10
B	11
C	12
D	13
E	14
10	15

As you can see, in the base 15 number system, the number fourteen is written as "E" and ten is written as "A"! Because this is different than the number system you're used to, it may be hard to comprehend. But don't worry, you don't need to learn how to count in base 15. It is only mentioned here as an example of a different number system than what you're used to.

SUMMARY:

We are all used to a base ten number system, which is a way of counting and performing math that includes these ten digits (symbols that represent a quantity): 0, 1, 2, 3, 4, 5, 6, 7, 8 and 9. This is also called the decimal number system because decimal means "made up of ten unique parts."

So, if computers don't use the decimal (base ten) number system, what do they use?

CHAPTER 4:
COMPUTER NUMBERS

"It may be conceded (admitted) *to the mathematicians that four is twice two. But two is not twice one; two is two thousand times one."*
-G. K. Chesterton (English writer, 1874-1936)

This brings us to the number system that computers use: base two. As covered in the last chapter, base refers to how many unique digits are used in a number system. A base two number system means that computers only use two unique digits to operate.

The only two digits computers use to operate are: 0 and 1.

The base two number system is called "binary." The word comes from the Latin word *binarius*, meaning "two together" or a "pair."

All quantities in binary are represented by numbers that use a 1 and/or a 0. In fact, *any* number can be written in binary.

Here is how to count to ten in binary:

0 (zero),
1 (one),
10 (two),
11 (three),
100 (four),
101 (five),
110 (six),
111 (seven),
1000 (eight),
1001 (nine) and
1010 (ten).

Written another way, here is binary converted to decimal (the base ten number system we are all used to):

Base 2	Base 10 (decimal)
0	0
1	1

10	2
11	3
100	4
101	5
110	6
111	7
1000	8
1001	9
1010	10

To further clarify this, here are places in binary:

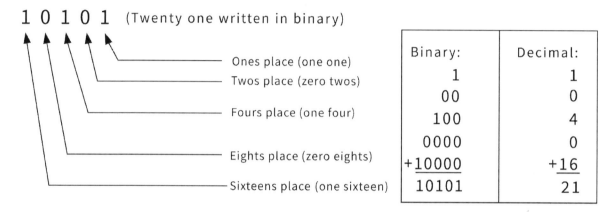

1 0 1 0 1 (Twenty one written in binary)

Ones place (one one)
Twos place (zero twos)
Fours place (one four)
Eights place (zero eights)
Sixteens place (one sixteen)

Binary:	Decimal:
1	1
00	0
100	4
0000	0
+10000	+16
10101	21

It is not necessary for you to learn to count or perform math in binary. You just need to understand the definition of binary (the base two number system that uses only 0 and 1 to represent all numbers) and that it is the number system that computers utilize.

SUMMARY:

Computers were built, initially, to work with numbers. Computer designers had a choice of how to represent numbers in these new machines they were designing, and they chose a number system called binary. Using only the two symbols 1 and 0, we can represent quantities and other types of data that use numbers.

So, how exactly do computers use binary to operate?

CHAPTER 5:
DISTINCT DIFFERENCES

"Never trust a computer you can't throw out a window."
-Steve Wozniak (Co-Founder of Apple, 1950-)

Digital things are made up of exact, distinct parts. These parts are always in one precise state. "State" refers to the condition of a thing – such as, "green," "empty," "50 years old," etc.

Things that are digital can only be in one of the available states for that thing, and not "in between" any of the states. A light bulb with a regular light switch is digital because it only has two states: totally on or totally off. A light bulb with a dimmer switch that could be set somewhere between "totally on" and "totally off" is not digital.

The photograph below is digital:

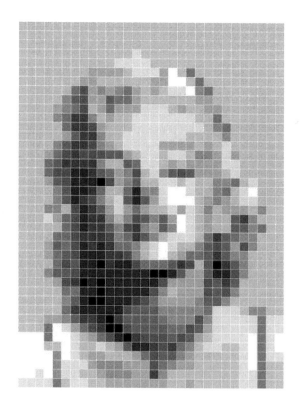

Each square in the photo is its own distinct part with its own distinct state – black, white, gray, dark gray, etc. This doesn't mean that every blurry photo is digital. Most digital photos are composed of so many "squares" that, to the eye, they look just like the real world shown in the photo.

One of the ways to understand digital is to compare it to a different term: "analog."

"Analog" refers to devices or objects that represent amounts in a continuous stream. It means that the item gradually increases or decreases or stays the same in a steady flow over time.

"Analog" comes from the Greek word *analogy,* meaning "analogous" (similar; related to). Due to the fact that "digital" means "distinct" and "analog" means "gradual," the two terms are commonly considered opposites. In fact, one of the definitions of "analog" is "not digital."

This car speedometer is an analog device:

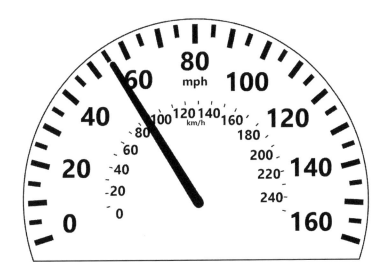

The needle changes position in relation to the physical movement of the wheels. On the other hand, this is a digital speedometer:

Many speedometers nowadays are digital because modern cars have computers built into them.

You commonly see a combination of both speedometer types, analog and digital:

These two types of speedometer provide a great way to really show the difference between analog and digital.

These devices operate with electricity. Small currents (flows) of electricity go through them. There are several words used to describe these small electrical currents, including: impulses, signals and pulses.

In both types of speedometer, a device will measure the speed of the car, create an electrical signal based on that speed, and send that signal to the speedometer. That signal is used to control the speed that is displayed. The two types differ in how they can represent that speed to the driver.

Let's say you're going *exactly* 54 miles per hour (MPH). Both types of speedometer (the digital number displayed and the needle on the dial) are showing 54 MPH.

Now, let's make it interesting. Say you start *slowly* increasing your speed, eventually getting to the point where you are going 55 MPH.

What happens as you're increasing speed from 54 MPH to 55 MPH shows the difference between analog devices and digital devices very clearly. On the analog speedometer, you will be able to watch the needle slowly move from 54 to 55 MPH. That needle is controlled directly by the electrical signal that indicates the speed of the car. As that signal changes, even by a small amount, the position of the needle changes. So at any given moment, the needle (analog display) is an accurate indication of the actual speed of the car – in other words, the needle movement is analogous (similar or comparable) to the actual speed.

The digital speedometer, however, has a problem: It only has certain exact states that can be used in representing data. In this case, it is restricted to only being able to display whole numbers – like 1, 2, 10, 30, 54, 55, etc. It is built that way. It physically can't display a number like 54.1, or 54.7, etc.

So as you are slowly increasing the speed of your car from 54 MPH to 55 MPH, and the electronic signal sent to the speedometer changes, that digital display isn't going to change right away. It is going to keep displaying 54 MPH until the actual speed is high enough that the device interprets it as 55 MPH, and only then will the display change. For example: the digital device may interpret anything below 54.5 as 54, and anything equal to or above 54.5 as 55.

This means that the speed shown on the digital device is not always an accurate indication of the actual speed of the car – in fact, it is only when the actual speed is a whole number like 54 MPH or 55 MPH that the digital display matches the actual speed of the vehicle. Now, that doesn't mean the speedometer is dangerous, or can't be relied upon. After all, the designers of that digital device built it to show speed in increments of one MPH, so the speedometer should be accurate enough to be useful to the driver.

Can you imagine, though, if they built it so it could only show speed in increments of twenty MPH? Now that speedometer becomes a lot less useful!

This is a factor in all digital machines: can they represent data with enough accuracy that they are useful, even though the way they represent data may not always be identical to the actual thing being represented?

As a further example of machines that can be either analog or digital, there are analog watches:

And digital watches:

And just as a loose final example, let's compare analog and digital to physical objects. A slide or a hill could be considered "analog" because the slopes are gradual. Whereas a staircase, with its distinct steps that are each separate from each other, could be considered "digital." This can be seen in the picture below – the waves are analog and the steps are digital:

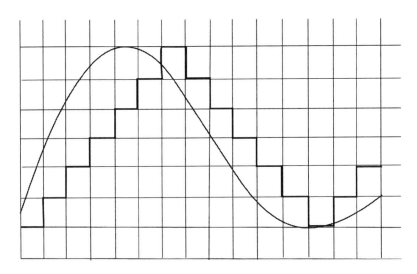

SUMMARY:

Digital refers to distinct differences in states, conditions, parts, etc. Analog refers to gradual increases or decreases.

Now, let's see how digital relates to binary (the number system that uses 1 and 0 to represent all quantities).

CHAPTER 6:
DIGITAL COMPUTERS

"Our technology, our machines, is part of our humanity.
We created them to extend ourselves,
and that is what is unique about human beings."
-Ray Kurzweil (American inventor, 1948-)

"Digital" often refers to devices or objects that represent amounts using the digits 0 and 1 (binary). This is because 0 and 1 are distinctly different numbers.

Binary devices are digital devices. And so, computers are digital machines.

In fact, there is an additional definition of "digital" that means "involving or relating to the use of computers or technology."

Computers, and technology in general, are referred to as "digital" due to the fact that computers operate on data that is represented using the whole numbers 0 and 1. There is no concept of "almost zero" or "halfway to one" in the binary system. Remember, digital devices operate on data that can only be in one of the available states built into the machine – and in computers, the available states are one and zero.

It is possible to design computers that operate off other number systems – systems that use more than two digits. It would even be possible to design a computer that uses the decimal system, with its ten digits. However, creating an electronic device that can represent ten exact, distinct states, one for each digit in the decimal system, would be very challenging. Early computer designers recognized that it is very easy to represent just two digits in an electronic device, simply by controlling whether electricity is present or not at a specific location in the computer. You will learn more about how this is done later in this book.

And so binary was the best number system to use in representing digital data and running digital machines.

We will take a deeper dive into exactly how computers use 1s and 0s to perform actions, but at this point in the book, it's only necessary for you to understand the definition of digital and binary, which you now know.

SUMMARY:

When you hear about a "digital" machine, you can know that it probably is a computer, or uses one in its operation. It is still just a machine, and as it does its work, it may operate using data that is close to, but not an exact match for, the thing it represents in the real world. But even with that factor, computers can be very useful, valuable and accurate. Binary was chosen because representing just two different digits (0 and 1) using an electronic device is easier and more reliable than trying to represent several different digits electronically.

The whole idea of digital can be further explained by a system of logic. But what does logic have to do with computers?

CHAPTER 7:
TRUE OR FALSE?

"No matter how correct a mathematical theorem (an idea generally accepted as true) *may appear to be, one ought never to be satisfied that there was not something imperfect about it until it also gives the impression of being beautiful."*
-George Boole (English mathematician, 1815-1864)

"Logic" refers to actions, behavior and thinking that makes sense. When speaking about computers, logic is the rules that form the foundation for a computer in performing certain tasks.

An example of computer logic is the guidelines the computer uses when making decisions, such as:

- If the maximum number of students has not been enrolled in the class, then allow another student to be added.

- If the maximum number of students has been enrolled in the class, then do not allow another student to be added.

George Boole (the English mathematician quoted above) developed Boolean logic. "Boolean logic" is a form of logic in which the only possible results of a decision are "true" and "false." There aren't any vague or "almost" answers to a calculation or decision – black or white, no gray.

An example of Boolean logic would be answering questions with only "yes" or "no."

Computers "think" this way:

5 is larger than 3 = TRUE

3 is bigger than 5 = FALSE

Boolean logic relates to digital in that digital devices only allow for one of two states. These terms both relate to the binary number system because 1 can be used to mean "true," while 0 can be used to mean "false" (two distinct states).

And so, Boolean logic is the foundation for the construction and operation of computers.

Boolean logic uses certain kinds of comparisons that revolve around something being true or false.

SUMMARY:

Everything in computers and all actions they perform come down to Boolean logic: yes/no, true/false, go/stop – which are all represented by 1 and 0 (binary).

Let's take a look at how computers can compare two or more pieces of data.

CHAPTER 8:
COMPARISONS

"Logic will get you from A to B.
Imagination will take you everywhere."
-Albert Einstein (German scientist, 1879-1955)

In computers, we can use two or more comparisons *to make an additional comparison*. This is done by using Boolean logic. We do this by getting the results of the two (or more) comparisons and then comparing those results in some way.

Some common examples of such Boolean comparisons are "AND" and "OR."

With the Boolean comparison called "AND," the comparison is true *only if all of the involved comparisons are true.*

Let's look at some examples to show how this works:

In the following AND comparison, the result is true:

```
5 is more than 3 AND 10 is more than 5
```

Let's break it down.

There are three comparisons happening here:

1. Comparing 5 and 3 to see if 5 is larger than 3 (is 5 larger than 3?)

2. Comparing 10 and 5 to see if 10 is larger than 5 (is 10 larger than 5?)

3. Comparing the results of those two comparisons, using the Boolean comparison "AND" (are both comparisons true?)

This is the overall comparison.

It is true that 5 is greater than 3, so the first comparison is true.

It is also true that 10 is greater than 5 – so the second comparison is true as well.

A Boolean AND comparison is true if the other comparisons are all true – so in this example, the overall comparison is true, since the first comparison is true *and* the second comparison is true.

In this next example, the result is false (not true):

```
5 is more than 7 AND 10 is more than 5
```

Even though 10 is more than 5, 5 is not more than 7 – so the overall comparison is not true.

A "condition" is an item that must be true before something else occurs. In the AND comparison above, these are the two conditions checked for:

1. 5 is more than 7

2. 10 is more than 5

They're conditions because the outcome is conditional upon (dependent on) these two comparisons.

A Boolean OR comparison checks for whether one *or* both conditions are true. Here is an example:

```
4 is less than 9 OR 8 is less than 7
```

The result would be true because at least one of the comparisons is true (4 is a smaller number than 9).

In the following example, the result would be false since neither is true:

```
8 is less than 4 OR 9 is less than 3
```

And in this example, the result would be true because one or both (in this case both) are true:

```
7 is less than 8 OR 2 is less than 5
```

As a note: in writing instructions for a computer, we would use the greater and lesser symbols (> and < respectively). For example: $7 > 3$ means "seven is greater than three," and $4 < 9$ means "four is less than nine."

So, for example, instead of "10 is greater than 2," we would write:

```
10 > 2
```

If we wanted to say "greater than *or* equal to," we could use the symbol >=.

For example:

```
10 >= 8
```

So, why does all this matter? With computers, Boolean logic is valuable because we can build very precise instructions that allow computers to make decisions extremely quickly (billions a second). Keep in mind that no matter how many actions a computer is performing, it all comes down to yes/no, true/false, on/off ("on" meaning, "electricity present; operating," and "off" meaning, "no electricity present; not operating"), etc. – it all boils down to Boolean logic, which is represented using the binary digits 1 and 0.

Another element of Boolean logic is the IF comparison. The IF comparison in computers checks for whether or not a Boolean comparison is true. If the comparison is true, then the IF comparison is true as well.

As an example, a vending machine could operate as follows:

```
IF customer paid in full, dispense their requested snack
```

Or said another way:

```
IF full payment true, provide snack. IF full payment false, do nothing
```

Here's a more realistic example of a computer putting Boolean logic to use:

Let's say we want the computer to determine who on a list of names is eligible to vote in the U.S. election. The Boolean comparison would look something like this:

```
IF [age >= 18] AND [U.S. Citizen = yes]: Can vote
```

What this is saying is: if the person is 18 or older *and* they are a citizen of the United States, they can vote. If only one or neither of these conditions were true, then the result would be false (meaning, the person can't vote in the U.S.).

SUMMARY:

We often use computers to make decisions a human could make, if the human had a well-established process for making those decisions. One of the main tools we use in this is Boolean logic, since it is similar to the process we go through ourselves when doing work. One of the main reasons computers are so valuable is that, once we set them up to make these comparisons and decisions, they can do so much faster than a person – but at the end of the day, they are just making simple comparisons that you and I could make.

TR✓E
or
F✗LSE

If a computer is off, it can't utilize Boolean logic. In fact, without an energy source, computers can do nothing. So, what is the source of energy for computers?

CHAPTER 9:
ENERGY

"Electricity is really just organized lightning."
-George Carlin (American comedian, 1937-2008)

Electricity is a type of energy that can be stored or can flow from one location to another, and computers cannot operate without it.

You've probably heard of negative and positive electricity. "Negative" and "positive" are the two main types of electricity, and as the saying goes, "Opposites attract." Positive energy is drawn toward negative, and vice versa. On the other hand, negative electricity pushes away other negative electricity and positive electricity repels positive electricity. Here is an illustration showing this (negative electricity is indicated by a minus sign, -, while a plus sign, +, is used for positive):

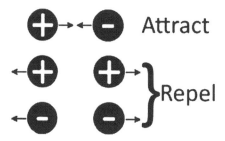

You can see the negative and positive written on batteries:

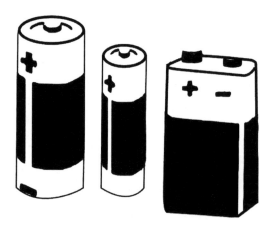

A "circuit" is a path that electricity flows along from beginning to end. Along that path, there might be certain machine parts that do work or control the flow of the electricity.

The electricity that travels through this circuit will come from a source (such as a battery or an electrical outlet in a wall), travel through wires and devices, and return back to that source.

Batteries utilize the negative and positive energy to draw electricity through circuits, as can be seen in this illustration:

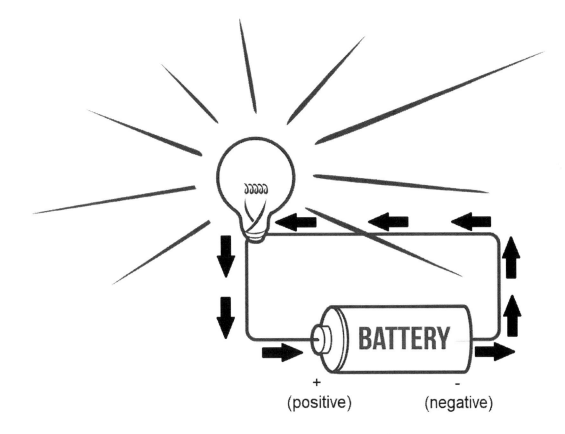

All of this directly relates to computers because they're connected to an electricity source (a plug in a wall; an internal battery) – and that electricity runs through circuits in the computer and performs functions along the way.

"Power" or "power source" is where a machine receives its energy (usually electricity) from. A "cable" is a wire or wires, wrapped in a protective casing (container), that are used to transport electricity. A power cable is the cord that provides electricity to something. Computer power cables look like this:

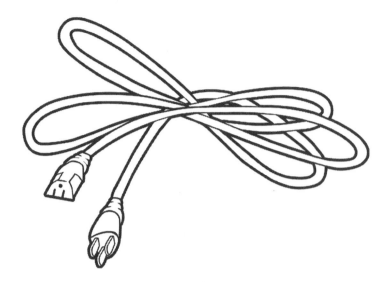

The power cable plugs into the power "supply" (the part of a computer that manages the electricity that is passed into the rest of the computer).

A power supply converts the power coming through the power cord into various different levels of electricity needed by the computer. It looks like this:

That picture shows the power supply of a computer separated from the main computer. Here is what it looks like as part of a whole:

You can see the power supply at the top of the picture; it has a place to plug in the power cord (on the left), and a vent to allow air flow (on the right).

The power supply performs important functions:

The first thing it does is to lower the amount of the electricity that goes into the rest of the machine.

Without getting buried in a bunch of electronics terminology, you should know this: you measure how much "force" electricity has by what's called "voltage." Higher voltage means more "force" in the electricity available to move through a machine.

When electricity moves through things, it produces heat. The higher the voltage, the more electricity is moving. Therefore, the temperature rises.

The parts in a computer can't tolerate a lot of heat. In fact, if we didn't use the power supply to drop down the voltage of the electricity that goes to the rest of the computer, we could break or melt those parts and the computer would be damaged.

A common source of electricity is a wall socket (a device you plug cords into):

A computer's power supply takes in the electricity that comes from the wall socket, through that power cord.

The voltage that comes out of a wall socket is around 110 "volts" (measurement of voltage). This is way too high a voltage for the parts in a computer, so the power supply drops it down to a much lower level: 5 volts. As a note: 5 volts isn't enough to even noticeably shock someone – it's very little electrical force.

That 5 volts is what comes out of the power supply and gets distributed to the parts inside the computer that need electricity.

The other thing the power supply does is to "regulate" (control) the electricity that it sends into the computer. This means keeping the level of the electricity constant. Even if the level of the electricity coming from the wall socket into the power supply varies a bit, the power supply keeps the electricity level it sends out constant at 5 volts, no matter what.

This is very important, because the computer relies on exact levels of electricity to represent data, and if the voltage level varies, the computer gets incorrect data and provides us with wrong answers.

Electricity is the source of "life" for computers.

As a note: in some laptops, the power supply and power cable are connected together as one unit, like this:

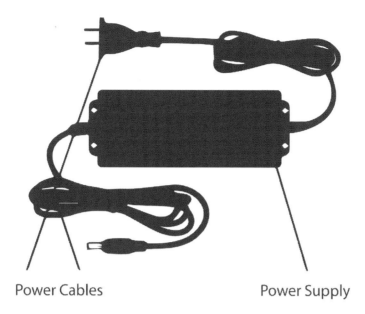

Power Cables   Power Supply

Here, the power cable delivers electricity from the wall to the power supply at 110 volts and the power supply passes electricity to the laptop at 5 volts.

As a note, the process of dropping the voltage down from 110 volts to 5 volts produces a good amount of heat. You may notice the power supply on a laptop gets warm. With a larger computer like the one we looked at earlier in this chapter, the power supply will have a vent and a fan to get rid of this heat.

SUMMARY:

Computers are machines and they need energy to do their job. The energy comes from electricity. When we send electricity into a computer, we need to drop the voltage (the level of "force" it has) to protect the delicate parts inside the computer. Power supplies do that – and they also regulate the level of the electricity they put out so the computer has stable electricity to work with. They produce heat as they do this work.

Now, how are Boolean logic, numbers and electricity connected to each other?

CHAPTER 10:
ONES AND ZEROS

*"There are only 10 types of people in the world:
those who understand binary, and those who don't."*
-Unknown

As we covered earlier, Boolean logic involves comparisons that end up being either true or false and those states are represented in binary, with 1 being true and 0 being false.

1 is also used in computers to mean "on" and 0 to mean "off." In fact, as you can see below, most power buttons on computers and other devices are a symbol made up of a 1 and a 0 (on/off):

If you're near a computer or laptop, go ahead and take a look.

You've also probably seen switches like this:

You click 1 and the machine is on – set it to 0 and it's off.

The ones and zeros in a computer are called bits (short for "binary digits"). Bits are held in the computer by using very small devices, each of which can change to represent either a 1 or a 0. Here is an example of what a device to store an individual bit can look like:

This is actually pretty large as computer parts go – it is about half an inch long. Computers nowadays use much smaller parts to perform the same function of storing a binary digit (a bit). We are using an older, larger device just to help illustrate the way this works. You would need a microscope to see the current devices in real life.

That is one of the biggest challenges in understanding how computers work – you can't see inside them to look at all of the various parts and get an idea of how they work together to accomplish the purpose of the machine (take in data, process it and send it out).

Let's take a look at the larger device pictured above, though.

There are three prongs (points) on this device: one for electricity to go in, one that controls whether or not the bit is on or off and one for electricity to go out. Specifically, the middle prong controls whether or not a signal is sent out (1; on) or not (0; off).

Here it is illustrated:

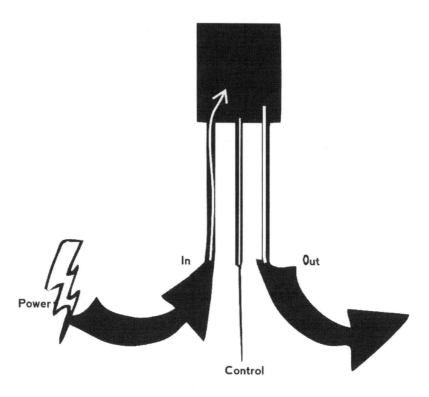

This device, representing a bit, is on (a binary 1) because electricity is allowed to pass through. If it were off (a binary 0), the middle prong would prevent any electricity from flowing out the third prong (nothing would come out the right prong) – like this:

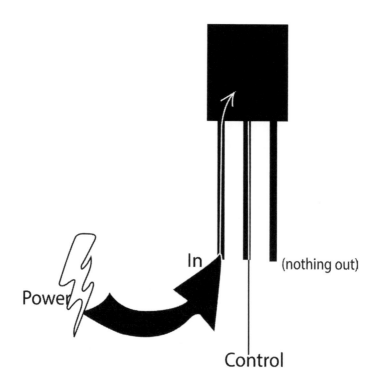

Bits are individually set to on and off based on instructions entered in the computer – it all comes down to 1s and 0s. Using bits, we are able to tell a computer true and false, on and off, yes and no, etc. Multiplying this by billions, we can make computers perform extremely impressive and complicated operations.

Remember, in modern computers the parts that store bits are VERY small. Computers have billions to trillions of bits, and each one can be individually on or off.

For example: this piece of a computer can hold about 128,000,000,000 (one-hundred-twenty-eight billion) bits on it (it's about four inches long):

Computers have their own language called "machine language." Computers are designed to perform actions based on instructions written in machine language. Guess what the only two symbols used in machine language are? 1 and 0.

What this means is that by typing these 1s and 0s into a computer, we can make it operate. For example: by typing 1100 0111, you could change the color of the text on the screen.

But wait – when was the last time you typed 1s and 0s into a computer to get it to do something? Probably never. Fortunately, the people who designed computers worked out how we can write the instructions for the computer in a language that looks a lot like English – and inside the computer those instructions are translated into machine language that the computer can understand.

For example, every letter you type has its own series of binary 1s and 0s assigned to it so the computer can "understand" what to display. The letter "A" could be binary number 01000001, and the binary number for a lowercase "a" could be 01100001. Here's an example illustration:

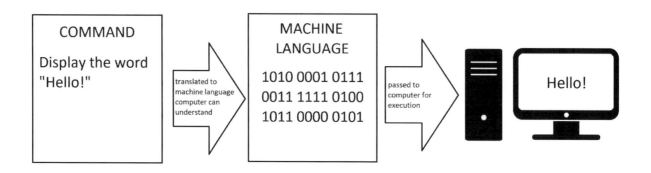

Commands written in machine language are called "machine instructions." When computers are manufactured, they're made so that they obey machine instructions. Some machine instructions are already built in and they automatically run so as to enable your computer to perform basic actions, such as starting up when you turn on the computer.

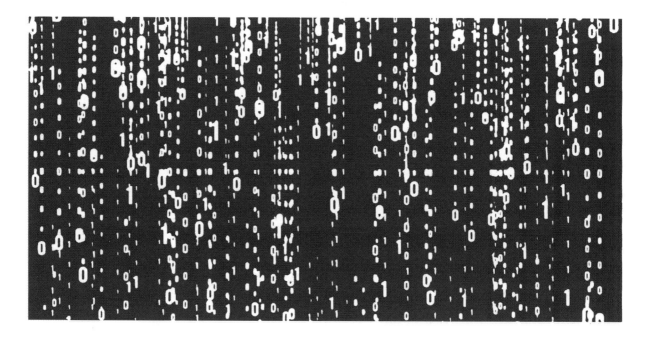

Information stored in a computer is stored in bits. Later in this book, we will cover how this works in more detail. What's important to understand at this point is that computers operate on binary, which is based on Boolean logic, and that it all comes down to bits being on and off in exact sequences.

SUMMARY:

Earlier, we covered the idea that a computer's main purpose is to take in data, process it, and output data. That data is represented in the computer as binary digits. Those binary digits always correspond to some physical item, and that physical item is capable of being changed to represent either a 1 or a 0. There is no "magic" to a computer; it just uses parts that are very small. It all comes down to using 1s and 0s to represent data and to represent the instructions for what to do with that data.

We've talked about some parts of computers and elements of how they work – now let's discuss computers in their own right.

CHAPTER 11:
COMPUTERS

"The most overlooked advantage of owning a computer is that if they foul up there's no law against whacking them around a bit."
-Unknown

The first documented use of the word "computer" occurred in the 1600s and it meant, "A person who carries out calculations and computations." Calculations and computations are actions taken to determine the number or size of something. For example: in the 1950s, workers on the U.S. space flight program who performed large numbers of complex math calculations had the job title "Computer."

The first functional computer device was designed only to perform mathematical calculations. By today's standards, it was a very basic calculator (machine that performs math).

The word "compute" means "to determine the answer." Humans can compute by evaluating a situation and coming up with a solution.

"Compute," as it applies to computers, means to figure out the solution to a problem using numerical data.

A computer is an electronic machine that stores and deals with information. It is made up of many different parts through which electricity passes.

Computers can store instructions to be done at a later point in time, so that people do not have to re-enter the same instructions over and over again.

"Complicated" literally means "consisting of many connected pieces; having lots of parts" and so, by definition, computers are complicated. There are billions of individual pieces that make up the modern computer – some have trillions. To put that number in perspective, if you were to stack 1,000,000,000,000 (one trillion) one-dollar bills on the ground, they would reach into outer space (about 1/4 of the way to the moon). The stack would be 67,866 miles high and weigh 20,000 pounds (about ten tons).

How do they fit billions to trillions of individual parts into a computer? By making the parts extremely small. How small? Well, on the order of nanometers.

"Nano-" means one billionth. A meter is about 3 feet and 3 inches. Here is a meter stick:

For reference, some examples of things that measure about one meter are chairs (from ground to top of the back of the chair) and guitars (measured from the bottom to the top). Doorways are around .8 or .9 meters wide.

There are 100 centimeters in a meter (centi- means "hundredth" or "hundred," and there are 1,000 millimeters in a meter (milli- means "one of a thousand equal parts of something"):

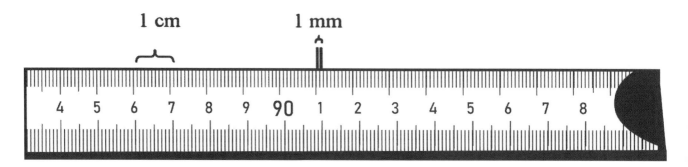

1 cm   1 mm

A pencil eraser is about five millimeters wide. A nanometer is one billionth of a meter, or one millionth of a millimeter. Here is an illustration:

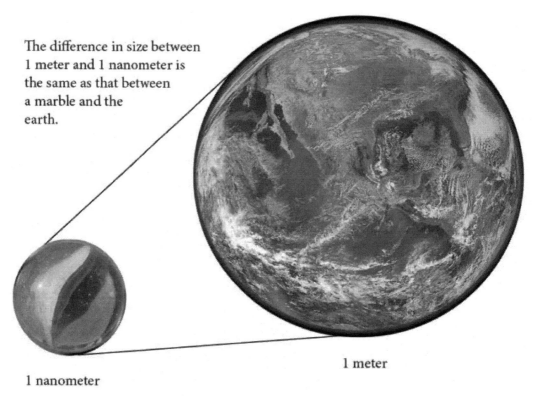

The difference in size between 1 meter and 1 nanometer is the same as that between a marble and the earth.

1 nanometer

1 meter

(this image is not to scale)

As of 2020, computers had some individual parts that were as small as 14 nanometers. Considering a human hair is about 75,000 nanometers wide, and a human red blood cell (tiny entities that carry oxygen through your blood) is about 7,000 nanometers, we've gotten computer components down to a microscopic size.

But here's the good news: even though it may seem overwhelming, computers are composed of only a few main parts. You will learn about all of them in this book. Earlier in time, these components were much larger and we will show those to you as well, so you can relate how computers got the way they are today.

Also, the "brain" of a computer can perform only one action at a time.

Here's an example of how computers operate: Suppose we have someone who works with weather patterns over time. Let's say they had written records of various kinds of data about the weather in a certain city – temperature, rainfall, humidity, etc.

They are given the task of calculating averages for all those types of data over a period of three years and then creating a chart showing those averages for every month during that period of three years.

This task involves taking in data, processing the data and outputting (sending out) data.

The person might do this by hand – go through all of the weather records, identify the data they need for this task, write that data down in a way that makes it easy to do math with the data, do the math to calculate all the averages for each month in that three year period, and then write a list of the averages.

This is a task that would take a long time. It would also be easy to make a mistake, because there is a lot of work that involves copying data from one place to another and performing mathematical calculations.

This is where computers are valuable. With a little work, you could set up the computer to do each of those things the person is doing by hand – searching through the weather records, identifying the needed data, calculating the averages, creating a chart and displaying it. It could do this much faster than the person, with few (or no) errors in each step.

Computers have expanded far beyond their initial use of performing math. Their usability extends about as far as human imagination. They are able to do virtually anything we decide we want them to do, within the laws of reality, of course.

They are a beautiful tool that can be used for good. And as we mentioned toward the beginning of this book, they are not alive and do not possess a mind. The true source of their beauty and usefulness is the people behind them.

SUMMARY:

Computers are digital machines that can take in, process and output data. They may seem quite complex, and the individual parts inside them may be very small, but the basics are really simple: we can store instructions in them, and then they can perform those instructions without stopping, faster than we can ever hope to, and without deviation. Yet as amazing as they are, it's how *we* set them up and use them that's truly amazing.

We've mentioned that computers follow instructions – well, how are they given those instructions?

CHAPTER 12:
PROGRAMMING

"Everybody in this country should learn to program a computer...
because it teaches you how to think."
-Steve Jobs (Co-Founder of Apple, 1955-2011)

The point where computers really started to become valuable to people was when it was worked out how to install programs on them. "Install" means to put something inside a computer that the computer can then use.

Programs are sets of written instructions, entered into a computer by people, that make it execute specific tasks. Installing a program means to put it into a computer so that the program can execute. For example: you could install a program by transferring the data that makes up the program from the internet to your computer.

Behind every action you perform on a computer, there's a program. Common programs you've probably used before include:

- Microsoft Word (a program that allows you to type documents)

- Google Chrome (a program that helps you search the internet)

- iTunes (a program used to organize and listen to music)

Let's say you were an early computer designer, and you worked out how to create a computer that was built for one purpose: to allow a user (a person that uses something) to create, edit and print documents. All of the instructions you built into it would revolve around that one purpose.

Now, say you got the idea of creating a computer that would help you monitor all of the equipment in a manufacturing plant. You then created a separate computer for that purpose. Its physical design might be different from the first computer, and for sure the instructions it performed would be different.

This isn't far from the actual history of computers. Often, early computers were created for one primary purpose, and they weren't suitable for other purposes unless those purposes were closely related.

The computers most of us use today are, instead, general-purpose computers. They were built to accommodate the installation, operation and removal of multiple programs, each created for specific purposes.

Programs are written in a programming language (an organized system of words, phrases and symbols that let you create programs). Just as there are many languages used by humans across the world, there are different types of programming languages. In fact, there are over a thousand programming languages (though only about ten account for the majority of languages used).

Just like hammers and ladders have different uses, each programming language has different uses. For example: some programming languages were designed mainly to improve websites (locations on the internet that can be viewed by people), while others were made for creating computer games.

The instructions inside these programs are referred to as "code." Most code looks similar to English and is translated down to instructions composed of the 1s and 0s that computers understand (machine language).

For example, to have a computer display the words "Hello!" using Python (a popular computer programming language used to create programs and websites), the code is written as:

```
print("Hello!")
```

When someone says "program a computer" or "do some coding," they're saying, "Write a set of instructions into a computer, using a programming language, that will result in specific actions being performed when that set of instructions is called for." A computer programmer is one who engages in computer programming (writing code that results in programs).

How does it work, then, when you put a program on a computer?

Since the instructions that make up programs come down to combinations of 0s and 1s, those instructions can be sent to the computer as electrical signals representing the 0s and 1s (for example: no signal = 0; 5 volts = 1), and the computer can sense those electrical signals and figure out the exact combination of 0s and 1s.

That data, stored in 0s and 1s, represents either one of the following:

1) Data to be worked with, or

2) The instructions for what to do with data.

Once the program has been transferred to the computer, the computer goes through the program and sorts out the data from the instructions. These instructions, by the way, can only be made up from built-in actions the computer can do – things like making an image appear on a screen, or doing math, or storing data somewhere. So, the person creating the program needs to be familiar with what actions the computer *can* perform. If a program is written that tells a computer to perform an action it wasn't designed to do, it won't do it because it can't.

When a user turns a program on, the computer performs the set of instructions found by reading the program – creating things on the screen; taking in data the user might type, printing documents to a printer, etc.

When a user is done using a program, they might end it and turn on another program – say, a card game.

So, your computer can store lots of different programs, and can operate multiple programs simultaneously. And all of the programs were created by people. You can even learn to create programs yourself – something that was unimaginable in the early years of the computer industry.

Always keep in mind that programs are written by people and people aren't perfect. Sometimes the frustration you feel while using a digital device (i.e. a computer) is actually because of an error made by computer programmers. For example, have you ever been playing a video game and you know you did something right, but the game said you failed? Maybe you were certain you tapped the button at the exact right moment or had aimed perfectly. Chances are you were actually right and there was some error in the game's design, or possibly with the machine you're using or some other factor that isn't your fault. Computers and computer programs aren't flawless 100% of the time and never will be.

SUMMARY:

Computers need to be told what to do. The set of instructions telling a computer what to do is called a program. Programs are written in one of many available languages, but the instructions in that language are converted to instructions the computer can understand and perform (machine language – 1s and 0s). You can install multiple programs on a computer, and run more than one program at a time. You can even learn to create programs that can go on your computer or other people's computers.

In order to understand where we are now, it's important to understand how we got here. So, what is the history of computers anyway?

CHAPTER 13:
THE FIRST CALCULATOR

"I didn't have a computer until I was 19 – but I did have an abacus."
-Jan Koum (Co-Founder of WhatsApp, 1976-)

Attempting to fully understand modern computers can be overwhelming if you don't understand how we arrived there. There are fundamental computer parts that were originally only one piece, that have now been divided up, made incredibly smaller, combined with other parts, etc. It is much easier to understand how that part worked at its most basic form. For example, one of the original computers performed one command a second. Modern computers operate the same basic way except they can now perform billions of commands a second. The basic concepts they started with have been multiplied through advancements and by making components smaller.

The first operational electronic computer was constructed in 1942. In order to see how we arrived there, let's look at its ancestors. Keep in mind that the following chapters are a relatively brief history, considering that an entire book could be written about the history of computers alone.

The abacus was technically the first computer. An abacus is a tool made up of rods and beads that can be used for calculating. It looks like this:

Each bead represents a different place value – the bottom row is 1s, the second row up is 10s, etc. Counting and math were made easier with the abacus. The term comes from the Greek word *abax*, which literally means "a board to draw on."

The abacus was used by the Egyptians in 2000 BC. It remained in use for about the next 3,600 years. Here is an ancient abacus:

It is one of the first instances of using a tool to perform math, which was the primary function performed by the original electronic computers and something computers do to this very day.

SUMMARY:

While a modern computer can seem almost overwhelmingly complex, the core elements of its design and operation are actually pretty simple. It helps to understand the history of those key elements. As for the common use of computers to perform math calculations, we have the abacus to thank. This was a mechanical tool, based on the principles of a number system, that let a human perform math calculations much faster and with less chance for error. Sounds kind of like a computer, doesn't it?

So, what was the next advancement?

CHAPTER 14:
RULER

"Do not worry about your difficulties in Mathematics.
I can assure you mine are still greater."
-Albert Einstein (German scientist, 1879-1955)

In 1622, an English mathematician named William Oughtred invented the slide rule – a ruler with a strip that slides and can be used to make rapid calculations, especially division and multiplication. Here's what a slide rule looks like:

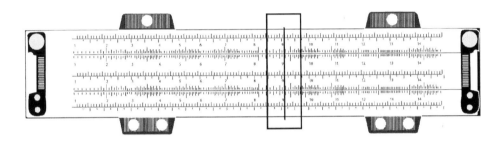

These forerunners to computers had the purpose of increasing efficiency and making calculations easier. The various numbers and lines on a slide rule can be used to perform math.

For an example: you can multiply 2 times 4 by using specific rows on the slide rule. You simply move the slide so that the line covers 2 and 4 in certain rows, and the line will also fall on the answer: 8.

The slide rule was an enhancement of the abacus, and allowed for faster and more advanced calculations. The abacus was useful mainly for addition and subtraction, but it didn't enable the user to perform division and multiplication, as the slide rule does.

The slide rule also influenced one of the primary elements of how we interact today with a computer using a visual display:

When using a keyboard, your computer screen displays an indicator that shows where you can type in text (data in the form of letters and numbers). This indicator is called a cursor – it looks like this: |

This black bar (the cursor) usually flashes – appears and disappears.

As a note, people often mistake "pointers" for cursors. Pointers are the various symbols used to show where the mouse is on your screen. Here are some pointers:

Cursors actually date back to slide rules. On a slide rule, the cursor is a clear slide that marks the point of attention on the rule. Here is a picture of it:

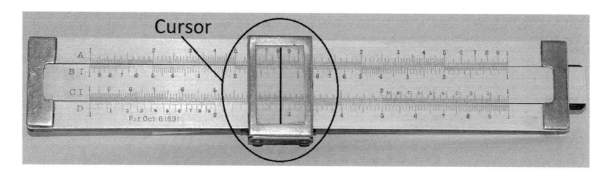

Cursor

SUMMARY:

The slide rule, allowing as it did for rapid performance of complex mathematical calculations, was a key tool in many scientific fields for hundreds of years, only falling out of use with the development of inexpensive electronic calculators that came later. It influenced the computer field in many ways, including inspiring the name for the cursor, the indicator to a computer user for where the focus is in the current program being used.

The next development wasn't in math but in an unrelated field.

CHAPTER 15:
PROGRAMMING MACHINES

"If you don't know history, then you don't know anything.
You are a leaf that doesn't know it's part of a tree."
-Michael Crichton (American author, 1942-2008)

In 1725, a French inventor named Basile Bouchon invented a way to control the operation of a loom (a machine that makes fabric) using perforated (pierced with holes) paper tape. This paper was used in an assembly (something composed of parts fitted together) that could be installed on a loom in order to automate certain parts of how the loom worked. This invention was later improved by another Frenchman, Joseph Jacquard.

The Bouchon loom looked like this:

It turns out that this was one of the most important developments influencing modern computers.

Here's some background on this:

Looms are used to create fabric. This fabric can then be turned into clothing, blankets, towels, etc.

Looms create fabric through a process called weaving. Weaving involves taking two sets of threads and interlacing them (crossing them together) to form one layer of fabric. You can see a simple illustration of that here:

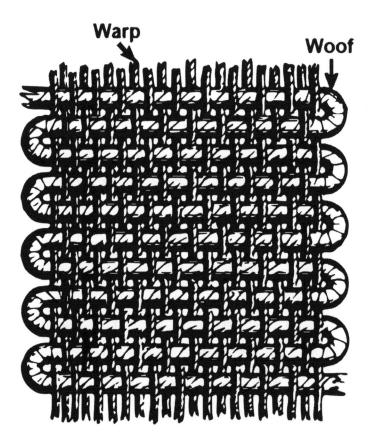

The threads that go back and forth are called the woof, and the threads that go up and down are called the warp.

You can see someone weaving by hand in the following picture:

Look at the warp threads (they run up and down). If you look closely, you can see that half of them are raised up, and there is a gap between them and the lower warp threads.

In hand weaving, to make a simple fabric, you would pull the woof thread through that gap, then reverse the warp threads (shift the ones that were above to below and vice versa), and then pull the woof thread through the new gap that was formed. This way you would produce an interlaced fabric like you saw in the simple illustration earlier.

A loom is just a machine that makes this work easier. Instead of a person's hands, a loom uses needles to control which warp threads get raised, and a small piece of smooth wood to pull the woof thread through the gap.

These needles typically have little hooks and look something like this:

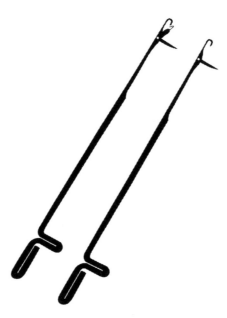

The needles were mounted at the top of the loom. There was one needle for each warp thread in the fabric you were making. Each needle could be set (using a lever, which is a handle used to operate part of a machine) to either lift a warp thread or not lift it.

The process of using a loom to make fabric was composed of doing the same thing over and over again:

1. Decide on the pattern of which warp threads should be raised,

2. Set the needles so that only those threads will rise,

3. Operate a lever to raise the selected warp threads, forming a gap,

4. Move the woof thread through the gap,

5. Move the lever back to its original position, bringing the warp threads back in line together.

Having a machine to help (the loom) made the work faster than doing it by hand, but it was still laborious work, and errors could easily be made in setting the needles up – which would then ruin the pattern you were trying to make in the fabric.

This is why the work Bouchon and Jacquard did was so important: It made the above process, which was repeated over and over again during weaving, much faster – and it also removed the possibility of error in setting up the needles for the desired design in the fabric.

Let's look at what Bouchon did along this line:

Bouchon's design used perforated (having holes) paper tape. This is also referred to as punched tape. A punch is a tool, usually a short metal rod, that is used to create holes in material. "Punched tape" is paper with holes punched (cut) in it. You can see punched tape in the first picture in this chapter (the photo of the Bouchon loom); it is the long roll of paper at the front of the loom.

Each hole in the punched tape matches up with a needle inside the loom. The holes instruct the loom whether or not to raise needles that exist inside the machine. So, depending on where you place the holes in the tape, the loom weaves differently.

The holes are read by a line of pins (short pieces of wood or metal) in the loom. Each of these pins is connected to a corresponding needle on the loom.

Here is where the magic happens:

When the pins are pressed against the tape, they are either blocked by the paper or allowed to go through. These pins then pass along the "data" to the corresponding needle (if a pin is inserted into a hole, the corresponding needle is raised).

The sequence is: data from the paper is passed to the pins, which are connected to the needles, which then control what thread is used and where it goes.

The issues with punched paper tape included that it was expensive to make, fragile and hard to repair.

In 1801, Joseph Jacquard invented a loom that used wooden cards with holes punched in them, called punch cards, to automatically weave fabric designs.

The holes in punch cards relay instructions to machines, depending on their placement and/or shape (just like punched tape).

The punch cards invented by Joseph Jacquard looked like this:

Here is a Jacquard loom:

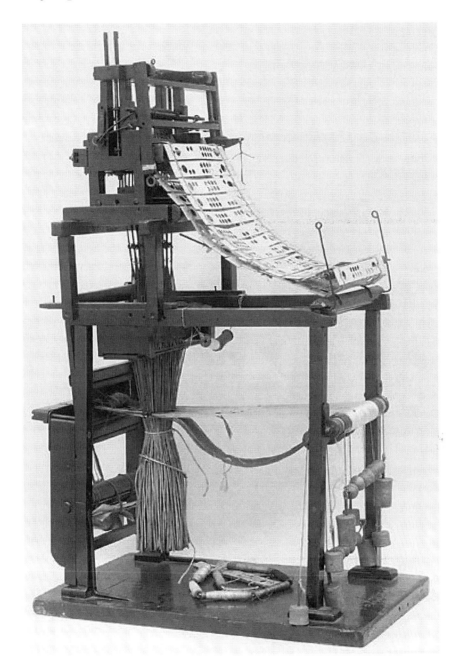

The chain of punch cards in Jacquard's loom were connected together in a sequence. You can see these punch cards in the pictures above (they are the rectangular pieces at the front of the loom that are connected together like a ladder).

Each card had rows of holes punched in it. The holes in the cards matched up with hooks (needles) on the loom. These hooks each raised or lowered a part of the machine that carried and guided thread.

The hooks would be raised or lowered depending on whether or not the corresponding hole was punched. The sequence of lowered and raised threads created the pattern.

The differences between the punched tape created by Bouchon and Jacquard's punch cards were:

1. Jacquard's punch cards automated nearly the entire process of weaving with a loom, whereas the punched tape only partially automated part of setting up a loom.

2. Compared to punched tape, the punch cards were cheaper to make and more durable, and so allowed for a higher level of efficiency.

Now, we just covered a lot of data about weaving and looms, and it's actually not that important to understand those concepts. What's important in this chapter is that machines can be automated using punch cards.

Jacquard's invention was important because early digital computers would use similar punch cards. In fact, the whole idea of a computer operating on "true or false," "one or zero," "on or off" directly corresponds to the Jacquard loom's punch card – if there is a hole, that's a "true" - raise the needle. If there isn't, that's a "false" – don't raise the needle. That is pretty much exactly how computers work, as you'll learn more about later in this book.

SUMMARY:

The invention of the Jacquard loom is huge as far as the development of computers goes – after all, early computers used the exact same device (punched cards) to control the data being entered into computers. But the true value of the Jacquard loom lies in its use as a learning tool – in it, in the physical universe you can see the basic purpose of a computer playing out in front of you:

1. Take in data (press rods against the current punch card, causing the needles to be positioned according to the desired pattern),

2. Process the data (pull the lever on the loom, raising up the desired warp threads, and move the woof thread between them),

3. Move on to the next set of data (return the lever to its original position, causing the thread needles to reset and moving the next punch card into position to be used),

4. Repeat those three steps, over and over, until fabric is complete,

5. Send out data (deliver fabric, with the desired pattern).

The next invention was another step forward in the development of computers.

CHAPTER 16:
MATH AND SWITCHES

"When you have mastered numbers, you will in fact no longer be reading numbers, any more than you read words when reading books. You will be reading meanings."
-W.E.B. Dubois (American historian, 1868-1963)

In 1820, a Frenchman named Charles Xavier Thomas invented a tool for doing math called the arithmometer – "arithmetic" (addition, subtraction, multiplication and division) + "meter" (measuring tool).

The arithmometer was the first digital mechanical calculator to be used on a wide scale and it looked like this:

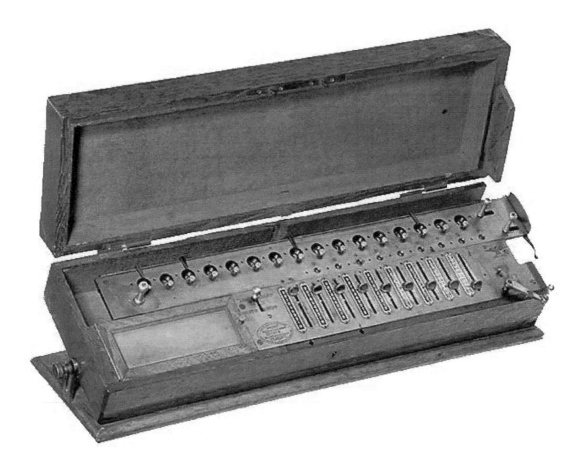

It consisted of switches, levers, gears and axles (a rod that runs through the center of a wheel or gear). Here is what it looks like on the inside:

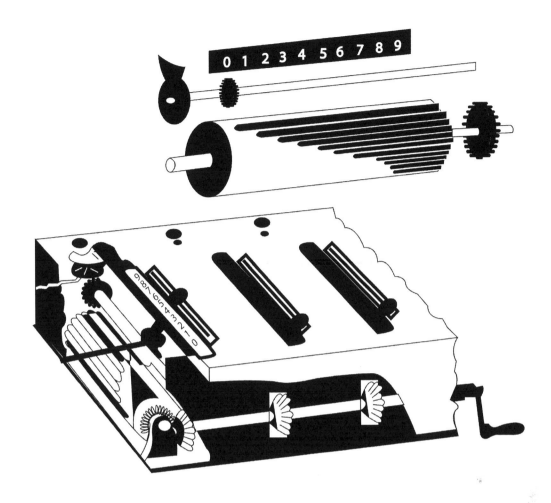

Each number lever has a corresponding line etched onto rods inside the machine. Based on selections made, you turned the crank until the gear stopped on the appropriate number(s).

For example: you could set one lever to 2, another lever to 3, and another lever to add (+). Then you crank the lever until it stops turning and the internal mechanism would cause a 5 button to pop up.

The arithmometer was a machine that performed math, and as such, is an ancestor of the modern computer.

SUMMARY:

Original computers were basically calculators and so, as the first mechanical calculator, the arithmometer made modern computers possible.

Contemporary computers aren't operated by using a lever, so let's look at the next development that affected computer design and operation.

CHAPTER 17:
FIRST ELECTRIC MOTOR

"The engine is the heart of an airplane,
but the pilot is its soul."
-Walter Raleigh (English professor, 1861-1922)

A motor is another word for engine. It is a machine, especially one powered by electricity or internal combustion (operated by heat), that produces motion for a vehicle or some other device with moving parts.

In 1821, a year after the invention of the arithmometer, a British Scientist named Michael Faraday constructed the first operational electric motor, which looked like this:

Using electricity, he was able to move the wire in the glass around. This was a major development because most modern computers have electric motors.

SUMMARY:

Modern computers run on electricity and so without the invention of this electric motor, computers as we know them today might not exist.

Now that brings us to the first computer design.

CHAPTER 18:
LOGIC

"Numbers are masters of the weak,
but the slaves of the strong."
-Charles Babbage (English mathematician, 1791-1871)

In 1822, an English mathematician named Charles Babbage began designing a machine that automatically performed mathematical operations. He is considered by some to be the "father of computers" because some modern computer components and designs are based on his work.

One of his inventions was the Difference Engine – an automatic calculator. In fact, his "Difference Engine No 1" (pictured below) was the first successful automatic calculator design:

Sadly, the machines he designed were never fully built during his lifetime – but in 2002 (after 17 years of work) construction of one of his machines was fully completed in London. And guess what? It worked! This meant his designs were correct.

The computer pictured above has 8,000 parts, weighs five tons and is 11 feet long. It can display letters and numbers!

Charles Babbage designed computers that would operate off of instructions on punch cards, following the principles invented by Joseph Marie Jacquard. In 1836, Charles Babbage wrote 24 programs for one of his computers, making him the first computer programmer in history.

Babbage's machines were made mainly of gears and were designed to use steam for the energy to move the gears and other moving parts. This meant using the force of steam from boiling water to move the parts of the machine. Babbage also designed them so they could be operated using cranks turned by people. A crank is a rotating lever that can be turned around and around using an attached handle (you can see cranks on the sides of the computer pictured above).

The punch cards worked by having rows of locations where there *could* be a hole. When a card was inserted into the machine, the machine would check each one of those available spots to see if a hole was present or not. Using this, data could be entered into the machine.

For example: let's say there was a potential for 10 holes in a row on a punch card. The 10 locations in that row could represent the numbers 0 through 9 as you moved from left to right.

If we wanted to represent the number 3, we would punch a hole in the fourth location from the left – remember, the first location would represent the number zero.

Here is a diagram of that example:

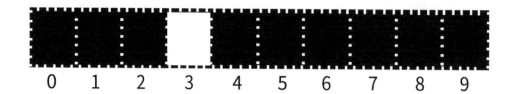

The location in each row of the punch cards inserted in Babbage's machine each corresponded to a rod inside the machine. These rods were in a row as well.

As the machine was operated, these rods would be pushed against the punch card. When a rod couldn't pass through the card (due to no hole to push through), the rod would move a lever (a switch that operates something inside a machine). These levers controlled which gears turned and which didn't. Based on this movement, numbers could be represented. A component or machine that can read (process) punch cards as described in this paragraph is called a punch card reader.

Here is a type of punch card reader (you can see the little rods poking through the holes in the punch card):

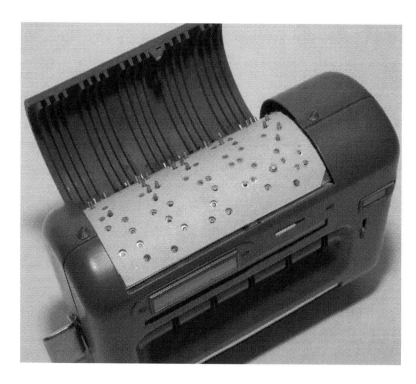

Another very important aspect of how these machines worked is this: The machine would only handle one row on the punch card at a time. It worked basically like this:

1. The card would be put into the machine, and a lever would move it forward so that the first row of holes was ready to be checked.

2. Then another lever would move the row of rods against the row on the card, effectively entering the information that was on the card into the machine.

3. Then the first lever would move the card forward again so the next row was ready to be checked, and so on.

In other words, this machine only did one thing at a time, and had to be directed one step at a time what to do. Modern computers are the same, as you will see.

These first computer designs included "memory" – which consisted of gears which were locked in a certain position to "store" numbers. Depending on which gear was turned and how far, a number was stored. For an example: if a gear is turned three notches (each of the ridges in a gear is a notch), that could be "3."

The machine also had a central set of gears which supervised and controlled the rest of the mechanism. This main set of gears could be considered the machine's "central processing unit" – they controlled all of the other gears in the machine. We will describe a modern central processing unit in further detail later in this book, but simply put, it is the main part of the computer that performs calculations and controls the various parts of the computer.

Like modern computers, you input data (in this case, using punch cards), the machine processed the data (executed commands), and output data (some action and/or data comes out the other end). The intended output for Babbage's original computers was a basic printer.

SUMMARY:

The "difference engine" from Charles Babbage was a really important development. Even though his machine was never constructed in his lifetime, key aspects of its design are still part of modern computers:

- Data was represented by the presence or absence of a physical thing – a hole in a punch card. In modern computers, the presence or absence of an electrical signal is used to represent data.

- The machine took in data one piece at a time, operated on that data and didn't move on to the next piece of data until directed to. In modern computers, only one operation is done at a time, and the computer needs an internal device to direct it to perform the next operation.

The next development was a key element in eventually building Babbage's machines and is used in modern computers.

CHAPTER 19:
RELAYS

"What is a soul?
It's like electricity – we don't really know what it is,
but it's a force that can light a room."
-Ray Charles (American musician, 1930-2004)

In 1835, an American scientist named Joseph Henry invented the relay – a switch controlled by electricity. Here, a switch means "a device that controls the flow of electricity" – think of a light switch. When the switch is in a position that allows electricity to flow, the switch is "on"; when the switch is positioned to stop electricity from flowing, the switch is "off."

You can think of a switch as a gate – if it's open, things can move through the gate; if it's closed, they can't.

What Henry did in creating the relay was make it so a person didn't need to physically move a switch in order to turn it on or off. Instead, they could use electricity itself to make the switch move. In other words, they could use electricity to control the flow of electricity, by remote control.

The relay looked like this:

This same year an English inventor named Edward Davy also invented a relay in his electric telegraph (a machine that sent messages over long distances by making and breaking electronic connections). Telegraph machines use Morse code (a code for representing letters through combinations of light or sound signals). Here is what a telegraph looked like:

Considering that the bits in computers (which can be on or off) are technically relays, this is a major development on the timeline of computers!

Here's how these first relays relate to modern computers:

A relay has *two* electrical signals it cares about:

1. The actual electric signal that is being controlled, and

2. The electrical signal that tells whether to open or close the switch.

The first electricity is what is doing the actual work we care about (turning a light on and off, for example); the second electricity is used just to change whether the first electricity is allowed to flow or not.

In a modern computer, as we covered earlier, very small devices are used to represent a binary digit – a "bit." The way these devices work to do that is simple: Electricity can go into them and out of them on very thin metal wires, and the device controls whether or not electricity flows from the input wire to the output wire. If it does, that represents a binary digit of 1. If electricity doesn't flow, that represents a binary digit of 0.

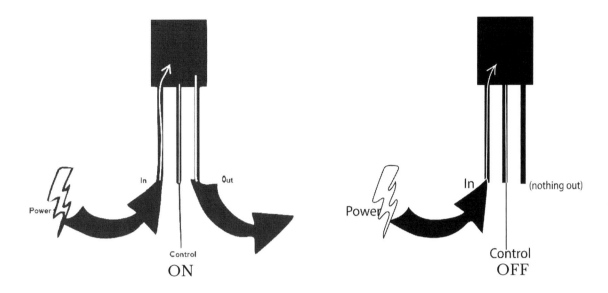

ON   OFF

In other words, each of these devices is essentially a switch.

And guess what? Each of these tiny devices has another electrical signal, coming in on a third small wire, that controls the operation of the device. If electricity is present on *that* wire, the device lets electricity pass through and you have a binary digit of 1. If electricity isn't present on that wire, the device doesn't let electricity pass and you have a binary digit of 0.

That wire, that controls the device, is even called the "gate" wire (the "control" in the pictures above).

So this development of the switch was key in the development of computers.

SUMMARY:

Being able to control the flow of electricity without having a human being move a physical device, but instead control it from a remote distance, was a huge scientific development and helped in the creation of many new technologies. It was key in the development of modern computers, though, because it allows us to make physical machines that rely on the presence or absence of an electrical signal to represent data, and to control that electricity without the need for a person to operate a device.

Men weren't the only people to assist in the development of modern technology. Women have been *vital*. If Charles Babbage was the father of computers, who was the mother?

CHAPTER 20:
FIRST FEMALE PROGRAMMER

"What is imagination?...
It is a God-like, a noble faculty (mental ability).
It renders Earth tolerable;
it teaches us to live, in the tone of the eternal."
-Ada Lovelace (English mathematician, 1815-1852)

In 1833, an English mathematician named Ada Lovelace met Charles Babbage. Babbage had invited her to see an early design for his Difference Engine. She was fascinated with it and in 1842 ended up writing her own computer program. You can see a copy of the original here:

Her program was designed to run on one of Babbage's computers – it accurately calculated a sequence of numbers.

Though she is sometimes referred to as the first person to ever write a computer program, that isn't technically accurate because Babbage had written programs about seven years before. But while Babbage's programs were found to have some errors in them, Ada's code was verified as being able to operate flawlessly – when actual Difference Engines were eventually constructed from Babbage's design, Ada's code was tested on Babbage's computer and her program ran correctly with no errors. So, in truth, Ada *was* the first computer programmer to write a perfect program.

She was also one of the first to view computers as more than just a calculator. She even mentioned the possibility of using computers to create art and music.

One of her inventions includes the "loop" – a sequence of instructions that are continually repeated until an exact condition is achieved. A loop works this way:

First, a series of instructions is created that is intended to be performed repetitively.

Second, a condition is defined that will mean that the series of instructions can stop being performed.

Finally, the loop is started – the series of actions is done, and the condition is checked.

If the condition is met, the loop ends – that series of instructions is no longer performed.

If the condition is not met, the series of instructions is performed again.

This is something we do in life all the time, though we may not think of it the same way. For example, let's say you are washing dishes. You have a set series of actions you take to wash a dish. This real-world "loop" could go like this:

1. Scrape excess food in the garbage.

2. Wash the dish with warm soapy water.

3. Rinse the dish in warm clean water.

4. Place the dish on a drying rack.

While doing the dishes, you would repeat this series of actions over and over until you were "done." Typically, this would be when you have no more dirty dishes to wash. So, this is basically a loop – the steps to wash a dish are your series of instructions, and "no more dirty dishes" is your condition for no longer repeating the loop.

Loops are used very often in computer programs. Here, a loop is where a certain set of instructions are performed by a computer program, then the program checks to see if it has reached the condition required for completion. If not, it starts over and repeats the set of instructions. If so, it exits the loop and moves on to the next consecutive instruction in the computer program.

In Ada Lovelace's program, she arranged operations into groups that could be repeated – the first computer loops in history.

Loops are another example of the difference between humans and machines because if you don't tell the computer when to stop the loop, it will continue looping (repeating) forever. Loops that incessantly repeat are called "infinite loops." Computers have to have every step, including "begin" and "end," spelled out to them. A person would lose their mind adding 1 forever, but computers are machines – they have no mind, and cannot feel. Again, they are inanimate objects made up of plastic, metal, electricity, etc.

SUMMARY:

Ada Lovelace is justifiably revered as one of the most influential figures in the history of the computer. Not only did she break down gender barriers in the male-dominated field of scientific research, but her breakthroughs in some of the core principles of computing laid the foundation for work done nearly a century later when electronic computers became a reality. She has been honored in many ways, not the least of which was the creation of a computer language called "Ada."

One of the important functions of a computer is to keep records. How did that become possible?

CHAPTER 21:
RECORDS

*"Somebody was trying to tell me that CDs are better than vinyl (records)
because they don't have any surface noise.
I said, 'Listen, mate, life has surface noise.'"*
-John Peel (English DJ, 1939-2004)

A "phonograph record" (also called "vinyl record," "record" or "vinyl") is a thin, plastic disk that carries recorded sound.

"Phono-" means "sound" or "voice" and -graph means a "record," "writing" or "drawing."

Vinyl is a type of plastic and records are made out of it.

Waves are a flow of energy that have low points and high points. They come in all sorts of types, patterns, and sizes. Energy moves through space in waves. They look like this:

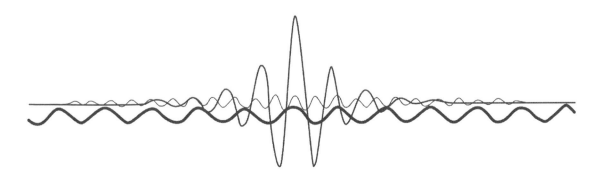

Music consists of waves of pressure moving through the air. Your ears "feel" these pressures and you hear them as sounds.

You can actually feel big waves (loud volume, in other words) of lower pitch (quality of sound), like a bass guitar or bass drum, as the pressure pushes and pulls on your chest.

If you are standing next to a drum set and someone kicks the "kick drum" (the largest drum on a drum set; it is hit by a hammer when the player taps their foot on a pedal), what you feel and hear is just a motion of air back and forth which then moves your eardrums. The sound itself is analog (natural and continuous).

Recording music, then, is capturing those constantly changing waves on some sort of a physical object so the waves can be re-created later.

The continuous groove in a record is actually the shape of this wave, cut into the vinyl material. Any small object that is moved along that groove will move in the same wave pattern as the music that was recorded earlier. You can take the movement of that object and use it to produce the sound waves of the original recording.

You can actually place any little pin, held in your fingers, on a spinning record and you will hear the song faintly. Tape that pin to a cone of paper, and you'll hear it clearly! What is happening is that, as the needle moves in waves (because of the groove), those waves are transferred to the paper cone. Those waves move through the paper, and the waves become larger and larger as they approach the large open end of the cone. That cone makes the air vibrate in the same waves, which reach your ear and you can hear the sound clearly.

The pin is not a magical computer; it's just a stick of metal. There is no system here that deals with numbers – the groove in the record is just a direct, mechanical impression of the original recorded sound. The sound that comes from this is a representation of the physical form of the groove in the record, just as the groove is a copy of the actual sound that was being created by a band when the record was being recorded.

In 1857, a Frenchman named Leon Scott created the phonautograph ("phono" meaning "sound," and "autograph" meaning "self-written"). This machine recorded sound waves on pieces of paper. His intention was to use these for visual analysis – not for playing back sound. It looked like this:

In the 2000s some engineers decided to try to play these phonautograph recordings and they played sound – the sound that was originally recorded back in the 19th century!

Also in 1857, an American inventor named Thomas Edison came up with the phonograph – a machine that could both record *and* play back sound. It looks like this:

SUMMARY:

Throughout history people have, for various reasons, tried recording things that happen in the physical universe so they can be used later. The early machines and technology created to record sound signals for later use led not just to exciting products, but to technology for recording data for later use in computers. And without the ability to do work with data stored for later use, computers would only have limited value. They would just be complex calculators, only able to work on data that had to be entered into them all over again every time the work needed to be done.

Remember punch cards, like the ones used in looms? The next technological development put them to use in a new way.

CHAPTER 22:
COUNTING MACHINE

"A businessman is a hybrid of a dancer and a calculator."
-Paul Valery (French poet, 1871-1945)

In 1890, an American inventor named Herman Hollerith created the tabulating machine ("tabulate" means to count or list). This machine ran off electricity and used punch cards to calculate the U.S. census (population count). The tabulating machine looked like this:

Prior to the creation of this machine, census data was counted by hand. With this machine available to the government, the population data taken down by census workers would be stored as punched holes on paper cards.

This machine would read those punch cards and store the numbers it read on a component called an accumulator. The accumulator would pass the data along to a display that the user could view to read the numbers. This made the census work much faster and more accurate.

Modern computers have accumulators that store data that's currently being processed by the computer.

Herman Hollerith established the company that would later become IBM (International Business Machines Corporation) – one of the top computer companies on Earth.

SUMMARY:

Punched cards had already proven valuable in storing data for the weaving industry – the holes (or lack of them) represented a pattern for the creation of woven goods. With the advent of Hollerith's census machine, punch cards held numerical data and brought us closer to a reliable method for inputting numerical data into an electronic computer.

We're getting close to having all of the technologies needed for modern computers. Some of the most important work, however, didn't involve physical technology – instead, it dealt with the thought behind what computers would be like and the kind of behavior we could build into them.

CHAPTER 23:
THE TEST

*"Sometimes it is the people no one can imagine anything of
who do the things no one can imagine."*
-Alan Turing (English mathematician, 1912-1954)

In 1936, an English mathematician named Alan Turing published a paper about a machine (called the Turing machine). His paper covered the idea that the Turing machine, which was a computer, could solve any problem that could be described by simple instructions written on paper tape. The basic idea was that a machine could execute tasks written as programs.

The machine Turing described could not actually be constructed at the time, due to limitations of available technology. Had it been constructed, the Turing machine would have looked something like this:

The theoretical machine Turing described would use a paper tape of infinite length – so obviously an actual Turing machine could not be constructed.

So, why was this valuable, considering an actual machine as described in his work couldn't even be made?

It has to do with *what* this machine was doing with that tape. On the tape would be symbols that represented built-in instructions – one symbol after another. The tape would move one symbol at a time into the machine. The machine would read the symbol, look up what instruction it represented, and perform an action based on that instruction.

Modern computers operate off the basic concepts covered in his paper, i.e. the computer is provided with executable instructions and performs them.

The Turing machine operated off of the same basic principles as the Jacquard loom (the programmable weaving machine) in that it read where there were holes in the tape and, based off of the placement of holes, performed instructions. Each unique pattern of holes represented one symbol.

Alan Turing had many other notable accomplishments in his life, including development of the Turing Test in 1950. This test consisted of testing two subjects (one human and one computer) to determine which was the computer. A human tester observed both of their responses to written questions without being able to observe which answers came from a human and which from a computer. If a computer "passed the Turing test," it meant that it couldn't be distinguished from a human.

Questions like "How did you feel during your first kiss?," "What was the most emotional moment in your life?," "What's the last food you ate that caused you brain freeze?" or "Is the other one I am questioning a computer?" are examples of questions from a Turing test.

SUMMARY:

Being able to enter numerical data into a computer is important, of course. But it's even more important to be able to enter instructions into a computer that tell it what to *do* with the data it's been given. Alan Turing's work on the principles behind a machine that could be given a set of pre-built instructions and then given a series of those instructions to perform was extremely valuable.

The next development actually made building these various computer designs possible.

CHAPTER 24:
SPEEDING IT UP

*"Once a new technology rolls over you, if you're not part of the steamroller,
you're part of the road."*
–Stewart Brand (American writer, 1938-)

A major step forward for electronics occurred in 1904, when an electrical engineer named John Ambrose Fleming invented the vacuum tube.

A vacuum tube is basically a relay. A relay is a switch controlled by electricity. As a reminder, a switch is simply a device that controls the flow of electricity.

A vacuum tube consists of a relay inside a glass tube that has had all the air removed from it. They are used to control the flow of electricity, like any relay. Here are some various vacuum tubes:

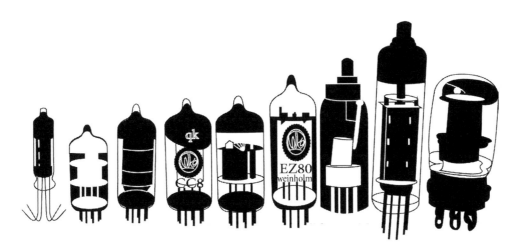

Vacuum tubes ranged from about ½ inch to a little over three feet in height.

Vacuum tubes solved a major problem with relays. Earlier relays controlled the flow of electricity through the physical movement of thin pieces of metal. Not only can these pieces of metal wear out over time, but they can only switch so fast, as they are dependent on the actual piece of metal moving through space. Even early computers required the ability to turn electrical signals on and off very rapidly. These early relays were not up to the task.

What was needed was a way to control the flow of electricity by having it move through space between two different points, without any moving parts.

The vacuum tube has two metal parts inside that are separated by empty space, and the flow of electricity between those two points can be controlled. If the tube were filled with air, the metal pieces would rapidly get destroyed, as electricity interacts with the elements (substances that cannot be broken down into smaller substances) in the air in a way that degrades metal over time. Instead, all the air is removed from the tube (that's why it's called a vacuum tube – a vacuum is a space where there is no air). That way the metal parts inside can last for a long time before they wear out.

This new invention, the vacuum tube, allowed for the controlled flow of electricity. Vacuum tubes acted as switches inside the computer and could turn on and off much faster than the switches that came before.

Through combinations of these "ons" and "offs" in vacuum tubes, binary could be represented and thereby computer logic.

You can see vacuum tubes inside a computer here:

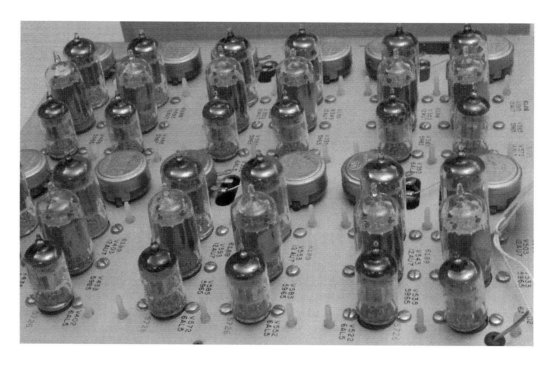

Electricity flowed through vacuum tubes like this:

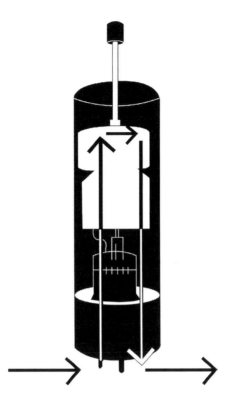

As a note: we will be covering exactly how, through the use of a series of "ons" and "offs," computers can perform actions (such as counting, displaying pictures, playing sound, etc. – the wide array of functions modern computers perform) later on in this book. One step at a time!

One of the characteristics of the vacuum tube is that it contained an automatic relay (a switch that controls the flow of electrical current without direct human contact). The relay that we spoke of earlier was invented in 1835 and required human contact to operate, i.e. a person had to push a button or flip a switch – the automatic relay performs these actions automatically (without manual contact).

The automatic switches inside vacuum tubes are called control grids. The control grid acted as a "door" (gate) that let electricity flow through it or stopped the flow. You can see this pictured here:

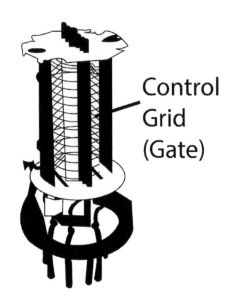

Control
Grid
(Gate)

The control grid either prevented electricity from passing on or let it pass through, i.e. it could be on or off depending on instructions given).

SUMMARY:

One of the most basic principles we use to create computers is the idea that, by controlling whether or not electricity is flowing, we can control the computer's operation and the data it uses. This is represented variously as "on/off," "true/false," "one/zero," etc. However, in the physical universe, all we're doing is controlling the flow of electricity.

Because of this, devices that control whether or not electricity flows are very important in computers and some of the most important advances in the field have come about when someone figures out a better device for that purpose. We have come from mechanical switches through to vacuum tubes that all come down to controlling whether electricity flows or not.

One of the downsides to vacuum tubes was that they would occasionally burn out and need to be replaced. It took about 15 minutes to replace one vacuum tube. An upgrade was needed...

CHAPTER 25:
A MAJOR UPGRADE

*"If everything seems under control,
you're not going fast enough."*
-Mario Andretti (Italian racing driver, 1940-)

In 1947, an upgrade to vacuum tubes happened when a research and development company called Bell Labs invented the transistor.

A "transistor" is a device that can alter the flow of electricity in a machine. It can let electricity flow through it, it can stop the flow of electricity, or it can increase the flow of electricity. In other words, it is basically a switch (device that regulates the flow of electricity). Here is what the first one looked like:

Transistors perform the same function of vacuum tubes, except better.

You can liken the flow of electricity in a computer to water through a hose. Imagine folding a garden hose to stop the flow of water, partially unfolding it to allow some through and unfolding it all the way to allow the water flow freely – the "folding action" is like what the transistor does to an electrical flow.

The transistor was a solid-state (having no moving parts) switch, and lasted much longer than vacuum tubes. They were a major advancement in computers. While the first transistor was about 3 ½ inches (about the size of the average palm), they quickly became smaller and smaller – they had them down to about a centimeter in the 1950s.

The smaller you can get the pieces, the closer you can place them together, which speeds up computer operations due to less space needing to be traveled by the electricity inside the machine. It also allows for fitting more components inside the machine.

There are many different types of transistors, each of which is created for one purpose or another. Here are some various types of transistors:

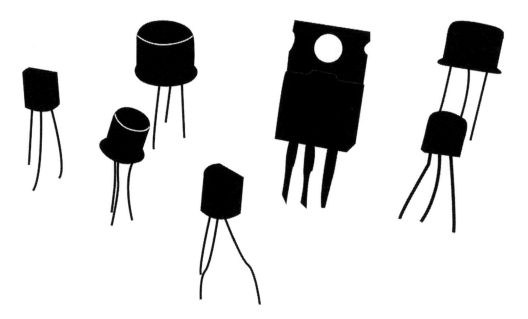

Transistors nowadays often look like this:

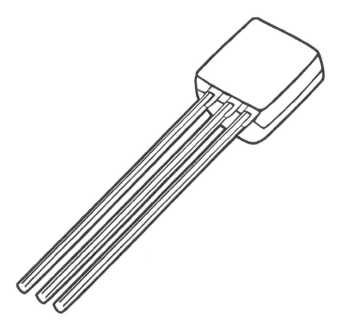

You may have noticed that these look exactly like the bit we mentioned earlier in the book. That's because this *is* a bit! The transistor (bit) can be on or off, as indicated by 1 or 0 in the computer.

Transistors of the type used in computers can now be created that are so small they can't be seen without a magnifying glass. And so, they have gotten these transistors down to microscopic sizes and there are billions-trillions of these in a computer.

SUMMARY:

Transistors were an improvement upon vacuum tubes for several reasons, including:

1. **They are smaller,**

2. **They are more durable and last longer,**

3. **They operate faster.**

So what are the different combinations of computer transistors called?

CHAPTER 26:
GATES

"It's supposed to be automatic, but actually you have to push this button. "
-John Brunner (British author, 1934-1995)

Remember Boolean logic (true or false) and its associated logic operations that we talked about earlier in this book? As a reminder, Boolean operations included the concepts of AND and OR (for example: "if you are tired AND you have a bed: sleep in the bed" or "if mattress OR couch is present: sleep on whichever is closer"). AND means that both of the options must be true for the answer to be true, while OR means that one or both of the options must be true for the answer to be true.

There is a way to represent these operations in physical form. This is done with logic "gates." Note that this is a different use of the word "gate" than the gate inside of a transistor (electronic components that can either be "on" [pass electricity] or "off" [block/hold electricity]) that controls whether that particular transistor is passing electricity or not.

A logic gate is a switch composed of transistors that are connected so they have one or more points that take in data ("inputs"), and one point that puts out data ("output"). There are various kinds of gates; each one implements a particular type of Boolean logic operation. It is called a gate because it opens or shuts the flow of electricity.

An AND gate is created with two inputs and one output. These inputs are actually small metal wires. If both the first two inputs are on (meaning electricity is present at both of the input wires), then the output is on (meaning electricity flows from the output wire). Here is a diagram of how the AND gate works, using light switches to illustrate what is happening (think of the light switches below as transistors – the top switch AND the bottom switch must be on [true] for the light to be on [true]):

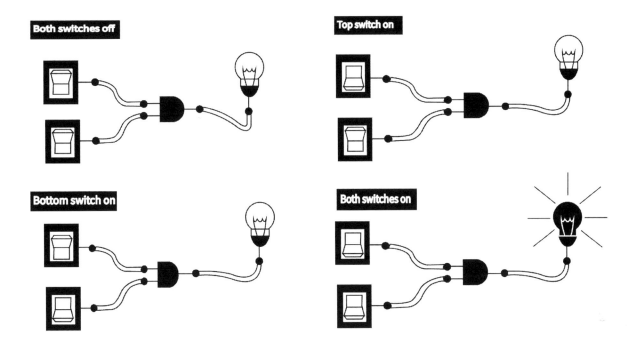

Each type of gate has its own symbol. The symbol for an AND gate is:

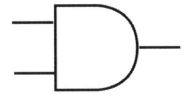

This symbol represents real items in the physical universe.

In this picture, the two lines on the left leading up to the center (inputs), and the line on the right leading away (output), represent wires. The part that looks like a letter "D" represents the collection of transistors that are arranged in such a way that they operate according to a Boolean "AND" operation.

The symbol for an OR gate is:

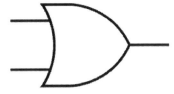

These symbols are only being shown in case you've come across them before or if you may see them in the future.

Here is a diagram showing how OR gates work (the wires are marked as "ON" or "OFF" to show whether or not electricity is present).

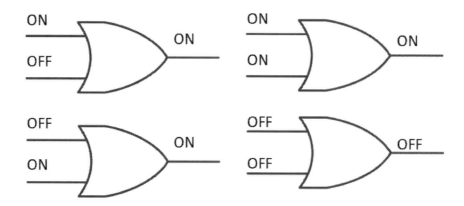

As you can see, gates pass or block electrical flow based on the flows coming in. The OR gate consists of three wires – each of these wires is a bit. Reminder: a bit is a "binary digit" – it has only two possible states: "on" (1) or "off" (0). Through complicated combinations of gates and bits programmed to either 1 or 0, computers can perform advanced actions.

To give you an idea, there are around 65,000,000 (sixty-five million) bits used to represent the average song in a digital form. What this means is that there are that many 1s and 0s behind one song. These are stored by the computer with that many components inside the computer being on or off (meaning in the case of a 65,000,000 bit song, it takes 65,000,000 dedicated transistors to store that song). We will get into further detail on how this works later, but for now, back to gates.

Tables are sets of figures or data displayed in an organized way. "Truth tables" are mathematical tables used in Boolean logic. They lay out the possible inputs for a logic gate, along with their corresponding output.

Here is a truth table for an AND gate. Note: INPUT A refers to the first wire in the gate – top left line in earlier pictures. INPUT B refers to the second wire – bottom left line in earlier pictures. OUTPUT refers to the wire on the right. False = off and true = on:

INPUT A	INPUT B	OUTPUT
FALSE	FALSE	FALSE
FALSE	TRUE	FALSE

TRUE	FALSE	FALSE
TRUE	TRUE	TRUE

(AND gate truth table)

Feel free to compare the truth tables in this chapter with the earlier symbols for each gate.

Now that you have a basic idea of how gates work, what use do they have in computers?

Well, let's say you want to use a gate to determine which students passed an exam. We'll set the failing grade at 69% (meaning, to pass, the student had to have gotten at least 70% of the questions right). Additionally, let's say the other aspect of the passing standard is whether or not the student submitted the exam on time (students who turned in their exam past the deadline automatically fail).

We can use an AND gate to see who passed (70% or higher) and who failed (69% or less). The truth table would look like this (in this case, false = no, and true = yes – reminder: > means "greater than"):

INPUT A: Submitted on time?	INPUT B: Grade > 69%?	OUTPUT: Pass?
FALSE	FALSE	FALSE
TRUE	FALSE	FALSE
FALSE	TRUE	FALSE
TRUE	TRUE	TRUE

There are other gates besides AND and OR, but they aren't necessary knowledge for the purposes of this book.

We can use these gates to form combinations of bits being on or off that instruct computers to "make decisions" based on data entered.

SUMMARY:

Now that we have tiny transistors that can control whether electricity flows or not, we can start to arrange them in combinations that implement Boolean

logic. Since Boolean logic is the main tool used to make a computer make "decisions" based on the data it is given, it's a pretty important concept.

Now that we know what gates are and the role that transistors play in them, what is the "secret ingredient" in transistors that made this all possible?

CHAPTER 27:
MAGIC SAND

"A basic truth that the history of the creation of the transistor reveals is that the foundations of transistor electronics were created by making errors and following hunches that failed to give what was expected."
-William Shockley (American inventor, 1910-1989)

Silicon is a very common material. Most sand is small pieces of silicon. Large chunks of silicon can be created by heating up sand. It looks like this:

Silicon has many uses. For example: it can be used to make glass.

But there is an important aspect to silicon that brought about a major enhancement in computers: Silicon can be modified so that its physical structure can be switched between two states when you heat it up or cool it down. This modification of silicon is accomplished just by adding a small amount of another metal to the silicon.

A "conductor" is a material that allows electricity to pass through in a relatively unhindered fashion – examples of conductors are metal and water. The opposite of a conductor is an insulator – something that stops the flow of electricity. Examples of insulators are rubber and glass.

A semiconductor is a material that operates at a level between that of a conductor and an insulator. In the case of silicon, it is a semiconductor because when you heat it up, it changes to a conductor, now passing electricity (1; on); when you cool it down, it becomes an insulator, now stopping the flow of electricity (0; off).

We use a small amount of electricity to warm the silicon up – remember, when electricity flows through materials, that material warms up. And it works the other way – when we remove the electricity from the silicon, it cools down.

And so, silicon can act as a physical representation of binary. When electricity is applied to it = on (1). When electricity is reduced/taken away = off (0). To function this way, silicon has to be put through a chemical process first but this process has been mastered and it is relatively affordable.

The fact that silicon's physical structure can be changed back and forth between two states, just by applying a small amount of electricity to it, makes it very useful in making the tiny parts of a computer.

Again, by increasing the temperature of a semiconductor (i.e. heating up the silicon slightly), more electricity passes through it. The reverse happens if you decrease the temperature.

Due to the fact that transistors contain silicon, they are semiconductors.

Semiconductors are also used in chips. "Chip" is short for "microchip" – "micro" meaning "small" and "chip" meaning "small piece." They look like this:

Chips are tiny electrical circuits (paths of electricity). They contain transistors (small devices that alter the flow of electricity), which are made of silicon. The transistors are placed inside chips, and some chips can fit billions. There are many types of chips but they all share the same basic function of handling different operations in a computer using electricity.

If we put a chip under a microscope, we may see transistors that look like this:

The placement of these transistors make up the complex gates that we covered earlier in the book, and allows the computer to store and process large amounts of data.

Chips can store data and execute instructions. There are different types of chips and you'll learn about the most-used in this book.

The first chip was created by American engineer Jack St. Clair Kilby and American physicist Robert Norton Noyce in 1958. It looked like this:

Semiconductors (transistors containing silicon) and chips are used in modern computers.

SUMMARY:

Even as the early computers were being developed, we knew we needed tiny, long-lasting switches, with no moving parts, that could be used to represent the "on/off," "true/false," "1/0" that a digital computer would utilize to represent both data and the instructions for what to do with that data. The discovery of how to modify silicon to become a semiconductor was a huge leap forward in this area, and made the modern computer possible. As they became smaller and smaller, they enabled us to create computers that were smaller and faster. Eventually, we learned how to create chips with many tiny transistors on them. These chips contained transistors that enabled the storage of data and instructions.

So, what is the most important chip in a computer?

CHAPTER 28:
THE COMPUTER'S BRAIN

"A computer once beat me at chess,
but it was no match for me at kickboxing."
-Emo Philips (American comedian, 1956-)

The "brain" of a computer is its central processing unit (CPU). It is the part of the computer that controls all the actions the computer does. The modern CPU is a chip that contains billions of transistors (bits). It looks like this:

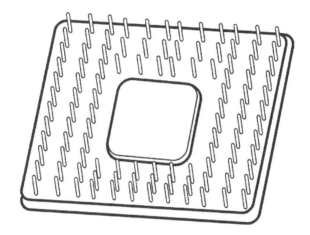

Most CPUs have a set of built-in "instructions" in them (transistors set in various permanent combinations of "on" and "off"). These instructions define the various actions the CPU can take – actions like taking in data from a keyboard, storing data in the computer, sending data to a display, etc.

CPUs are also called processors. The basic job of all processors is to execute various combinations of those simple instructions built into them. It only ever performs one of these instructions at a time, but (as mentioned earlier) modern computers can perform billions of instructions per second.

All actions you can make a computer do are composed of various combinations of the actions built into its CPU.

Here's an example of how a CPU operates: if you have a list of students in a computer file and you give the computer an instruction to put the list in alphabetical order, it is the CPU that receives your instruction, performs the analysis, puts the list in a new order, and then tells your screen to display the results.

The CPU is one of the main parts that affects the speed of your computer – the newer and better the CPU is, the faster your computer performs.

The first CPU was developed by Intel (the largest computer parts manufacturer in the world) and released to the public in 1971. It was called Intel 4004 and looked like this:

This brings us back to the basic functions of a computer: take in data, change it, and output data. There are all kinds of data we might want to use with computers – numbers, letters, images, videos, etc.

A computer can work with those kinds of data, and many others – but the data has to be in a form that computers can take in, work with and send on to other devices.

As we've covered, computers actually work with data that's made up of just two digits – 0 and 1 (bits). You can convert almost any type of data into a combination of ones and zeros.

If you set up a system where a unique combination of ones and zeroes are used to represent a specific letter, or number, or other piece of data, you can then use that unique combination of ones and zeroes in the computer as the "data" the computer is operating on.

As a reminder, if there are 5 volts (measurement of electrical force) present, that's a "one." If there isn't any voltage present, that's a "zero." So, you can represent all these combinations of ones and zeros with just "there are five volts" or "there are zero volts."

Now back to the CPU. One of the primary duties of the CPU is controlling devices. A device is a tool that you use for a particular purpose. Specifically, it is a machine that is external to a computer that can be connected to and work with the computer. Devices are also the physical parts of the computer that you can see, touch and interact with – such as the computer screen, the keyboard, or the mouse.

These built-in instructions that the CPU has might include "get data from an outside device (like a printer)," or "do this math operation," or "send data to an external device," etc.

Here are some common devices (printers, phones, cameras, etc.):

The most common devices are input/output devices (written as "I/O devices"). They're machines that people use to communicate with a computer.

"Input" refers to putting data into a computer. For example: A microphone connected to your computer is an input device.

"Output" refers to taking data from a computer. For example: A printer is an output device because it receives data from the computer.

I/O devices are controlled by a component inside the computer called the "I/O control." It looks like this:

The CPU takes in data, processes it, then sends it out.

It does this using a set of instructions that are built into it when it's manufactured.

So what do these instructions look like? They are a series of ones and zeroes.

For example, the instruction for "add two numbers" might look like this:

11001100

The instruction for "read data from an input device" (like a keyboard) might look like this:

11001101

These are just examples. The important thing here is that each instruction has a unique pattern of ones and zeroes and that these instructions are built into the CPU. So if you were creating a computer program, and you wanted the computer to add two numbers, you would enter this into the CPU:

11001100

To recap: the CPU is the main chip in the computer that processes data:

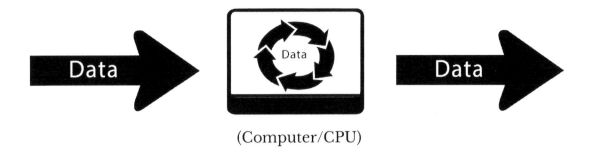

(Computer/CPU)

Remember, when we say computers, we are referring to more than just the computers you use at work and home – we also mean the computers inside of commonly-used modern machines, like your cell phone. Computers have CPUs in them. And so, for example, your cell phone (which nowadays basically is a computer) has a CPU inside of it.

SUMMARY:

The primary purpose of a computer is to take in data, process data, and output data. The chip that controls this overall operation is called the Central Processing Unit (CPU). It interacts with Input/Output (I/O) devices (like mice and printers) to get and give data, and it uses built-in instructions to process that data.

So, what's the most common input device?

CHAPTER 29:
KEYBOARDS

"Websites are designed to keep young people from using the keyboard,
except to enter in their parents' credit card information."
-Douglas Rushkoff (American writer, 1961-)

In 1868, an American inventor named Christopher Latham Sholes invented the first workable typewriter (a machine used for typing letters, numbers and symbols directly onto paper).

The main part of a computer keyboard is much like a typewriter – it has keys for alphanumeric (made up of a combination of letters and numbers) input. This includes keys for the letters A through Z, a Space bar to insert an empty space, the digits 0 through 9, and a Shift key to modify the output of the letter keys from lowercase to uppercase.

Keyboards have been the primary input device used with computers nearly since computers were first created. This was a logical move, since typewriters were in common use in society at that time, and since alphanumeric data was a common type of data needed by computer programs.

Keyboards can often have a "Caps Lock" or "Shift Lock" key that can toggle (switch) between two states. If the Caps Lock hasn't been pressed, the A-Z keys are lower case. If the Caps Lock key is pressed once, the keyboard is in a different mode, and the A-Z keys will be upper case without needing to use the Shift key. When the Caps Lock key is pressed again, the keyboard returns to the previous mode, and the A-Z keys are lower case again. The Caps Lock key doesn't affect how the number keys operate.

Over the years, computer manufacturers have worked together with keyboard manufacturers to add additional keys to keyboards that provide certain functionality (actions able to be performed) beyond just input of alphanumeric data (text). Not all keyboards have these additional keys, and some keyboards can have others. Keyboards often come with a manual that describes the use of these additional keys.

These additional keys are often used in combination with other keys to perform special actions. This involves holding down one key while pressing one or more other keys. This action is usually described as a "keyboard shortcut" because they're quicker than more complex interactions involving the mouse and the various programs on the computer.

The most common computer keyboard is called the "QWERTY" keyboard (which refers to how the keys are laid out – look at the letters on the top left of a keyboard). The placement of keys on the keyboard was based on feedback from telegraph (machines that send messages over long distances) operators in the past. Keyboards were incorporated into telegraphs to help type out messages.

SUMMARY:

If we're going to get data into a computer, it makes sense to use a familiar device for the purpose. The keyboard is a logical device. There are lots of other ways to get data into a computer, as you'll learn, but the keyboard is the most human-friendly of them. They let us use the letters and numbers we communicate with to get the data to the computer.

With so many keys on a keyboard, what are the most common keys and what do they mean?

CHAPTER 30:
KEYS

"Give a person a fish and you feed them for a day;
teach that person to use the internet and they won't bother you for weeks."
-Unknown

A "key" is a button on a machine that performs an action when pushed. The pushing of a key is called a keystroke – the pressing down of a key.

TAB KEY

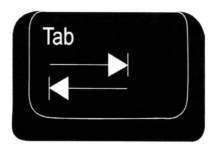

In order to describe the TAB key, you must first understand what a "spreadsheet" and a "table" are. A spreadsheet is a visual grid (lines that cross each other to form a series of squares and/or rectangles) structure that allows you to organize, modify and analyze data. The data is stored in individual containers called cells. These cells are organized into vertical (up and down) columns and horizontal (side to side) rows (each rectangle in this picture is a cell):

		Rows			
Columns					

Here is a spreadsheet:

	A	B	C	D
1	Country	Sales		
2	United States	7583		
3	United Kingdom	4359		
4	France	45995		
5	Germany	3933		
6	Spain	8738		
7	Italy	5239		
8	Greece	38282		
9				
10				

Sheet1 / Sheet2 / Sheet3

A set of rows and columns is called a table. In a more general sense, a table is information stored in a grid.

The "tab" in TAB key is short for "tabular" or "tabulator." "Tabular" means "of or related to a table," and it refers to data presented in columns or a table. A "tabulator" is a person or thing that arranges data in columns or tables and then works with that data.

Even before the development of computers, spreadsheets were used to organize and work with data in table form; people used printed grids on paper.

Spreadsheets are used in some of the most popular programs on computers; instead of the grids being drawn on paper, they are displayed on a screen.

The TAB key moves the cursor (flashing bar on screen that indicates where to type) forward on the screen a set number of spaces – usually this is set to 4 - 8 spaces. You may be familiar with this behavior from using computers.

However, the TAB key can also move the cursor over one cell to the right in a spreadsheet.

When pressed in combination with other keys, the TAB key performs other functions as well.

ESC KEY

This is short for "escape key." It is used to stop a computer action. This can take many forms, depending on how the computer programmer decided to make use of the Escape key (yes, programmers can instruct computers as to what effects various keys have when pressed inside their program).

For example, you may be using a computer program to connect to another computer so that you can access the files on the remote (separate; located at a distance) computer and could use the Escape key to stop the connection process.

CTRL KEY

This is short for "control key." This key doesn't do anything by itself. Instead, it is used in keyboard shortcuts (keys pressed in combination with other keys).

Instructions to do something like this are written as follows: CTRL-[Other key to be pressed]. For example, "CTRL-P" means to hold down the Control key and press the "P" key, then release both keys. This key combination, by the way, is a common shortcut to activate the "print a document" function in various computer programs.

"F key" is short for "Function key." Many keyboards have several Function keys, and they are usually numbered – that is, one key is the F1 key, the next is the F2 key, and so on.

These are used to provide keyboard shortcuts. Shortcuts aren't always two keys – a shortcut can also be just one key that you press for quick access to something. It is common for one computer program to make use of the Function keys in a different manner than another program.

For example, in a program for writing documents, the F3 key might be used to search a document for a specific word or phrase. In a video game, that same F3 key might be used to pause the game. Occasionally, a keyboard might have a single, non-numbered Function key in addition to the numbered Function keys; this usually operates as a modifier key (a key used in combination with other keys to perform various actions) in the same manner as the Alternate key, which is described next.

ALT KEY

Short for "Alternate key." Like the CTRL key, this key is usually used in combination with other keys, and it provides a way for one key to have two different functions. Often, a key will have its primary output written on it (say, the number 1), as well as a secondary output (say, an exclamation point). Normally the key will produce the primary output when not accompanied by another key. However, in the earlier example, when the 1 key is pressed while the SHIFT key is being held down, it will perform the secondary function: !.

Back to the ALT key – sometimes it can be used to access a menu of some sort on a computer program.

END KEY

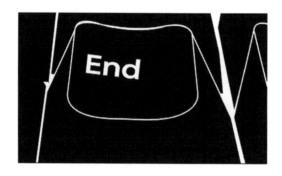

This key is used to move the cursor to the end of the current line of text. Depending on the computer, the END key can also take you to the very end of a document when pressed in combination with another key.

HOME KEY

This key is used to move the cursor to the beginning of the current line of text. It is the opposite of the END key. On some computers, it can take you to the very beginning of a document when pressed in combination with another key.

ENTER (RETURN) KEY

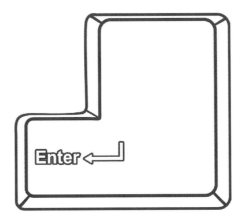

This key can function in several ways, but they all involve telling the computer to perform a certain operation after the user has had a chance to provide some input.

The original use was for entering individual instructions into a computer, back when all instructions had to be typed one at a time, and there was no visual interface (something that lets you communicate with a computer) on the screen to represent the various files and programs on the computer. It was the computer operator's (user's) responsibility to type out a specific instruction for the computer and then press the ENTER key. The computer would execute that instruction, and when it was done doing so, the user could enter another instruction.

Over time, the ENTER key has become the primary way a user tells the computer to start doing whatever function is being presented to the user. This could mean that after the user enters data in a form on the screen, pressing ENTER could cause the data in the form to be sent to the program being used.

On some keyboards there is a RETURN key instead of an ENTER key. It generally performs the same functions as the ENTER key.

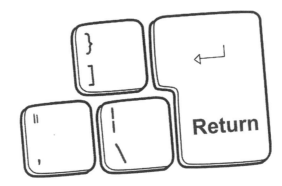

The origin of the name "Return" is from typewriters. The "Return" key on a typewriter would move the typewriter down one line of text and back to the far left of the page – in other words, the typewriter would "return to the home position." Hence, this symbol, meaning "move down and to the left": ⏎ or ↵

BACKSPACE KEY

Often abbreviated just BACK, it is used to move the cursor back one space. It can delete text just written.

Computer programmers have often made use of it for other functions in various different types of computer programs – for example, in a program that lets you access the internet, the BACK key might be used to navigate to the last web page you were visiting.

INS KEY

"Ins" is short for "Insert key." It is used to change the text input mode. Before it is pressed, the computer is in "insert mode" – new characters (letters, numbers, etc.) that are typed are added to the right of the cursor, forcing any existing text over to the right.

If the Insert key is pressed, it puts the keyboard into "overtype mode" or "replace mode," where new characters will overwrite (delete and replace) the character(s) to the right of the cursor position. Pressing it again will return the computer to "insert" mode.

ARROW KEYS

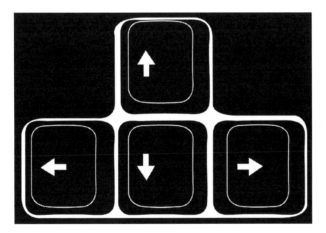

These are used to move the cursor around in a text document. There are four arrow keys – left, right, up, and down. They are often used in other ways, depending on the computer program being used. For example: a computer game that lets the user direct the path of a vehicle might use the arrow keys to "steer" the vehicle on the screen.

CMD KEY

Short for "command key," this key exists on some keyboards and is most commonly used in combination with other keys (shortcuts). For example: pressing CMD and the letter B at the same time, can make text **bold**.

The command key is found on Apple (major technology company) laptops.

Originally the Apple logo was going to be listed on the key, but Apple's Co-Founder (Steve Jobs) decided that having it displayed would be overuse of the company's logo.

(Apple logo)

An American designer named Susan Kare came up with using a looped square instead:

Most CMD keys have that symbol displayed.

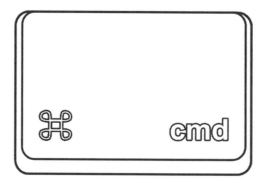

FN KEY

Short for "Function key." The FN key is also sometimes called the "F-Lock key."

The FN key executes the second option on a key. For example: look at this key:

There are two things written on this key: 1. F5, and 2. A mute symbol (a speaker with a "no" symbol).

Often, the F5 function key restarts a process.

In this example, if you press just F5, the program running on your screen refreshes (starts over and loads again), but if you press the FN key and F5 together, it turns your computer's sound off.

The main purpose of the FN key was to enable your keyboard to perform more actions without needing to add several more keys.

PG UP/PG DN KEYS

Short for "Page Up key" and "Page Down key." These buttons jump you up or down a full page within a document. Whereas the up arrow and down arrow on the keyboard moves you one line at a time, PG UP and PG DN move you several lines.

NUM LOCK KEY

Short for "Numeric Lock key." On some keyboards, there is a second row of numbers on the right hand side. This is called the "number pad" or "numpad." It looks like this:

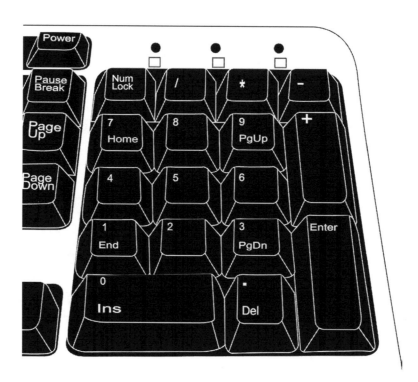

When the NUM LOCK is activated (pressed), the numpad types numbers when you press the keys. When it is deactivated by pressing it again, the numpad performs the other actions listed on the key. For example, if you turn NUM LOCK on and then press 1 on the numpad, you type a 1. If you turn NUM LOCK off and press 1, the END key executes and you're taken to the end of that line of text.

CAPS LOCK

As mentioned earlier, this key turns capitalization of letters on and off. When on, there is usually an indicator light that turns on (in the picture above, the small bar is the indicator light that can be turned on and off).

Keys on the keyboard that remain on after being pressed (as opposed to those like the SHIFT key that are only on while the key is held down) are referred to as toggle keys. "Toggle" means "to switch between." The CAPS LOCK key and NUM LOCK key are examples of toggle keys.

SUMMARY:

Keyboards have moved from simple input devices with only alphanumeric (letters and numbers) keys to complex devices with many specialized keys to make them more useful to computer users.

What's the other most popular I/O device?

CHAPTER 31:
MICE

"If I want to tell you there is a spot on your shirt,
I'm not going to do it linguistically (using language):
'There's a spot on your shirt 14 centimeters down from the collar and
three centimeters to the left of your button.'
If you have a spot – 'There!' – I'll point to it.
Pointing is a metaphor we all know.
It's much faster to do all kinds of functions,
such as cutting and pasting, with a mouse,
so it's not only easier to use but more efficient."
-Steve Jobs (1955-2011, Co-Founder of Apple)

One of the primary I/O devices is the mouse. You've most likely used one.

Doug Engelbart invented the first computer mouse around 1964; it was made of wood. It looked like this:

A mouse is a device that allows the user to interact with the visual display screen of the computer. It is a movable device about the size of a small hand.

Keep in mind that even though the mouse was invented in the 1960s, it wasn't widely used until the 1980s. Prior to the 1980s, data was only manipulated (controlled; handled) with a keyboard.

There is a pointer on the computer's display screen that moves in unison with the movement of the mouse. This allows the user to specify an item or items on the screen that they want to interact with. They do this by moving the pointer to the desired location on the screen:

Once the pointer is in the desired location, the user will want to take some action with the item or items that are at that screen location. A mouse has one or more buttons that can be used to control the action to be taken. The common physical actions you can perform to control actions are: "Click" (press the button down and release it right away); "Double-click" (perform two clicks in rapid succession); and "Drag and Drop" (press the button down and hold it down while moving the mouse pointer; then release the button when you want).

If you decide to abandon a "Drag and Drop" operation you're doing with the mouse – you can press the Escape key while dragging an item you selected with the mouse pointer; the Drag and Drop operation would be abandoned, and the dragged item would return to its original location.

Click and Double-click operations are often used to start programs on the computer. They are also sometimes used to select an item on the screen that you wish to do some sort of work on. Drag and Drop is often used to move various items around on the screen.

Most mice have two buttons side-by-side – the left button and the right button. Each of the two buttons can do those same operations – Click, Double-click, Drag and Drop. The terminology used is "Right" or "Left," followed by "Action." For example: "Left Double Click" or "Right Click." As the left button is the primary button, you will often see an instruction that neglects to specify which button to use – for example, "Click the picture on the screen." This means to move the mouse pointer over the indicated picture and then click the left button.

Some mice have a wheel that allows users to scroll (move up or down) a page:

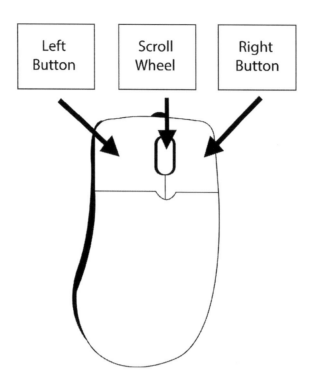

There are many ways to set up how the mouse and its buttons can be used, and they vary based on the manufacturer of the mouse or the computer, as well as the way a specific computer program is created.

Programmers can specify what mouse actions they will use, and what will happen in the program based on those mouse actions. They can even have the program make use of a combination of key presses on the keyboard with a simultaneous action of the mouse – for example, "Hold down the Shift key and double-click the image."

Another thing that can be specified by a programmer is what will happen, if anything, when a mouse pointer is positioned on an item on the screen but a mouse button isn't being clicked. This action is called "hovering." A common possibility here is that some short text item might be displayed when the mouse pointer is hovering over an item. For example, if you made the mouse pointer hover over a picture of a bird, the programmer might have set it up so that some text appeared near the mouse pointer that said, "American Eagle in a nest" or similar text. This text is called "hover text." Hovering can also cause the pointer to change to something like this:

SUMMARY:

As we moved away from purely text-based displays for computers, and started using graphical (composed of images and pictures) elements on the display to represent various data and programs on the computer, we needed a better input device than the keyboard for certain actions. The mouse has emerged as the most common input device for interacting with these displays, and therefore with the computer.

The mouse and keyboard are the most-used input devices. What's one of the most popular output devices?

CHAPTER 32:
PRINTERS

"A printer consists of three main parts:
the case,
the jammed paper tray
and the blinking red light."
-Dave Barry (American author, 1947-)

A printer is a machine connected to a computer that takes blank paper and prints documents, pictures, etc. on the paper. It is an output device because it puts out data.

Printers can be plugged into a computer or connected wirelessly.

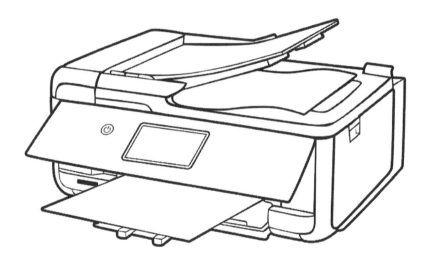

Printers have been used in conjunction with computers since the 1950s.

They're one of the oldest peripheral (external; outside of the computer) devices. Original computer printers looked like this:

Printers are useless without ink. The two most popular types of ink are:

1) Liquid, and

2) Toner.

Liquid ink is typically used by "inkjet printers" which are printers that literally spray the liquid ink from tiny jets inside the printer.

Toner is ink in the form of powder or powder suspended in liquid.

Another type of printer is a "laser printer." The first thing to understand about lasers is frequency.

As a reminder, a wave is a flow of energy that has a repeating variation in terms of how much energy is present at any one point in time. The energy amount will cycle from low to high, and back to low again – and so on. Waves come in all sorts of types, patterns, and sizes. Waves are how energy moves through space. The length of time between when the wave hits one point in its cycle and the next time the wave hits that exact same point in its cycle is called a wavelength. How many times this cycle repeats in a second is called the frequency of the wave.

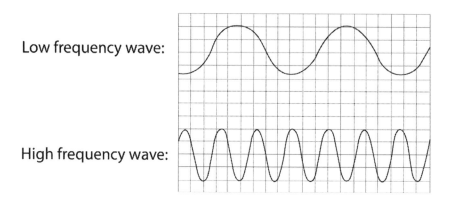

Low frequency wave:

High frequency wave:

A laser is an extremely focused beam of light. The difference between a laser and normal light is this: Normal light sources, like light bulbs, emit (sends out) light that has several different frequencies. In a laser, the light that is emitted is all the same frequency. Laser light contains a lot of energy, and that energy is absorbed by materials the laser hits against.

A laser printer is a printer that prints using toner and lasers. The lasers fix toner on the page with a high degree of accuracy through a heating process.

The keyboard and mouse are input devices, while the printer is an output device, and they are all monitored and obeyed by the CPU.

SUMMARY:

One of the main uses for computers is to output data. When we want that data in printed form, we use a printer.

The CPU is composed of various parts, so let's dive deeper into it. For example, what tells a CPU when it is supposed to take its next action?

CHAPTER 33:
TICK TOCK

"To err is human –
and to blame it on a computer is even more so."
-Robert Orben (American writer, 1927-)

The system computers use to control the timing of when a CPU receives a new instruction and then performs that instruction is called a "clock." The clock is a special electronic device that can put out an exact amount of electricity, for an exact period of time, at very precise intervals (spaces in time). It helps the CPU to know when to start doing its next action, and can operate in a precise, knowable way.

When the clock is "high," it is putting out electricity. When it is "low," it is not. The moment the clock goes "high," the CPU detects that this has occurred, and then knows it should acquire and execute its next instruction.

The first CPU clocks were made from a quartz crystal – quartz is a type of silicon that looks like this:

Like other parts of the computer, the clock is microscopic.

The faster your computer's clock can operate, the better your computer can perform.

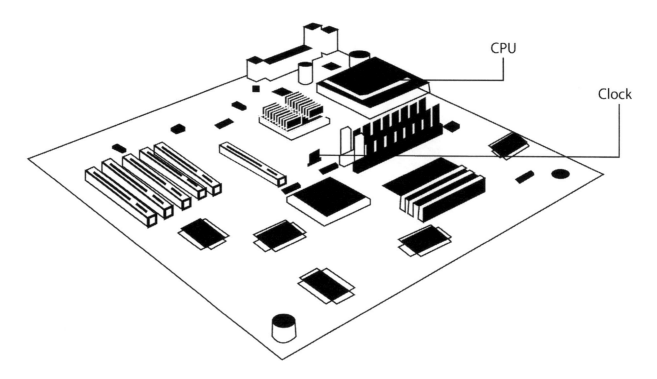

"Clock rate" is the rate of operation for the clock – that is, "how many times per second does the clock put out a signal?" Each of these signals is called a clock tick.

As covered earlier, a wave is a flow of energy that has a low point and a high point. Energy moves through space in waves.

The space between one point in a wave and the next exact same point in the wave is called a wavelength.

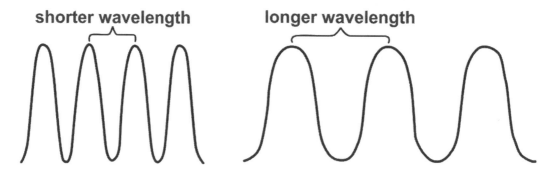

So what do waves have to do with clock rates? Clock rates are measured in "Hertz." Hertz is a measurement that refers to how many wavelengths occur in one second – literally how many "ups and downs" occur in an electric flow per second.

It was named after Heinrich Hertz, a German scientist who lived in the 1800s.

Hertz did some of the early research that led up to the radio, and as part of this research he studied the behavior of electricity. Again, Hertz (abbreviated Hz) means how many "ups and downs," or "cycles" in an electric flow that occur per second.

Modern clocks can operate at billions of Hertz a second.

And remember, the computer can only do one thing at a time. A computer receives instructions, one at a time, and performs them.

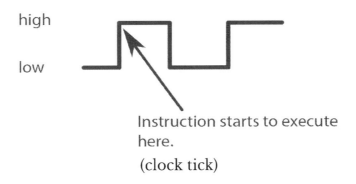

high

low

Instruction starts to execute here.
(clock tick)

And the computer can't do anything on its own – so we need a way to tell the computer that it is supposed to do the next instruction.

The clock sends a signal to the CPU, telling the CPU that it's allowed to perform the next instruction it's been given.

As soon as you turn on the computer, this clock turns on and begins sending out a regular electrical pulse – bang, bang, bang, bang... It runs like this, without stopping, for the entire time the computer is turned on.

That pulse (electrical signal) goes right to the CPU. When the CPU gets the pulse, that's its signal for it to do the next instruction it has been given.

Here is how the CPU and clock work together: A series of these instructions gets entered into the computer (this is called a program). One at a time, these instructions are fed to the CPU.

Inside the CPU, it looks like this:

1. The CPU gets a signal from the clock.

2. The CPU looks at the next instruction from the program – whether it's getting data from a keyboard, or adding two numbers, or sending data to a screen, etc.

3. The CPU does that instruction.

4. The CPU sits and waits, doing nothing, until the next clock signal arrives.

5. The CPU gets a signal from the clock.

6. The CPU looks at the next instruction from the program.

7. The CPU does that instruction.

8. The CPU sits and waits...

And so on, as long as the computer is turned on.

This reinforces a few things about computers:

a. They can only do one thing at a time

b. They can only do something a person thought of and placed in the computer as an instruction

c. They can never act on their own

What makes computers *seem* so powerful and complex is that they process BILLIONS of bits every second.

The CPU has a place on it where instructions can be stored. That way, when the clock sends a signal to do another instruction, the CPU looks at that place, sees the instruction, looks it up against its built-in list of instructions, and does what it's supposed to.

To go back to an earlier subject that is similar: remember the weaving loom that used cards with holes in it to control when various threads were woven in an exact pattern? Those looms needed an operator to move a lever each time the loom was supposed to check the next series of holes in the card. If the lever wasn't moved, the loom stopped. The clock is the same way – each time it gives the CPU a signal, it's like the lever being operated in those old looms.

The CPU and clock are the team that executes instructions.

SUMMARY:

We've covered the idea that we can enter a series of instructions into a computer. We want these instructions to be performed in order, one after the other. The clock is the device that tells the CPU when it can get its next instruction and perform it.

The CPU and the clock are considered "hardware" – so let's take a look at what hardware is exactly.

CHAPTER 34:
HARDWARE

"Hardware: the parts of a computer that can be kicked."
-Jeff Pesis (American, unknown age)

Hardware refers to the physical components of the computer – the parts that can be touched.

"Hard" means "solid" or "tangible" (able to be seen and felt), and "ware" means "something created."

The computer screen, mouse, printer and keyboard are all hardware.

SUMMARY:

Hardware is the tangible, physical parts of a computer system – including the computer itself, the display, the mouse, the keyboard, etc.

So, what is the opposite of hardware?

CHAPTER 35:
SOFTWARE

"Software is a great combination between artistry and engineering."
-Bill Gates, (Co-Founder of Microsoft, 1955-)

The opposite of hardware is software. Software are computer programs – sets of instructions that tell a computer what to do. Software is created by people to make the computer perform certain functions and achieve a certain output.

Computer games, like Solitaire, are examples of software.

The word software came about in the 1960s to emphasize the difference between it and computer hardware. Software are the instructions, while hardware implements the instructions.

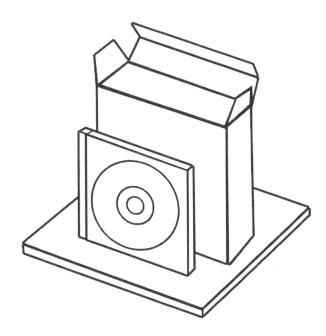

In an earlier chapter we covered what the I/O (Input/Output) control does – as a reminder, the I/O control is the hardware component that controls peripheral (outside of the computer) devices.

There is another definition of I/O control that relates to software. In software, an I/O control is computer instructions (code) that controls the computer hardware. For example: an I/O control could instruct the computer to go to sleep (place itself in a low-power mode where certain parts are turned off completely) – an action that would require the hardware to perform various functions.

SUMMARY:

Software is a set of instructions, loaded into the computer, that can control how the computer operates. Without software, the computer would just sit there, not doing anything.

So, if computers aren't alive, how can they "remember" anything?

CHAPTER 36:
MEMORIES

"Sometimes you will never know the value of a moment until it becomes a memory."
-Dr. Seuss (American author, 1904-1991)

"Memory" is a physical device used to store information on a computer. It holds recorded electronic data that can be accessed in the future.

A computer makes use of physical data storage devices in order to do its job of processing data. A data storage device could be thought of as a collection of boxes. Each box can contain data. Each box has a memory location (a number) so that the computer can keep track of it.

A memory location is also called an "address." The computer can "read" or "write" to these memory locations – "read" means to get the value (type; characteristic; amount) of the data in the location; "write" means to set the value of the data in the location.

"Volatile" literally means "likely to change." Memory storage devices are either volatile or persistent. Volatile devices lose their data when they are not powered on; persistent devices maintain their data even when they are not powered.

When you save a file, it is saved in the persistent memory of the computer.

In terms of storing data in the computer, a bit is used to represent the state of a location in the computer's memory storage device (1 for on, 0 for off).

Let's say you want to save a document on your computer that says, "Remember to buy milk at the store."

This small note might be around 1,000 bits in size. To save this document, 1,000 transistors inside memory would be set in a special sequence of "ons" and "offs" that tell the computer what letters and symbols to display, their size, where to place them on the screen, etc.

Here is an example of what a popular type of computer memory looks like:

SUMMARY:

In the early years of the computer industry, computer operators had to enter the instructions of their programs into the computer each time they wanted to have the computer do those instructions. It quickly became clear that we needed a way to store those instructions, and the data they would operate on, in the computer. Devices built for this purpose are called "memory." While there have been many types of memory devices, they all allow storage of electronic information for later use.

Now let's talk about an early type of computer memory.

CHAPTER 37:
TAPES

"Science and technology revolutionize our lives,
but memory, tradition and myth frame (formulate) *our response."*
-Arthur M. Schlesinger (American historian, 1917-2007)

You've most likely seen cassette tapes like this:

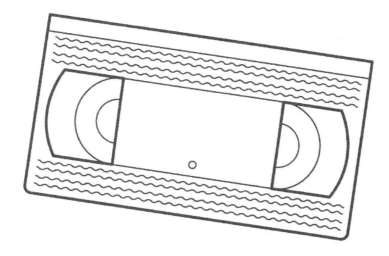

Such tapes were mainly used in the 1970s-1990s to play music or watch videos. They are also called VHS tapes. "VHS" stands for "Video Home System." They contained a long, thin magnetic tape that was wound around two spools.

A spool is a cylindrical device that something can be wrapped around:

As the name sounds, magnetic tape uses magnetic materials and magnetic energy. Magnetic materials either pull to each other or push each other away, and magnetic energy refers to the same fact – energy that has magnetic properties (attracts or pushes).

The main uses of magnetic tape are:

1. To store digital data.

2. To store sound.

3. To store video.

Let's look at how it is used to store data. Magnetic tape is able to be "programmed" like this:

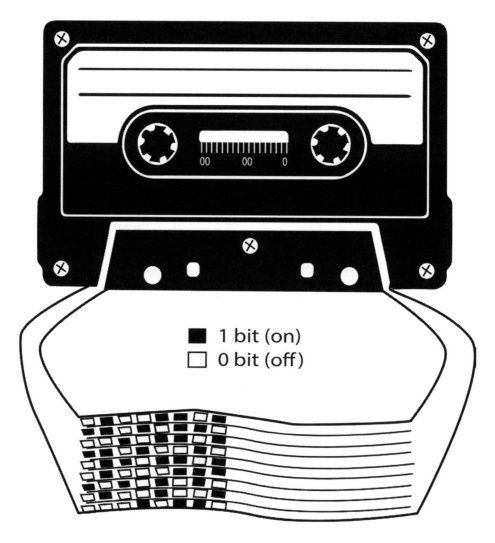

The black squares represent areas on the tape where a particular quality of magnetic energy was stored by stacks of magnets. The marks left by these magnets can be read by machines using heads (machine parts that pick up [read] and transfer electronic signals). They operate in the same, basic fashion as punched cards and tape.

You can see a past computer technician looking over magnetic tape below:

Data is stored on this tape and read by a computer.

The first magnetic recorder was developed in 1898 by Danish inventor Valdemar Poulsen. It was called the telegraphone and it looked like this:

The telegraphone was able to record speech magnetically on a thin steel wire.

The storage of sound later transitioned into magnetic tape made of plastic film.

Sound can be recorded on magnetic tape similar to how we create a record. "Copies" of the sound waves are made on the tape, just like copies of sound waves are made on records. Records record sound waves by making grooves that mirror the sounds waves of the physical universe – magnetic tape records the sound waves by making magnetic copies of the sound waves. Or said another way, the magnetic energy on tapes reflects the sound waves being fed into it.

Here it is diagrammed:

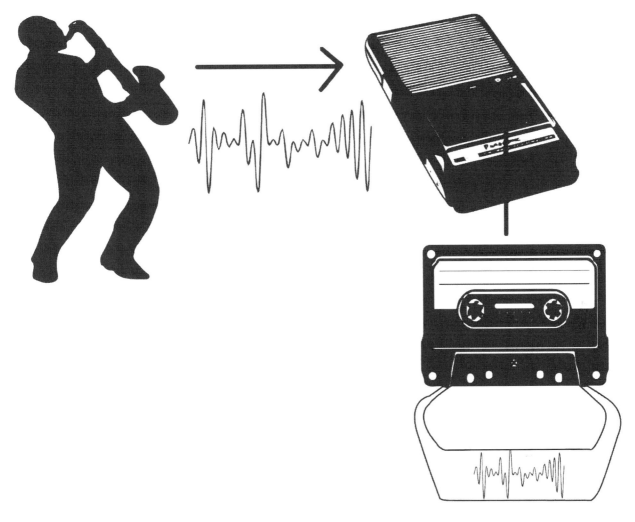

Alright, so we've covered how tape can store data. When used to record the 1s and 0s that computers use, it is considered "digital" (made up of distinct parts that can be processed as bits). When used for sound as covered above, they store analog data (continuous waves).

The third most common use of tapes is for videos.

Video works the same way as pictures that are taken by cameras. The light waves are stored by a reaction that happens with chemicals on the film.

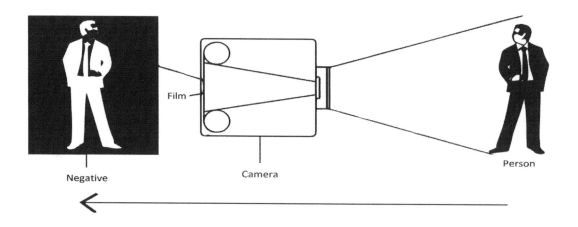

Negative   Film   Camera   Person

The stored images on film are called negatives because the image stored is the opposite colors as the actual scene. For example: on a black and white negative, black is white and white is black. The reason for this is if you want to make a copy (print) of the picture, you can shine light through the negative and the light and shadows interact with the chemicals on the picture paper. The picture paper starts out white, and gets darker when light hits it.

Let's say there is a black circle on the negative. When light hits the black circle in the negative, less light will pass through it than the white portions of the negative. This will result in the circle on the copy paper being lighter due to less light hitting it and the space surrounding the circle being darker because of more light hitting it.

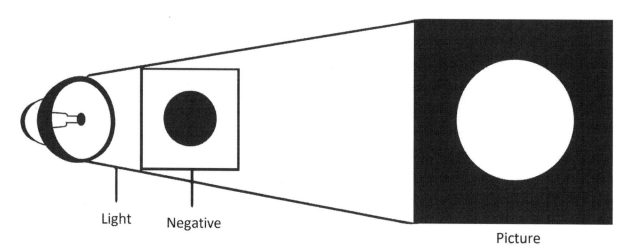

Light   Negative   Picture

Back to video on tape. Video on tape is actually lots of little negative pictures (each one called a frame) that is displayed by light passing through it because, remember, videos are just a series of pictures.

SUMMARY:

In order to get data into a computer, and to record the data it put out, we needed storage devices. These devices needed to be able to record the 1s and 0s the computer operates with. We developed magnetic tape and ways to change individual spots on the tape so they were in one of two available states. In this way, we could get data into and out of a computer that represents digital information.

Storing information on physical objects (as covered in this chapter) was an important step in the development of computers. Let's look at another step forward in the development of computer memory storage.

CHAPTER 38:
DRUMS

"My iPhone has 2 million times the storage of the 1969 Apollo 11 spacecraft computer.
They went to the moon.
I throw birds at pig houses."
-Unknown

In 1932, an Austrian inventor named Gustav Tauschek developed "drum memory" – a way to store data on a drum (metal cylindrical objects).

Drum memory is a magnetic data storage device that looked like this:

For many early computers, drum memory was used to store data. The drum was coated in magnetic iron (a type of metal).

Magnets are incredible. Entire books have been written about them. We've spoken about them a little already, but let's explore them a little further.

Magnets are surrounded by a magnetic field. This is the space around a magnet that contains the magnetic force (push and pull). Outside of the magnetic field, there is no magnetic effect (no push or pull).

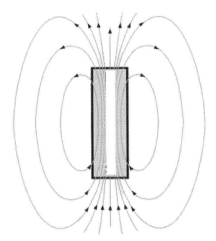

Iron is a very common type of metal often utilized in combination with other metals to make them suitable for different uses. You can make iron (and some other metals) magnetic by exposing them to a strong magnetic field.

The machine developed by Taushcek that used drum memory included a device called a head. A head can do two things:

1. Read a magnetic signal that is recorded on the drum, and

2. Change the signal that is recorded on the drum.

These two actions are commonly referred to as "read" and "write," and you often see them used in computers.

SUMMARY:

Being able to store data for later use by a computer is important. It was necessary to find physical objects that could be switched back and forth between two different states in order to make computers implement binary digits as data. Magnetic material, which either repels or attracts, was ideal for this purpose. Early data storage mechanisms used magnetic material because of this.

Due to their involvement in the development of computers, let's take a closer look at magnets.

CHAPTER 39:
MAGNETS

"Being a nerd is not about what you love; it's about the way you love it."
-Wil Wheaton (American actor, 1972-)

A "magnetic core" is a piece of material that has a strong magnetic field. This material can be used to hold in and guide magnetic fields – which comes in handy in the field of electronics.

In 1955, a man named An Wang invented magnetic core memory.

Core memory had an arrangement where wires were run through the hole in the middle of a round magnetic ring. The round magnet was called the "core." It was shaped like a doughnut and looked like this:

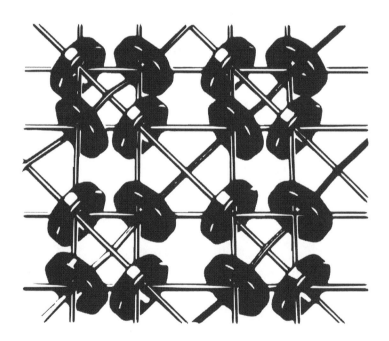

Older computers used these cores as memory to store data in, since you could set the magnet up in one of two distinct states, and that state wouldn't change unless you used electricity to make it change. In one state, energy would flow clockwise through the ring; in the other state, it would flow in a counter-clockwise direction.

And so, data could be stored by passing small amounts of electricity through the cores. The bit (magnet) was stored as either on (1) or off (0), depending on the direction of flow of the electricity (for example: on could be a clockwise flow of energy through the magnet, and off counterclockwise).

Erasing all of the contents of magnetic core memory was called a "core dump." Even though computers don't use this type of memory any longer, the memory of a computer is sometimes still called "core." The CPU is called "core" sometimes as well. Both of these uses have their roots in the original term.

Drum memory was replaced by core memory, which was a better choice in terms of size, cost, speed, and reliability.

SUMMARY:

As computer technology advanced, engineers were continually looking for better ways to store digital data. One important development along the way was magnetic core memory, in which wires were run through round magnetic cores. By controlling the electricity flowing through those wires, we could control the data stored in each core – either a one or a zero.

We're getting closer and closer to the modern computer. Let's look at some early computers that helped us arrive where we are now.

CHAPTER 40:
EARLY COMPUTERS

"You could say I was too lazy to calculate, so I invented the computer."
-Konrad Zuse (German inventor, 1910-1995)

In 1938, a German inventor named Konrad Zuse finished construction of the Z1 computer. The Z1 was a programmable computer that operated on binary (meaning, it used Boolean logic). Here is a picture of it:

It was composed of thin metal sheets that looked like this:

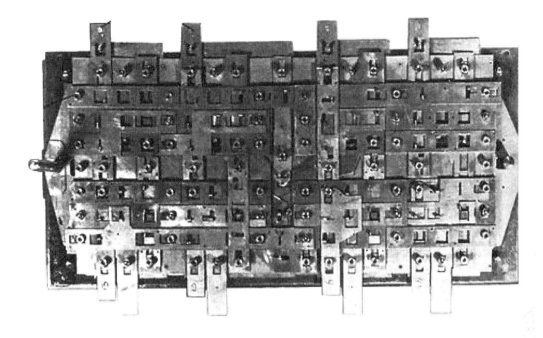

It had a keyboard that was used as an input device.

It didn't operate reliably, so Konrad Zuse continued developing computers, and in 1941 he perfected the Z3; a programmable, binary computer. The Z3 was controlled by programs and looked like this:

Zuse's computers read programs contained on punched plastic tape.

One thing to note is that the original computers designed by Charles Babbage a century before, operated on the decimal number system (0-9). Using binary is more efficient than decimal because it only requires two states of digital information (on or off), whereas a decimal computer means digital information must have 10 possible states (10 different levels of electricity).

These "Z" computers had input, memory, a central processing unit and output.

As covered earlier, the CPU has a set of built-in instructions that define the various actions the CPU can take. These built-in instructions are called machine instructions. Machine language is instructions to a computer written in a form the CPU can understand.

In modern computers, machine language is data that is composed of a series of 1s and 0s (binary). For example: "10010100 01101011 01011011 01010110" could tell the computer to "Delete the file entitled 'Vacation'."

It is difficult for people to read and write in machine language, since the instructions are just unique patterns of ones and zeroes. Punched cards and tape originally held instructions written in machine language. Machine language is a "low-level language" in that it operates at the level of the computer hardware. It directly represents the on or off states used in both the computer instructions and the data the computer operates on.

The opposite of a low-level language is a high-level language – code written in a way that is easier to read and write because it somewhat resembles English, such as:

```
Print "Hello";
```

(Here, you are telling the computer to display the word Hello on the screen).

Another major accomplishment from Konrad Zuse was inventing the first high-level programming language, Plankalkül (meaning a "formal system for planning").

SUMMARY:

In 1938, the Z1 computer was developed. It was the first computer to have many of the elements we see in modern computers – it operated on the binary

number system; it had a keyboard for data input; it had a CPU, and it operated on programs (sets of instructions fed into it on punched cards). Konrad Zuse also created the very high-level (similar to human language) programming language, Plankalkül. And so, he was a very important figure in the development of computers.

This brings us to one of the next major computers.

CHAPTER 41:
ELECTRONIC COMPUTERS

"The only constant in the technology industry is change."
-Marc Benioff (American businessman, 1964-)

In 1942, two American scientists named Clifford E. Berry and John Vincent Atanasoff constructed the Atanasoff-Berry Computer (ABC). This was the first automatic electronic digital computer – meaning, it contained automatic electronic switches (devices that control the flow of electricity).

The computer was able to perform advanced math but it wasn't programmable. It also had issues, such as an inability to store data. It weighed about 700 pounds and looked like this:

It was able to convert binary numbers (0-1) to decimal numbers (0-9) and it had a card reader that could receive mathematical instructions. The basic concept of inputting data, having the data processed (in this case, using vacuum tubes that could be on or off), and outputting results was performed by this computer.

In 1945, the ENIAC (Electronic Numerical Integrator and Computer) was constructed by two American engineers, John Mauchly and J. Presper Eckert. Some consider this to be the first digital computer because it was fully functional. The ENIAC operated on the binary number system and it was huge – it filled a 50-foot long room and weighed about 30 tons. There were around 20,000 vacuum tubes in it. Punch cards were used to input and output data. Here's a picture of the ENIAC:

The ENIAC was able to solve many types of numerical problems – such as addition and subtraction. It was primarily used to calculate data for firing and launching weapons for the United States Army.

It was a major advancement for computers because it could calculate certain math problems in 30 seconds that previously would take one person 20 hours.

An interesting side note about these massive computers: you've probably heard the term "bug," right? "Bugs" refer to issues and difficulties, and can even mean "something broken." One of the reasons the term bug is used to describe computer problems is that (according to people who worked on these old machines) sometimes when these huge computers broke down and were opened up, an actual bug (such as a moth) was found inside it as the source of the problem!

SUMMARY:

As we entered the 1940s, the first reliable electronic digital computers started to appear. ENIAC (Electronic Numerical Integrator and Computer) was the most famous of these; it was used mainly by the military and it could perform complex mathematical calculations much faster than a human.

A vital element to computers are programming languages (organized systems of words, phrases and symbols that let you create programs), so let's discuss a woman who was essential to the development of modern programming languages.

CHAPTER 42:
A TECH LEGEND

"A ship in port is safe, but that's not what ships are built for."
-Grace Hopper (Computer Scientist, 1906-1992)

An officer in the US Navy, Grace Hopper was instrumental in the creation of what is considered one of the first programming languages.

In 1943, she helped create the first compiler – a special computer program that is used to convert computer instructions written in higher-level programming languages (those that read much like English words) to a form that the computer can actually use (the binary code that represents the instructions built into the CPU).

Nowadays, when a computer programmer makes computer programs, the programs are usually written in a form that looks almost like English. For example, it might look like:

```
if age > 18 then print "You are an adult"
```

(the character ">" in this case means "greater than"). This line of code means that if the user's age is over 18, display the words "You are an adult" on the computer screen.

Computers can't understand language like that because they operate on machine language (1s and 0s). And so, the high-level language used above would have to be changed into a form that the computer does understand.

As we just mentioned, a compiler converts the code that looks nearly English (high-level language) into a form that the computer can understand and operate off of (machine language). The product of a compiler would be a set of instructions understandable to the computer and that the computer could execute. This would make the computer do what the "nearly English" code described. This collection of compiled code is called an "executable," because the computer can actually execute the instructions contained in it.

A compiler is a sort of translator between the computer and the programmer.

One important aspect of how a compiler works, is that it takes all of the instructions in the program and turns them all into language that the computer can understand, before actually executing the program. There are other methods of converting high-level languages to computer-readable form that don't involve converting the entire program before it is executed; in these other methods, each instruction is converted and executed one at a time, but that is not how a compiler works.

Grace Hopper's developments led to the first widely used computer programming languages and she's considered one of the most important contributors to technology in history.

SUMMARY:

Admiral Grace Hopper was hugely influential in the development of the modern computer. One of her most important contributions was her work in creating modern computer languages, which helped make the creation of computer programs much easier.

Most computers until this point were used by companies and the military. Let's look at the first computer available to the general public.

CHAPTER 43:
FIRST PUBLICLY AVAILABLE COMPUTER

"Bill Gates is a very rich man today... and do you want to know why?
The answer is one word: versions."
-Dave Barry (American author, 1947-)

In 1951, the UNIVAC I (Universal Automatic Computer 1) was produced by J. Presper Eckert and John Mauchly (the same two American engineers mentioned earlier that produced the ENIAC), along with a team. It became famous when in 1952, it was used to accurately predict that Dwight D. Eisenhower would win the US presidential election.

The UNIVAC I could store 12,000 characters (letters, numbers and symbols). Like other computers at the time, it was massive:

It operated similarly to its predecessors – data was input with a keyboard, processed inside the computer and output on the other end.

A couple of the developments of the UNIVAC included:

1. It was the first computer to utilize magnetic tape. Input, programs and output could be recorded on this tape and read by the computer.

2. It was the first computer to use buffer memory. Buffer is an area where data is stored for later use. Buffer memory is usually needed when data is being put into a computer faster than the computer can process it.

There may also be a case where not enough data has arrived for the computer to perform the requested action. In this case, as well, the incoming data is stored in a buffer for later use. In modern times, you've probably seen videos on your computer that say "buffering." This is a related concept of data loading before it is displayed or used.

Buffering...

The UNIVAC was the first commercial (available to be sold to the public for business use) computer and was a major step forward in the industry for many reasons – not the least of it was enhancing the social acceptability of computers.

SUMMARY:

The UNIVAC (Universal Automatic Computer) was an important device in the development of the modern computer. Besides its innovative use of magnetic tape for data storage and use of a data buffer to store electronic data for later processing, it was the first commercially available computer, and versions of it were purchased by businesses around America.

A computer without programs is like a car with no steering wheel. So let's go over some of the original programming languages.

CHAPTER 44:
ORIGINAL LANGUAGES

"That's the thing about people who think they hate computers.
What they really hate is lousy programmers."
-Larry Niven (American author, 1938-)

Two extremely popular programming languages that existed in the 1950s and 1960s were FORTRAN (FORmula TRANslation) and COBOL (COmmon Business Oriented Language).

FORTRAN was invented by IBM (International Business Machines) in 1954. It was mainly developed for scientific use. FORTRAN can perform complex calculations and solve math, physics and engineering problems. For example: It has been used to predict weather based on various numeric equations (math problems).

Here is how FORTRAN was typed on a punch card:

COBOL was designed by Grace Hopper and a team in 1959 as part of an effort to create one programming language that could work on several different types of computers. Up until that point, each manufacturer of computers often had designed their own programming language for their computers. COBOL was quite popular, and is still in use in certain industries today. For example, it is currently used in the financial analysis area of business. Here is a COBOL punch card:

```
ABCDEFGHIJKLMNOPQRSTUVWXYZ0123456789.$,+@%*<+,c<!
```

With COBOL and FORTRAN, programmers could instruct the computer to perform a basic equation by inputting this:

5 + 5

and the computer would calculate 10. This is opposed to having to write a series of binary instructions like this in machine language:

```
0010  0001  0000  0100
0001  0001  0000  0101
0011  0001  0000  0110
0111  0000  0000  0001
0000  0000  0000  0101
0000  0000  0000  0101
0000  0000  0000  0000
```

COBOL and FORTRAN sped up coding and made it accessible to more people.

SUMMARY:

Today there are thousands of programming languages but FORTRAN and COBOL, are worth mentioning as part of the history of computers because they were two of the first widely-used languages that allowed programmers to write code that was closer to English (and easier to write) than the 1s and 0s of machine

language. They were also designed for use on computers from multiple manufacturers.

Now, let's look at how computer code communicates letters, symbols and numbers to the computer.

CHAPTER 45:
CHARACTERS

"Letters are signs of things, symbols of words, whose power is so great that without a voice they speak to us the words of the absent; for they introduce words by the eye, not by the ear."
-Saint Isidore of Seville (Ancient Scholar, 560-636)

In the written form of a language, a character is a symbol that represents one of the various parts of that language. Characters are the various letters, punctuation marks and symbols that are used to lay out a language in written form. As an example, the English sentence "Speed limit 65 MPH!" makes use of uppercase letters (such as "S" and "M"), lowercase letters (such as "p" and "t"), a punctuation mark ("!"), a space to separate words, and numbers (like "6" and "5").

Character sets are fixed collections of these various symbols, usually containing all needed symbols for a specific language. If we took the English alphabet as an example, it is a character set containing almost 100 symbols. This includes 26 upper-case letters of the English alphabet, 26 lowercase characters of the English alphabet, the numeric digits 0 through 9, and a collection of punctuation marks.

As we have covered earlier, computers work with two main types of information:

1) The instructions that tell them what to do as they work, and

2) The information (data) they are to use in doing that work.

Since computers are often used to represent data in written form, they must be configured (set up) to represent the various characters for written languages. Early computers were primarily created by engineers whose primary language was English, so their efforts in this direction concerned the representation of English characters using computers – specifically, representing the nearly 100 characters described above.

In the 1960s, the ASCII (American Standard Code for Information Interchange) was created in order to standardize a system to represent English characters using computers. It contains 127 symbols, including numbers and letters. ASCII was designed for languages that use the English alphabet only.

In simple terms, each character in the ASCII character set has an associated unique number. When that number is given to a device meant to use written characters – such as a monitor (computer screen) or a printer – the computer can look that number up in the ASCII tables, get the specific symbol it represents from that table, and then print or display that character.

For example, the ASCII code for an uppercase "S" is the decimal (using ten digits – 0-9) number 83, while the code for a lowercase "s" is 115.

Since computers operate in binary, the characters in character sets must each be translated into binary.

Using the ASCII codes, the earlier sentence "Speed limit 65 MPH!" would be represented in decimal numbers in this manner:

83 112 101 101 100 32 108 105 109 105 116 32 54 53 32 77 80 72 33

Using the ASCII codes, that same sentence would be represented in binary numbers in this manner:

01010011 01110000 01100101 01100101 01100100 00100000 01101100 01101001 01101101 01101001 01110100 00100000 00110110 00110101 00100000 01001101 01010000 01001000 00100001

Those binary numbers are the actual data that would be given to the computer in order to create the sentence "Speed limit 65 MPH!."

Here is some of the ASCII chart:

Decimal	Binary	ASCII	Decimal	Binary	ASCII	Decimal	Binary	ASCII
33	00100001	!	65	01000001	A	97	01100001	a
34	00100010	'	66	01000010	B	98	01100010	b
35	00100011	#	67	01000011	C	99	00100011	c
36	00100100	$	68	01000100	D	100	01100100	d
37	00100101	%	69	01000101	E	101	01100101	e
38	00100110	&	70	01000110	F	102	01100110	f
39	00100111	*	71	01000111	G	103	01100111	g
40	00101000	(	72	01001000	H	104	01101000	h
41	00101001	)	73	01001001	I	105	01101001	i
42	00101010	*	74	01001010	J	106	01101010	j
43	00101011	+	75	01001011	K	107	01101011	k
44	00101100	.	76	01001100	L	108	01101100	l
45	00101101	-	77	01001101	M	109	01101101	m
46	00101110	_	78	01001110	N	110	01101110	n
47	00101111	/	70	01001111	O	111	01101111	o
48	00110000	0	80	01010000	P	112	01110000	p
49	00110001	1	81	01010001	Q	113	01110001	q
50	00110010	2	82	01010010	R	114	01110010	r
51	00110011	3	83	01010011	S	115	01110011	s
52	00110100	4	84	01010100	T	116	01110100	t
53	00110101	5	85	01010101	U	117	01110101	u
54	00110110	6	86	01010110	V	118	01110110	v
55	00110111	7	87	01010111	W	119	01110111	w
56	00111000	8	88	01011000	X	120	01111000	x
57	00111001	8	89	01011001	Y	121	01111001	y
58	00111010	,	90	01011010	Z	122	01111010	z
59	00111011	;	91	01011011	[	123	01111011	{
60	00111100	<	92	01011100	\	124	01111100	l
61	00111101	=	93	01011101	]	125	01111101	}
61	00111110	>	94	01011110	^	126	01111110	~

As a note, you could find each of the above codes used to represent the sentence "Speed limit 65 MPH!" in the above chart and see how each code corresponds to a character in the sentence.

SUMMARY:

ASCII provided a standardized way for computers to work with characters, something that is one of the most common functions of computers today.

ASCII does not contain symbols or characters like: è, ñ, ©, or characters from other languages like Chinese or Arabic. As there are many different written languages in use on Earth, a system was needed that accommodated more than just the English language.

CHAPTER 46:
WORLDWIDE LANGUAGE

"But words are things; and a small drop of ink,
Falling, like dew, upon a thought, produces
That which makes thousands, perhaps millions, think."
-George Gordon Byron (British poet, 1788-1824)

Unicode (short for unique, unified and universal encoding) is another standard for representing letters and symbols in computers. The idea for Unicode came about in the late 1980s during discussions amongst various technology professionals. It was released to the public in 1991.

Unicode is intended to represent all languages across the world, not just English. Each letter and symbol of the various languages of the world has a specific number in the Unicode system.

This is important because computers are much more useful if they can display data in the language of the user.

Unicode was developed because computer programmers needed a way to clarify what letters or symbols to use in their programs if the user wanted the data displayed in another language. It was necessary that all computer manufacturers agree on this system so that computers could be used everywhere.

As an example, in Unicode, the letter "A" could be represented as 0041.

Whereas the standard ASCII character set can only support 128 characters, Unicode can support about 1,000,000 characters.

"UTF" stands for "Unicode Transformation Format." UTF is a system that utilizes Unicode in various ways for data storage, compatibility (working together without errors) with various computer languages and interoperability (ability to operate together) between computer systems.

The most popular type of Unicode is UTF-8. Here, the 8 means that each Unicode character is represented by one or more 8-bit binary numbers. As a note, a set of 8 binary digits is called a byte. For example, whereas 1 is a bit or 0 is a bit, 0101 1100 is a byte

Meaning, in UTF-8, only one byte is used to represent common English characters. Hebrew, European, and Arabic characters are represented with two bytes. Three bytes are used to represent Chinese, Korean, Japanese, and other Asian characters. There are other Unicode characters that can be represented with four bytes.

Another useful aspect of UTF-8 is that it is backwards compatible (able to be used with an older piece of hardware or software without special adaptation or changes) with ASCII.

We covered all of this for two primary reasons:

1. It helps to know how a computer "understands" and "translates" characters.

2. You may run across these terms at some point. For example, some websites have (UTF-8) displayed in their address and so it is beneficial to understand what that means.

SUMMARY:

Computers are used to take in data, process it and then output data. Since much of the data we want to use computers for is in written form, we needed a way to represent text data that was common to all computers in the world. This is done by programming computers with a character set that is basically a "lookup table" showing the decimal and binary number that corresponds to each character needed in the computer. This means that when we see a character printed on the display, the actual data stored and used by the computer for that character is in binary, the only data that the computer can understand. Every displayed character on your computer screen is stored within your computer on a physical device containing transistors that are either on or off. Various character code systems exist that cover nearly every language used on earth.

Now that we've covered how the computer can "think" with text data, let's look at how it can present that data to us in visual form.

CHAPTER 47:
SCREENS

"One of the great challenges of our age,
in which the tools of our productivity are also the tools of our leisure (relaxation time),
is to figure out how to make more useful those moments of procrastination (putting off
work) *when we're idling in front of our computer screens."*
-Joshua Foer (American journalist, 1982-)

A television screen is the part of the TV that displays the pictures. It is the same thing with a computer: the computer monitor is the part of a computer where you can view things. Other terms for this part include "display" and "screen." They usually look like this:

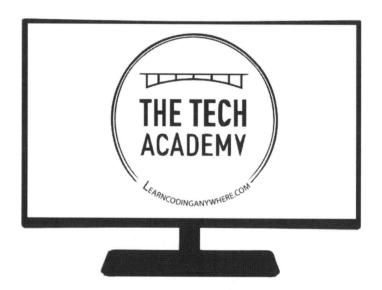

Occasionally, people mistake the monitor for the computer itself. The computer is not a display device; it is a data-processing machine that can make use of a display. The monitor is connected to the computer, but it is not the computer itself. It is only an I/O (Input/Output) device for the computer.

So, how do monitors work?

The original computer monitors were used mainly to facilitate (allow for; make easier) the input of data, while output was typically printed out on paper or tape.

For an example, a programmer could enter in a math problem using a keyboard and display, and then the answer would be printed out. Here is one of the original computer monitors:

The first computer to use a monitor was a US military computer in the 1950s.

To understand how digital displays work, we first need to discuss "pixels."

A pixel is the smallest single component of a digital image. It can be thought of as a small dot that helps to make up an image on a computer display, television or similar display device. Each pixel gets set to display a specific color and when many pixels are arranged together, an overall image is displayed that is a composite of the individual pixels.

If you are looking at a picture on a computer, that image is actually made up of many small pixels of different colors. Together, they combine to form the picture.

When you can see the individual dots on a screen, this is referred to as "pixelated." If we zoom in on this deer's ear, the ear is pixelated (meaning, the pixels are visible):

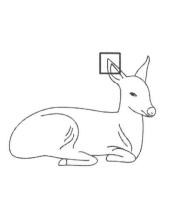 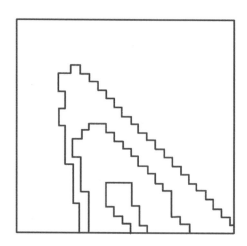

Original computer monitors usually had a black background with white, yellow or green pixels. Because text was only displayed using one color, this type of monitor was called a "monochrome" monitor, from the Greek "mono," meaning "one," and "chroma," meaning "color." You could see what looked like little squares on the screen, like this:

With a black and green monochrome screen, for example, each spot on the screen has two possible states: on (green) or off (black).

Simply put: these monitors work by computers instructing them which lights to turn on.

For example, the spot at the very top left of the screen can be turned on by code entered by a computer programmer. Programmers can command that the spot "five rows down and six spots to the right" be illuminated. Through combinations of lighting up various spots, pictures can be formed.

Modern computer monitors not only contain more than a million pixels, but each of those pixels can display millions of different colors. The basic idea is the same, though – each "dot" on the screen can be programmed to display colors. Through millions of combinations of these pixels, extremely clear and vibrant (bright) pictures can be displayed.

SUMMARY:

Monitors were a big step forward for computers as they offered a visual representation of what the computer is doing. Early computer monitors used one color to display information on the screen. These screens are made up of many spots, in a grid, and each one can be turned on or off to display the color. Using this grid of spots, we can represent text and images.

Let's look at some early monitors.

CHAPTER 48:
EARLY DISPLAYS

"Being a geek means never having to play it cool about how much you like something."
(Simon Pegg, English actor 1970-)

Early monitors used "cathode ray tubes." That sounds like something from a comic book, right? They're a type of vacuum tube (reminder: vacuum tubes are containers, from which virtually all air has been taken out, that can be used to control the flow of electricity).

Cathode ray tubes can produce light. They look like this:

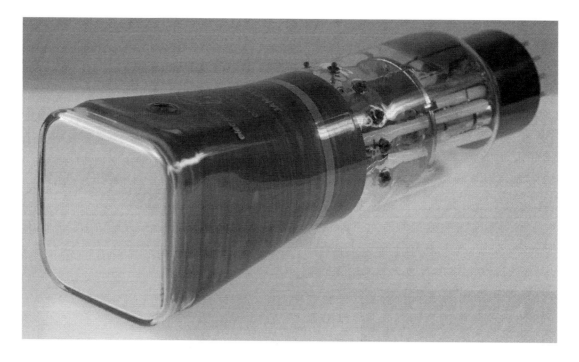

A cathode is the part of an object or device where electricity enters or exits. As the name states, there is a cathode inside cathode ray tubes:

Cathode ray tubes display images on screens by shooting out a tiny beam (ray of energy) from left to right on the screen. The screen contains several lines and the ray moves as shown in the picture below (left to right, diagonal down to the left, then to the right, etc.):

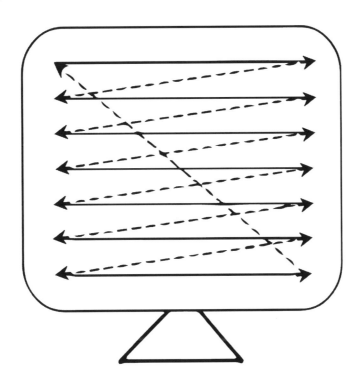

The cathode ray tube completes this whole cycle ("painting" the image on the screen top to bottom with a beam) several times a second – very quickly!

In the beginning of monitors, these rays could only be on or off and so you had black and white images. The ray literally turned on and off extremely quickly as it moved across the screen.

Computer programmers could instruct cathode ray tubes when and where to turn on and off, and thereby display data on a screen.

The cathode ray tube was invented by a German scientist named Karl Ferdinand Braun in 1897. His work made computer monitors possible!

SUMMARY:

Early computer monitors, like early televisions, used a device called a CRT (Cathode Ray Tube) to control the information displayed on the screen. The CRT uses a ray that moves rapidly across the screen from behind it. The ray could turn on and off, thereby controlling whether spots on the screen were on or off.

Considering cathode-ray displays aren't used much in the present, let's take a look at some popular modern displays.

CHAPTER 49:
MODERN DISPLAYS

*"I decided to make my password 'incorrect' because if I type it in wrong,
my computer will remind me, 'Your password is incorrect.'"*
-Unknown

In this chapter we are going to describe some of the most popular technologies used to display data on monitors. We will attempt to keep these explanations basic because full scientific descriptions of each of these would be very lengthy and aren't required for the purposes of this book. The intention is for you to understand the definition of these terms and have a basic understanding – not that you can go build a monitor from scratch!

"LED" stands for "Light-Emitting Diode." Emit means to send out. A diode is actually a specialized type of transistor. As a reminder, a transistor is a switch that controls the flow of electricity.

A diode is an electronic device that will allow electricity to pass through it in one direction only. Diodes can be modified so that when electricity passes through them, they give off light. They are then called Light Emitting Diodes.

An LED light is a small electronic device that can give off light.

LED lights generally use less electricity than other types of devices (such as light bulbs) and are usually less hot and, therefore, run a smaller chance of causing a fire.

Here are some LED lights:

LED monitors use LED lights to display data.

The first LED was developed in 1962 by an American named Nick Holobyak Jr.

Another type of screen that's popular are LCD monitors. "LCD" stands for "liquid crystal display."

Liquid crystals are a type of liquid (flowing substance) in a state between liquid and solid. They change shape like liquid does but have some similarities to crystals in appearance.

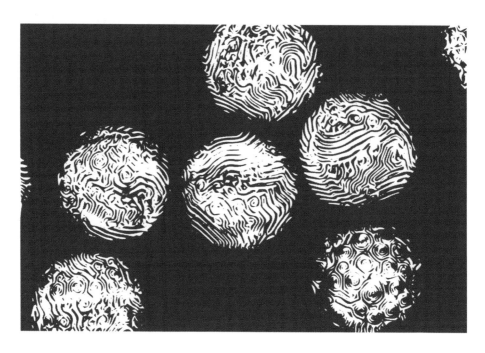

LCD displays utilize liquid crystals to display data. Electricity is used to control how much light passes through the crystals and how they're positioned.

Calculator displays have used LCD displays for a long time:

In the above picture, the liquid crystals are the "|" marks that block the light from coming through and thereby display the numbers. For example: the number 2 contains 5 liquid crystals:

LCD TVs operate in the same way, except with color and with much smaller liquid crystals.

An American named George H. Heilmeier is credited with having invented LCD in 1964.

Another type of LED display you might hear about is OLED. This stands for "Organic Light-Emitting Diode." To explain this we need to get a little scientific. "Organic" refers to a compound (something composed of multiple parts) that contains carbon. Carbon is an element (a substance in its most basic form that cannot be broken down – silicon is another example of an element). Carbon dioxide (a gas released by various things – for example: the gas released from cars as a result of burning gasoline) is *not* an element because it can be broken down into carbon and oxygen (the two components that make it up).

Every living substance on Earth contains carbon. Carbon is also found in many non-living materials, such as diamonds and coal.

Inside OLEDs is an organic (containing carbon) compound layer that emits (sends out) light. In OLED displays, the pixels each provide their own illumination. This is different from LED displays, where light comes from the back of the screen (called a backlight). Since there is no backlight on OLED displays, they can be made thinner than LED screens.

Here is a diagram that shows that OLED displays have fewer layers:

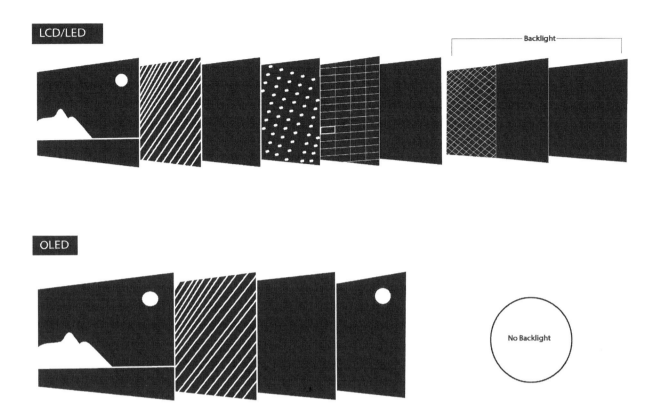

LCD/LED

OLED

Backlight

No Backlight

You can see that these screens are composed of several layers – each layer performs an exact function. Examples of layers in various displays are: crystal or glass.

OLED technology was developed by Ching W. Tang (a Chinese chemist) and Steven Van Slyke (an American chemist) in 1987. Isn't it interesting that so many of these technologies existed long before they entered general use?

Another type of display that is very popular is plasma screens.

Plasma is a type of gas (a substance that has no fixed shape or size, and that will expand freely to fill whatever container it's inside). Each pixel is illuminated by a tiny bit of plasma (a small section of gas with electricity applied to it).

Plasma video display was created by three Americans named Donald Bitzer, Robert Willson, and H. Gene Slottow in 1964 at the University of Illinois.

SUMMARY:

Since the main way we have computers present information to us is through a visual display, the technology used in computer displays has continually

evolved. As each new technology came along, it used less electricity, or had a more accurate and colorful display method, or both. Common technologies used in modern displays are LED (Light-Emitting Diode), LCD (Liquid Crystal Display) and OLED (Organic LED).

In the future, other types of displays will be released. The basic function of 1s and 0s specifying *what* to place *where* on screens will remain the same.

Now that you have the basic idea of how computers display data, let's dive into how computers connect to and communicate with other computers.

CHAPTER 50:
<u>NETWORKS</u>

"The most compelling reason for most people to buy a computer for the home will be to link it to a nationwide communications network.
We're just in the beginning stages of what will be a truly remarkable breakthrough for most people – as remarkable as the telephone."
-Steve Jobs in 1985 (Co-Founder of Apple, 1955-2011)

A network is a system where two or more computers are connected to each other. The computers can be connected by a cable (i.e. a wired connection) or connected wirelessly (through the air). Network is the word used to describe the link between things that are working together and is used in many different ways with computers.

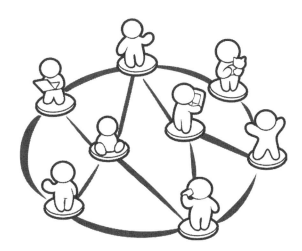

Information can be shared from computer to computer through the use of a network.

Prior to networks, computers operated independently (separately).

A Local Area Network (LAN) is a type of network where the computers are located near each other (in the same room or building, for example). The fact that the computers are connected via the network allows them to share access to files and devices (such as printers).

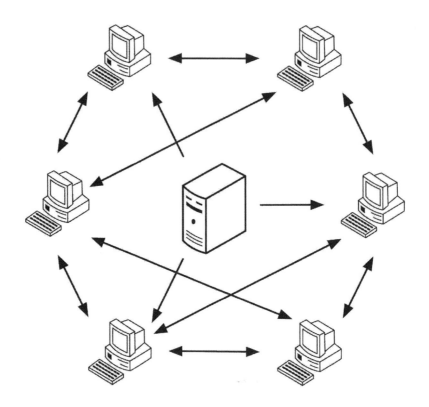

In the gaming community, gamers sometimes bring their computers to a central location for a large gaming activity called a "LAN Party." All the computers will be connected together for the duration of the event, and the players can play multiplayer computer games.

The first instance of a computer-to-computer link was established on the Advanced Research Projects Agency Network (ARPANET) in 1969. It occured between two computers at the University of California, Los Angeles (UCLA). The message "LOGIN" was sent, though only "L" and "O" were received – the network crashed (stopped functioning) before the rest of the message was relayed. The network soon expanded to include computers located at several schools and military facilities.

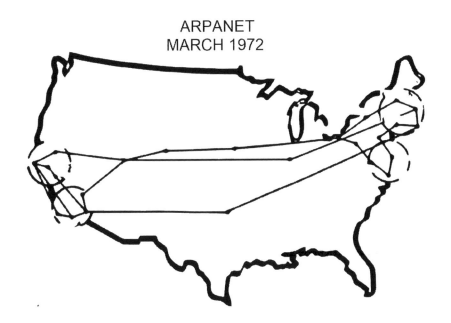

ARPANET
MARCH 1972

Information can be sent over a network as "packets." Packets are small clusters (groups of related things) of digital information broken up from larger messages. The purpose of packets is to speed data transmission by sending it in smaller pieces, as opposed to a larger whole.

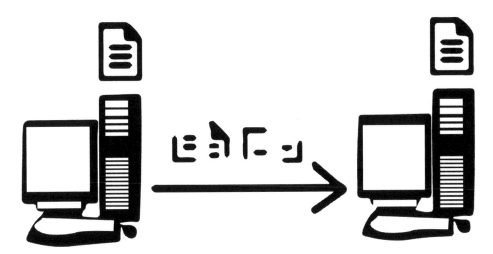

By sending the packets of data over multiple networks, one could increase the speed of data transmission.

Networks were originally developed for educational purposes, such as allowing the sharing of research.

Another purpose of the networks was to allow computers to use the processing powers of other computers via a network. Let's say you wanted to perform a function on your computer that would take a long time; using this network you could "piggyback" off another computer on the network, thereby increasing speed.

The U.S. government became involved in networks as well, in the interest of increasing the defense and security of their nation.

The idea was to create a network which allowed communication through computers throughout the United States. A key aspect of this network's design was that it could still operate even if a section of it was knocked out. As a dark example: if an attack destroyed a portion of the East Coast, this network could continue to operate by sending the data over different sections of the network. There became so many networks that if "Section A" ceased working, the data could simply be sent over "Section B."

SUMMARY:

Networks allow computers to "talk to" one another. ARPANET (Advanced Research Projects Agency Network) was the first computer network. One of the most common ways for data to be sent over a network is through packets – small clusters of digital information broken up from larger messages.

We will now go over a vital machine used in connection with networks.

CHAPTER 51:
ROUTING

"The internet's not written in pencil, Mark, it's written in ink."
-The movie "The Social Network"

A router is a machine that sends data to one or more locations. It is most commonly used to transfer information to various computers that are connected in a network.

Routers typically look like this:

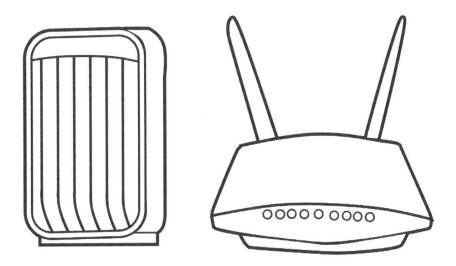

If you had a network where one computer had a set of data that was commonly accessed by the other computers in the network, a router would help manage the requests by those computers for that data. This would be especially important in the event that two simultaneous requests were given to access the same computer – the router would make sure that the requests were both handled.

Routers are commonly used to allow a user's computer to connect to the internet, which is a huge network of computers around the world.

The first routers were created the same year (1981) in separate locations – one at the Massachusetts Institute of Technology (MIT) by Noel Chiappa (a European inventor) and the other at Stanford University by William Yeager (an American engineer).

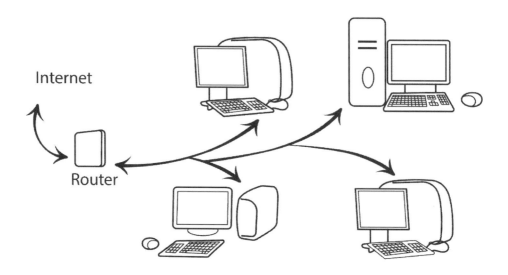

A router is the conductor of the computers on a network.

SUMMARY:

When you connect multiple computers together to form a network, they often need to send messages back and forth between themselves. A special piece of equipment called a router helps to manage the traffic of these messages between the computers. Routers also connect computers to the internet.

And this brings us to the most popular network of all time!

CHAPTER 52:
INTERNET

"We're still in the first minutes of the first day of the internet revolution."
-Scott Cook (American businessman, 1952-)

Internet is a combination of the words "interconnected" and "network."

The internet is an interconnected network of many computers around the world. It is the largest network in existence and allows computers to pass data to one another.

There are lots of different types of data that can be sent back and forth between computers connected to the internet – like electronic messages, electronic documents, healthcare records, etc.

In addition to referring to the connected computers that make up this network, internet also means the set of agreements, or protocols, for how to transfer different types of data between those computers.

A "protocol" is an official procedure. In technology, it is a formal description of how a certain type of information will be formatted and handled. Basically, it's an agreement that the various people who work with that type of information all adhere to. Protocols are usually described in written documents, and are very precise. They are created by experts in the applicable industry.

An example of a type of data where a protocol would be valuable is healthcare information. If various organizations in the healthcare industry were to transfer healthcare data back and forth between computers as they perform their work, it would be important that they all agree about things like the exact format of the information, how to keep private data safe, etc. All of that would be laid down in a written protocol. Several such protocols do exist in the healthcare industry.

One or more protocols have been created for each type of data that can be transferred around on the internet. Violation of these protocols results in an error and the data will not be transferred properly or at all.

So to recap: the internet is an interconnected network of many computers around the world, and a set of agreements, or protocols, for transferring different types of data between those computers.

The internet finds its roots in the earlier-mentioned ARPANET.

The protocols (sets of rules governing the exchange between devices) used by the ARPANET that assisted in the development of the internet were called Transmission Control Protocol and Internet Protocol (TCP/IP).

These protocols cover the required format of data sent over the internet and allow delivery of data that is broken into smaller packets. These protocols are used to set up the connection between the sending and receiving computers on the internet.

Remember how we talked about data being sent in packets? We take the data, break it up into pieces (packets), send it across a network and then reassemble it on the other end. The TCP/IP protocols handle all that.

The purpose of this book isn't to make you an expert in protocols; they're mentioned here as a key development that led to the creation of the internet. The inventors of the internet include Robert E. Kahn (American electrical engineer) and

Vint Cerf (American inventor) who are both sometimes referred to as the fathers of the internet.

Another term related to the subject of Internet Protocol (IP), is Internet Protocol address (IP address). An IP address is the numbered address of a machine, in the format used on the internet. Each computer that uses the internet is assigned its own IP address so that it can be identified by the other computers in the network. IP addresses are written as a series of numbers with periods in between them. They designate an exact computer and are written like this: 128.192.12.9.

In the 1980s, researchers began to assemble the "network of networks" that became the modern internet.

SUMMARY:

The internet is a worldwide network of connected computers that use various protocols, or formal agreements, to transfer different types of data between those computers.

It wasn't until a later development occurred that the internet was widely used. So what was it that boosted the popularity of the internet?

CHAPTER 53:
WWW

"The World Wide Web is the only thing I know of whose shortened form takes three times longer to say than what it's short for."
-Douglas Adams (English author, 1952-2001)

The internet became widely used after Tim Berners-Lee (British computer scientist) invented the World Wide Web in 1989. And no, the World Wide Web and the internet are not the same thing.

The World Wide Web (abbreviated "www" or the "web") is a collection of linked electronic documents, organized into groups called websites.

A website is composed of one or more individual webpages, where a "page" is an organized, separate document containing text, images, video and other elements.

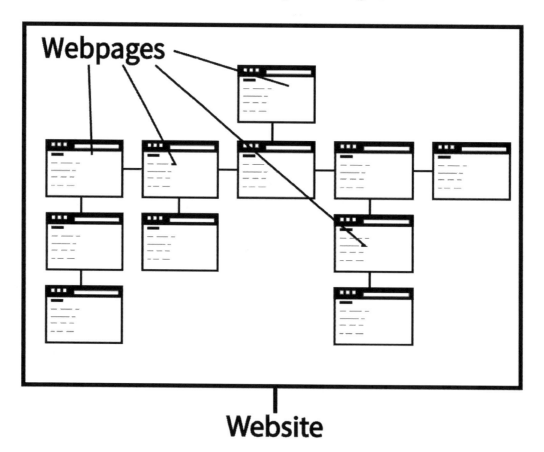

The electronic files that make up a website are stored on specialized computers called web servers (computers used to store and transmit data). Web servers accept requests from other, remote computers for specific webpages, and deliver those files needed to make the webpage display on the remote computer. The type of program you would use to view webpages is called a web browser. The web browser is the program that would make the requests to the web server for the website files.

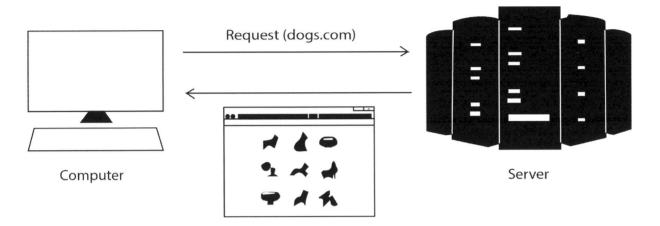

As of 2020, there were around two billion websites.

You've heard the term "surfing" the web, right? Well, it originated in 1992, courtesy of a New York librarian named Jean Armour Polly. "Surfing" means to move from website to website on the internet. Even now, the term is used quite often, but other words such as "browsing" have also become a popular addition.

So, what's the difference between the internet and the World Wide Web? The internet is the hardware and protocols for exchanging information, whereas the web is one type of information that is accessed over the internet. The web is a collection of linked electronic documents called webpages.

The internet is the infrastructure (physical framework), while the web is the code that is transmitted and displayed. In a way, the internet is the hardware and the web is the software.

The web is the largest collection of data ever assembled by mankind. By far.

A single example of this is the fact that Wikipedia is the largest encyclopedia ever created.

A wiki is a website that allows the people viewing it to add things and change the website. Wikis are a team effort where anyone can alter the website, as long as they follow the basic rules established by the operators of the wiki.

"Wiki" means "quick" in Hawaiian. The first wiki was created in 1994 by an American computer programmer named Howard G. Cunningham. He was the one who chose to use that word.

Wikipedia is a free encyclopedia on the web, created through the collaborative effort of a community of people known as Wikipedians. Anyone who signs up for the site can create and edit articles in the encyclopedia.

Though there are strict guidelines for posting data on Wikipedia, not all information on Wikipedia is completely accurate or true because virtually anyone can post on it. Note: the word "post" refers to placing something online. A post is a public message, article, picture, etc. placed on the web.

SUMMARY:

The internet and the World Wide Web (the "web") are not the same thing. The internet is a worldwide network of connected computers that use various protocols, or formal agreements, to transfer different types of data between those computers, whereas the web is a collection of linked electronic documents that are stored on some of the computers that make up the internet. These documents, called "webpages," are accessed by using a special program called a web browser. There is a protocol, or agreement, that describes how these webpages are to be sent between the computers on the internet. There are other protocols that describe how to handle other types of electronic data as it is transferred between these computers.

Let's take a deeper look at protocols.

CHAPTER 54:
RULES

"Really, if you think about it, it (the World Wide Web) doesn't need the //.
I could have designed it not to have the //.
Look at all the paper and trees that could have been saved if people had not had to write or
type out those slashes on paper over the years – not to mention the human labor and time
spent typing those two keystrokes countless millions of times in browser address boxes.
But there you go, it seemed like a good idea at the time."
-Sir Timothy John Berners-Lee (Inventor of the World Wide Web, 1955-)

The double slash (//) mentioned in the above quote refers to the // you see in website addresses. Here's an example: http://dogs.com

You've probably seen web addresses like this thousands of times. We are going to break down every part of it in this chapter, starting at the beginning.

"HTTP" stands for "Hypertext Transfer Protocol."

Hypertext is text in a document that, when accessed, takes you to another document. Since hypertext documents are the content that makes up the World Wide Web, it's accurate to say that HTTP is the transmission (the act of passing or sending out) protocol that makes the web possible.

As the name states, Hypertext Transfer Protocol is a protocol (an agreed-upon system for formatting and transmitting various types of data).

HTTP is the agreed-upon system for organizing and transmitting hypertext documents.

Most computers are designed so that they can use HTTP, so HTTP is an important way of ensuring computers can communicate with each other via the internet and that the World Wide Web keeps working. If you try to make a webpage without following HTTP (the protocols required in making a webpage), your webpage won't work correctly.

Note: HTTPS means the same thing as HTTP, except HTTPS is more secure (the "S" stands for secure). This means that the website has successfully completed certain required actions to be considered a secure website. By secure is meant that sensitive data (payment info, personal data, passwords, etc.) is more likely to be kept confidential than on non-secure websites. There are certain requirements one must meet in making a website compliant with HTTPS. Secure websites usually have a locked lock symbol next to their title, whereas unsecure sites (sites only containing http, with no "s," at the beginning of their name), have an unlocked lock symbol next to them.

Back to the original website address we used as an example (http://dogs.com) – the next point to define is the ":" symbol. This has a special meaning in this case.

":" is a colon. The colon is used when separating the protocol (HTTP) from the rest of the address of a website. It is placed after http to create a separation point to help the computer find the address you want to go to. It is basically telling the computer, "using the Hypertext Transfer Protocol, find the following website."

The colon is used in a browser's address bar to separate two things. To the left of the colon, you'll find the protocol the browser is using in requesting, receiving, and displaying information found using the internet. To the right of the colon, you'll find the source of the particular information being requested and displayed.

Colons are used in lots of ways in the computer industry, but at its root meaning, it is nearly always used to separate two things that have some sort of a relationship to each other, but that are different.

The next item to define in our website address (http://dogs.com) is the / (slash).

A slash is a symbol most commonly used in the following ways:

a. To show choices – meaning literally "and or"; for example "small/medium/large" on a menu.

b. To show a ratio (comparing figures) of things. For example: miles/day in traveling would be how many miles you travel per day; it could be spoken as "miles per day."

c. To separate sections in the addresses of websites. When you have a website, the name of it follows http://. To go to an individual webpage, an additional / is added between the website name and the specific webpage on that site that is being requested.

Let's say that we want to view a webpage just about boxers (type of dog) on dogs.com. That could be written out as: http://dogs.com/boxer

The "/boxer" separates the website from the webpage.

This brings us to the double slash.

The double slash was originally created in the 1980s to help separate the different parts of the address, but two slashes aren't actually necessary. One slash is adequate and there is actually no difference. Try it: type a website address out and write only one slash after http: – it works!

With that said, when following "http:," it is common practice to have //. If you type a website in with only one /, it will usually automatically format (adjust content) to //. Basically, // is used following http: to separate it from www. or the name of the website, and it holds the same meaning as a single slash. Just as with a single slash, it is simply meant to separate different parts of the address – it separates the protocol and the website name.

Back to http://dogs.com.

Even the dot has a meaning! The dot (.) is used in computers to separate multiple pieces of data, where the whole set of data is meant to be processed by the computer.

The "." character is used by the computer to show where one piece of data ends and another begins.

When you type google.com, you are telling the computer that the name of the place you want to go is "Google," and that Google is a "com" (stands for commercial – something that exists for profit) entity.

"Google" and "com" are different things. One is a name, the other is a type of thing, and the "." separates the two. Again, "com" at the end of website addresses indicates that it is a company that exists to make money (as opposed to a charity).

SUMMARY:

In order to locate a specific webpage on a specific website, you need to tell the computer what protocol to use (HTTP), what website to look for, what page on that website to look for and what type of website it is (e.g. .com). An example is: http://www.dogs.com/boxer. Here, the protocol is HTTP, the website is www.dogs.com, and the webpage is boxers.

Now you should be able to read through most website names with understanding! So, what is the official word for website names?

CHAPTER 55:
ADDRESSES

"There's a theory that if you gave a million monkeys typewriters and set them to work,
they'd eventually come up with the complete works of Shakespeare.
Thanks to the internet, we now know this isn't true."
-Ian Hart (English actor, 1964-)

A Uniform Resource Locator (URL) is a unique name for a web resource. A "web resource" is an identifiable thing that can be found on the internet. Examples are: webpages, other computers, printers, etc.

Along with the name, URLs contain a description of how to access web resources. This is needed because different types of data need to be accessed in different ways.

The most common use for URLs is seen in web addresses – the unique name of websites.

The website name we discussed in the previous chapter (http://dogs.com) is the URL. URLs list out the protocol (in this case, http), the name (dogs) and the domain (.com). So, what is a domain?

Well, literally, a domain is a location or area.

In computers, domains are the various categories of websites that are available on the World Wide Web. Typically, these are categories like "websites for commercial companies," "websites for educational institutions," etc. These categories are given two- or three-character names.

In the example just mentioned, "com" is the domain – the commercial domain.

Educational institution URLs end in "edu" – the educational domain.

Governmental institution URLs end in "gov" – the government domain.

Organization URLs sometimes end in "org" – which is short for "organization." Originally, the org domain was set up for nonprofit organizations and charities, but nowadays anyone can use it.

Businesses sometimes use the "net" domain, which is short for "network." Websites ending in .net sometimes exist because the URL using .com was already taken. For example: computers.net is a different website than computers.com, though both sites are about the same subject.

Some companies purchase multiple domains for their website and have them all send people to one website. For example: google.net takes you to google.com.

There are other domains, like "us" for United States, "ca" for Canada, "eu.com" for Europe commercial, "co.uk" for commercial United Kingdom, "biz" for business, "info" (short for "information") for informative websites, and even "fun" for anyone who considers their website fun. Whereas certain domains require proof that a website falls under a particular category (such as .gov), many require no proof and can be purchased by anyone (such as .info and .fun).

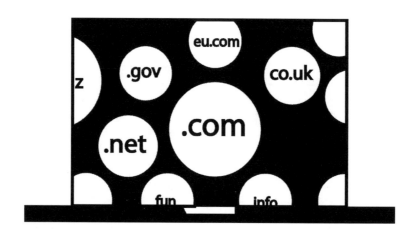

The Domain Name System (DNS) is a naming system for computers connected to the internet. Typically the names for a computer are represented in the DNS by a series of four numbers, separated by periods – for example, 127.0.0.1 is a DNS name. Remember, each resource on the internet needs a unique identifier so it can be located by the other computers in the network.

DNS is something that works in the background when you are on the internet. DNS changes domain names from human language (e.g. doughnuts.com) to computer language (e.g. 131.235.98.45). It does this because your computer doesn't understand "doughnuts.com." Your computer and the internet communicate with numbers.

DNS is sometimes compared to a phone book. You tell your computer where you want to go on the internet, DNS translates that to your computer and the internet, and voila!, you are taken there. DNS helps people navigate the internet.

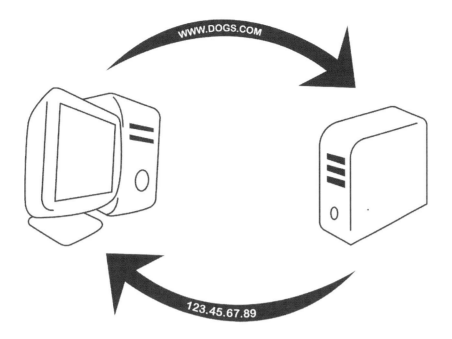

To recap, URLs contain the protocol, website name and domain – it tells your browser how and where to find the information to be displayed.

SUMMARY:

Anything you can connect to over the internet (webpages, printers, computers, etc.) has a unique identifier so it can be located by the other computers on the internet. This unique identifier is called a URL (Uniform Resource Locator). URLs are a series of four numbers. For example, 123.45.67.890. In order to make these URLs easier for humans to understand, a system on the internet called the Domain Name System is used to provide a unique text name that corresponds to each URL. An example is www.dogs.com.

Websites stored on the internet are organized into various domains, or areas, based on the type of data on the websites. For example, websites used by for-profit companies are in the "com" domain, while websites used by governments are in the "gov" domain. A full URL gives a computer all the information it needs to locate a specific resource on the internet.

You now have a basic understanding of what website addresses mean. Now let's take a look at another popular protocol used on the internet.

CHAPTER 56:
MAIL

"Electric communication will never be a substitute for the face of someone who with their soul encourages another person to be brave and true."
-Charles Dickens (English author, 1812-1870)

"Email" stands for "electronic mail." It is used for sending "mail" to someone using your computer.

Email is written communication sent person-to-person using computers. You type out what you want to say, and then send it to another person. The other person receives the email and then can read it and reply if they choose.

As of 2020, about 300,000,000,000 (three hundred billion) emails are sent out over the internet each day.

Email is sent using "Simple Mail Transfer Protocol" (SMTP). SMTP is a protocol for formatting and exchanging email messages between computers, whereas HTTP is a protocol for sending websites over the web.

When emails are sent to large groups all at once, they are called "bulk emails."

Email spam, also known as junk mail, is unsolicited bulk emails.

It is estimated that 90% of all emails sent out are spam emails.

Spam got its name from an episode of Monty Python (a British television show from the 1960s) where the canned meat product called Spam is described as "horrible, ubiquitous (existing everywhere) and inescapable."

An interesting note on how the internet operates: an email might be split into several packets of data and transmitted from one computer across a bunch of separate telephone lines. The packets aren't sent in any sequence and don't all follow the same route. Along with the packets are instructions on how to reassemble them at the receipt point (another computer).

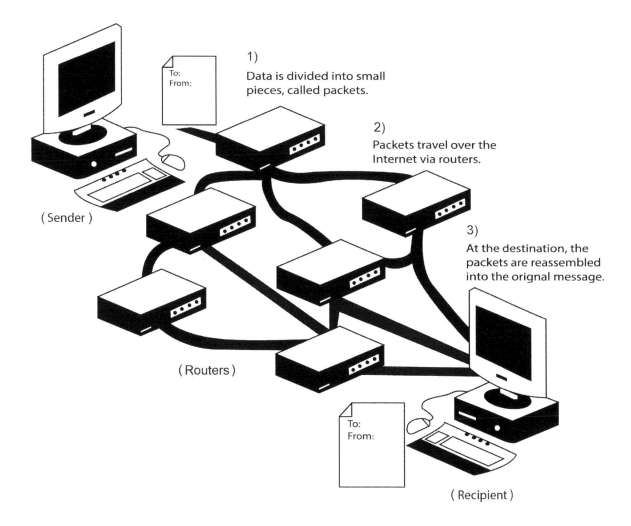

1) Data is divided into small pieces, called packets.

2) Packets travel over the Internet via routers.

3) At the destination, the packets are reassembled into the orignal message.

(Sender)

(Routers)

(Recipient)

Emails occasionally have "attachments." An attachment is information connected to an email. For example, if you sent someone an email and included a picture in the email, the picture would be an attachment.

SUMMARY:

One of the primary uses of the internet is to send electronic messages from one computer to another. These messages are called "email" – electronic mail. The protocol used on the internet to send these messages is called Simple Mail Transfer Protocol. When these messages are sent from one computer to another, they may be broken up into separate pieces, sent over various wires to the destination computer, and reconstructed when they all reach the destination computer according to instructions included with the email on how to reassemble the data to its original form.

Nowadays, most devices are connected to the internet and can send emails – let's look into this further.

CHAPTER 57:
SMART OR DUMB?

"Every time there's a new tool, whether it's internet or cell phones or anything else,
all these things can be used for good or evil.
Technology is neutral; it depends on how it's used."
-Rick Smolan (Professional photographer, 1949-)

A "smart" machine is a machine that can connect to other machines and and/or networks. They are usually interactive (allowing a flow of information that goes both ways – from computer to user and vice versa) and can operate independently.

Smart is put in front of machine names to indicate that they are a computer + that machine type. For example: a smartphone is a computer + phone. A smartwatch is a computer + watch.

An element of "smart" devices is that they typically can connect to the internet. This allows you to control them over the internet.

Examples of this are a smart washer or a smart heating system, both of which you could activate remotely (from a distance) over the internet.

SUMMARY:

We are no longer using the internet just for allowing computers to connect to each other. Now, we can install small computers into various other devices, such as home appliances, and allow those devices to use the internet to communicate with the other computers and devices connected to the internet. These are called "smart devices."

As you know, you aren't required to connect your smartphone, or even your computer, to the internet with a wire. So, how does that work?

CHAPTER 58:
WIFI

"Imagine if trees gave off wifi signals, we would be planting so many trees
and we'd probably save the planet too.
Too bad they only produce the oxygen we breathe."
-Unknown

Wi-Fi (also written WiFi or wifi) is a technology for linking up computers or other devices in a network without the use of physical connectors like wires.

As we covered earlier, computers can be connected over a network by a cable (wired) or connected wirelessly.

Wifi is used to connect computers and devices to the internet wirelessly.

To understand how WiFi works, you must understand radio waves.

Radio waves are a form of energy that moves at the speed of light. It can be sent through objects and can be used to transmit information (like data and sound).

Here is a radio tower sending out radio waves:

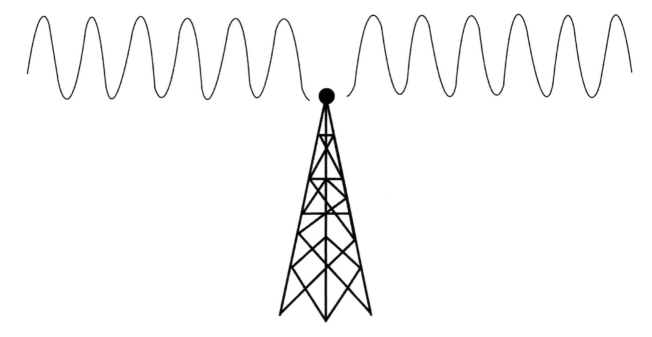

The word "radio" comes from "ray" or "beam."

How it works is that a transmitter (a device that can put out radio waves) sends out the data. The data travels through the air and arrives at a receiver (a device that can receive radio waves).

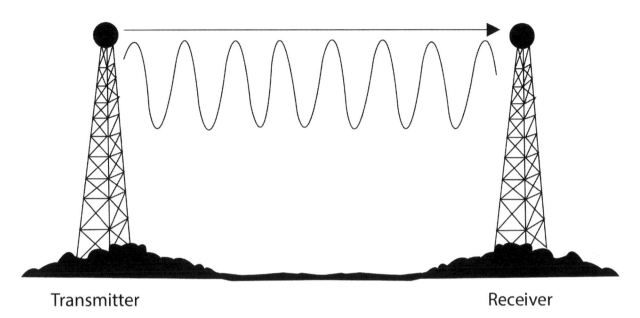

Transmitter   Receiver

Your cellphone has a transmitter and receiver built in.

Wifi uses radio waves to send data through the air. WiFi-compatible (meaning, able to connect to the internet via WiFi) computers are able to translate data to radio waves prior to sending it out via WiFi, and can translate received radio waves into digital data that it can process.

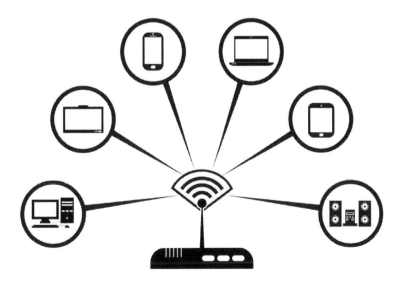

The name WiFi was chosen as a pun on the word "hi-fi" (high fidelity). Fidelity

refers to how exact a copy is made, compared to the original item. High fidelity sound is sound, played from a recording, that has very little distortion and sounds very similar to the original. Some say that WiFi means "wireless fidelity," but that isn't true.

WiFi was created in 1997 by an Australian named John O'Sullivan and a team of workers.

The term used to describe the potential speed of an internet connection is "bandwidth." Bandwidth is the capacity for traffic flow on the path that information travels on to and from a computer. The more bandwidth there is, the faster information can be sent. Bandwidth determines how fast information can be transferred from computer to computer. If something takes a lot of bandwidth up, it means that it is comprised of a lot of information and it takes up a lot of the "path."

You can think of bandwidth as similar to a pipe, in that the wider the pipe (bandwidth), the more water (data) can flow through.

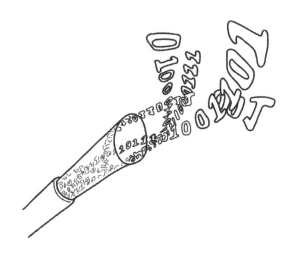

Even though wifi is extremely popular, wired connections are more secure and can transmit data faster.

SUMMARY:

Early computers that were joined together in a network relied on physical wires to make the connections that would be used to transfer information between those computers in the network. New devices were created in the 1990s that used radio waves to pass this information between computers without the use of a physical connection. These devices are called "WiFi" devices. They use

transmitters to send data, and receivers to receive data. Many computers still rely on physical wire connections to allow data transfer over a network.

Let's discuss some of the most popular wired connections.

CHAPTER 59:
WIRED CONNECTIONS

"Being the richest man in the cemetery doesn't matter to me.
Going to bed at night saying we've done something wonderful, that's what matters to me."
-Steve Jobs (Co-founder of Apple, 1955-2011)

Another popular way to connect computers to the internet is called ethernet. The word "ether" refers to the upper regions of space; the clear sky; the heavens.

Ethernet is a set of technologies for creating computer networks that relies on physical wires to connect computers to the network. It was developed in the late 1970s by two American inventors named Robert Metcalfe and David Boggs.

An Ethernet cable is able to handle the transfer of information in both directions simultaneously. These cables look like this:

When you say a computer is hardwired in, you're saying that the computer is connected to the internet with a physical cable, like an Ethernet cable.

And then there is DSL, which stands for Digital Subscriber Line. A subscriber is someone that requests to receive information from a particular source. DSL is another way to access the internet at a high speed – it uses telephone lines to transmit data.

Subscribers connect to the internet through the telephone line leading to their building or home.

Prior to DSL was dial-up internet. Dial-up was when a computer dialed a phone number to connect to the internet. Establishing a connection took around 10 seconds. People using the internet in the 1990s probably remember the interesting beeping and electronic noises made while the computer was connecting in this way.

Dial-up internet connection was relatively slow and also prohibited users from using their landline phones because it tied up the phone line while the computer was using it.

DSL was a better option than dial-up because it allowed users to make calls and utilize the internet simultaneously, and the internet connection was faster than a dial-up connection. Here is a DSL router with the cable used to connect it to a computer:

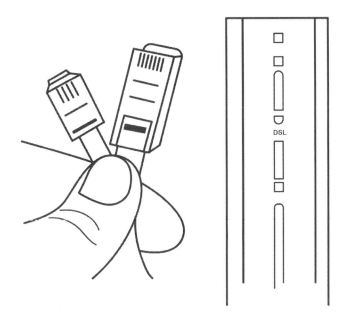

As of 2020, the fastest possible type of internet connection is fiber optics.

Fiber is a physical cable that can be used to transfer information over long distances. It is made out of glass or plastic, formed into threads (fibers).

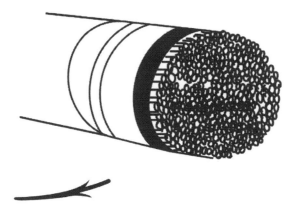

Optics is the study of visible and invisible light.

Fiber optic cables can carry pulses of light which represent data. These pulses of light move at the speed of light – 186,000 miles per second. When computers are connected by fiber optics, data transfer between them happens very quickly.

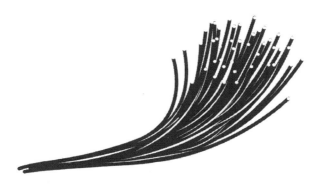

SUMMARY:

There are various technologies and equipment used to physically connect computers in a network like the internet. The most common are Ethernet, DSL (Digital Subscriber Line) and fiber optics (the fastest connection available).

Now that we've covered popular wired connections, let's go over some additional wireless connections.

CHAPTER 60:
WIRELESS CONNECTIONS

"WiFi went down for 5 minutes.
I had to talk to my family.
They seem like nice people."
-Unknown

Another way to connect devices is Near-Field Communication (abbreviated NFC). This is a technology that allows two computers to communicate with each other when they are brought within four centimeters (1.6 inches) of each other (this distance may expand in the future).

One of the uses of NFC is to allow people to pay for things using their mobile phones simply by moving their phone close to a payment device. It can also be used to share videos, files, photos, etc. Like WiFi, NFC transfers data via radio waves.

Another wireless transmission method is LiFi. This is a way of transferring data by light. It was invented by Harald Hass (Germann professor) in 2011 and is actually faster than WiFi!

How it works is that the light changes brightness imperceivably fast (so quickly you cannot see it with the human eye) and is picked up by a detector that processes the changes in light. Whereas WiFi can be sent through walls and barriers using radio waves, LiFi can only travel as light does – it doesn't pass through walls or solid barriers.

And then there's Bluetooth. Bluetooth technology was invented by Jaap Haartsen (Dutch engineer) in the 1990s. It is a wireless way to pass data using radio waves but the two devices involved have to be within around 33 feet (10 meters) or less of each other. As a note: there are some newer versions of bluetooth that can transmit data hundreds of feet and this will probably continue to improve with time.

Bluetooth components in small devices take up very little space and use a tiny amount of power. Devices can simultaneously be connected to and utilize both WiFi and a bluetooth connection without any effect on each other.

Bluetooth is totally different than Blu-ray. Blu-ray is a standardized way of storing video and audio data on plastic discs so the data can be used by computers. It is also used to refer to the discs themselves. These are a type of Digital Video Disc (DVD – a disc used to store data, usually videos).

Blu-ray allows much clearer and higher-quality videos and sound than earlier technologies, and can store much more data.

Apple has a product built into some of their phones and devices called "AirDrop." This utilizes Bluetooth and wifi to transfer data over short distances.

All of these various data transmission methods come down to passing signals through space to computers that can be converted into binary (1s and 0s), which in turn cause the computer to set various internal transistors to on and off.

SUMMARY:

There are several different types of wireless technologies used to allow data transfer between the devices connected to a network like the internet. Examples are NFC (Near Field Communication), LiFi, Bluetooth and AirDrop (a technology from Apple).

Speaking of Apple, let's discuss some of the major tech companies you've probably heard of.

CHAPTER 61:
TECH GIANTS

"Be nice to nerds. Chances are you'll end up working for one."
-Bill Gates (Co-Founder of Microsoft, 1955-)

The major tech companies that contributed to where we are today are too numerous to list.

With that said, in no particular order, here are four computer companies you should know about:

1. Microsoft: Founded in 1975 by Bill Gates and Paul Allen, Microsoft is one of the largest technology companies in the world. Microsoft stands for "microcomputer software." "Micro-" means "small." Microsoft makes software and electronic devices. They offer a wide range of services and products and are one of the most valuable companies on the planet. They are based in Washington state.

2. Intel: Founded in 1968 by Gordon Moore and Robert Noyce, Intel is one of the most successful computer hardware manufacturers on the planet. Intel makes specialized parts for computers and is based in California.

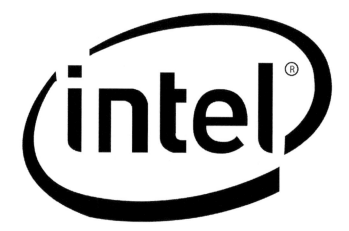

3. Apple: Founded in 1976 by Steve Jobs and Steve Wozniak. At the time this book was written, Apple was the top computer and electronics company on the planet.

It is based in Cupertino, California.

4. IBM (International Business Machines): Founded in 1911 by Charles Ranlett Flint and Thomas J. Watson Sr., IBM sells software and hardware. They're one of the largest companies on Earth.

It would take dozens of books to cover everything about these companies. Suffice it to say: we are fortunate they exist.

There are *many* other noteworthy technology companies, such as Facebook (a website for connecting with friends and family), Amazon (online retailer that has expanded into many other major industries), Google, and SpaceX (an outer space exploration company), but the above are mentioned as *computer-specific companies*. Again, while there are many more, we are mentioning these ones because they're covered several times in this book.

SUMMARY:

There are millions of companies around the world involved in the computer industry in one way or another. These technology companies have a great influence on society. Some of the most successful are Microsoft, Apple, Intel and IBM.

Now let's look at some of the various types of computers.

CHAPTER 62:
TYPES OF COMPUTERS

"My laptop has freed me to travel."
-Steven Pinker (Canadian-American author, 1954-)

There are many types of computers but the three most used by the general public are:

1. Desktop computers (computers that aren't very portable and are meant to be used at one's desk).

2. Laptops (small, lightweight portable computers that can be flipped open and shut).

3. Mobile devices (hand-held, portable computers).

Desktop computers are computers that are typically created for use in one location, such as a desk in an office (hence the name). These differ from laptops, which are typically created for use wherever the user wishes.

Desktops typically consist of a display screen, a tower (the computer itself), a keyboard and a mouse.

Here is what a tower looks like:

Here's a desktop from the early 1990s:

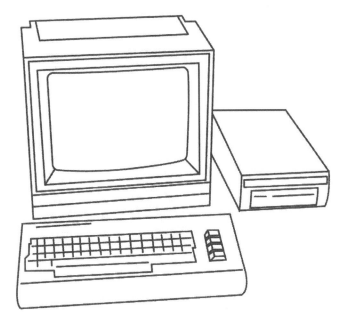

Many companies provide desktops to their employees.

Laptops can be carried around and usually weigh less than 8 pounds. They're powered by rechargeable batteries and are called laptops because you can fit them on the top of your lap.

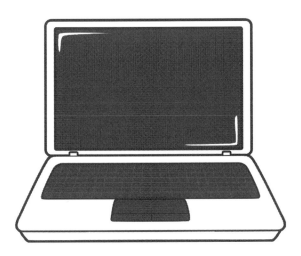

Mobile means "not requiring a fixed location in order to operate." The word literally means "able to move around."

Mobile telephones are an example of a mobile device.

Another term for mobile phones is "cell phones". Here's why:

A cell is the smallest functioning part of your body.

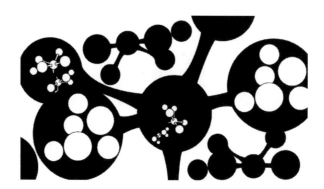

This term is part of how the phrase "cell phone" came about. It is related to how the phones interact with the towers that allow them to send and receive information.

Here are what cell phone towers look like – you've probably seen them around:

Each tower has a range around it in which it can send and receive data to various computer devices, as long as the device has the correct receiver and transmitter in it. Once you go beyond that range, the device and the tower can't detect each other anymore. In most places around the world now, before you pass out of the range of one tower, you pass into the range of a new tower.

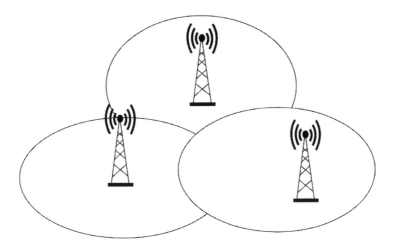

This area around a tower in which the signal is effective is called a "cell," from its resemblance to a physical cell in a body.

Towers are physically placed close enough to each other that these cells overlap – so that information can be passed from one cell to another. That way information can go from your cell phone, across this network of cells, to the cell phone of the person you're talking to.

You can be on a phone call while you are in a car and the call can continue for quite some time, as the connection to your phone is transferred from one cell tower to another, based on your changing location.

A cellular network (or mobile network) refers to the total coverage of cell towers. Nowadays most carriers (cell phone service companies) have cellular networks that span entire countries.

The first cell phone was created in 1973 and looked like this:

Cell phones didn't become available to the general public until the 1980s.

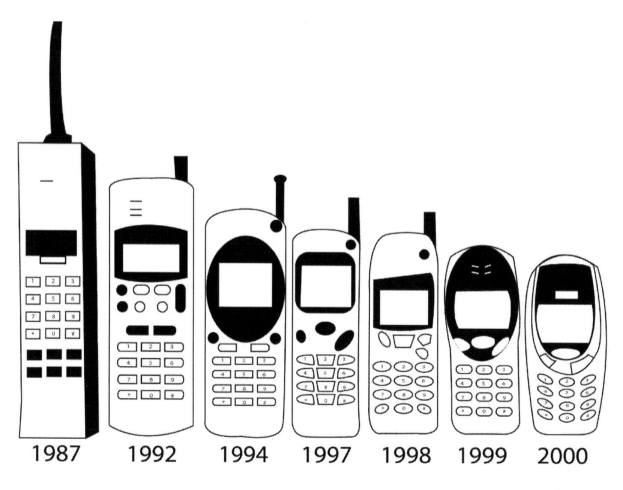

A smartphone is a handheld mobile computer that can connect to the internet. This makes it so the smartphone can function as a cell phone, but also as an internet-connected computer. You can use a smartphone to access websites, perform work tasks, play games, etc.

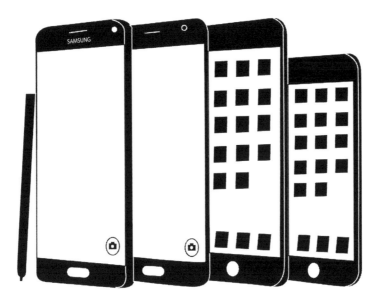

Nearly all cell phones being manufactured today are smartphones. The first smartphone was created by IBM in 1992. It was called the IBM Simon and it looked like this:

The IBM Simon could send emails and faxes. It also had a touchscreen (a display screen that acts as both an input and output device; you can touch the screen to interact with the computer) and basic programs built in, like calculator, to-do list and calendar.

A tablet is a computer that you use with your fingers or a stylus (plastic rod that you use to interact with a display). You click on things by just tapping on them with your finger or a stylus. Tablets are usually rectangular and measure between 5 and 11 inches diagonally. In terms of size, a tablet is between a computer and a mobile phone.

The history of tablets started with computer pads that you could write on with a stylus. They looked like this and actually came into existence in the 1980s:

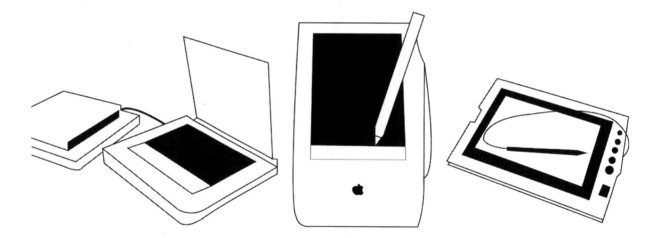

As time goes on, mobile devices (like all technology) will continue to improve.

One term you may come across is "phablet." A phablet is a mobile device in between the size of a smartphone and a tablet. It's a combination of the words "phone" and "tablet" – hence, "phablet." Phablets range in size between 5-8 inches diagonally. Nowadays, mobile phones, phablets and tablets can virtually all perform the same actions and the main difference is just the size.

We predict that in the future, there will be some devices that are transparent (able to be seen through) and eventually will be implemented as holographic (images projected mid-air). You see such things in science fiction, and science fiction can inspire technology. The founder of Amazon (Jeff Bezos) stated that Amazon's Alexa (a device that uses voice recognition to perform various functions for users) was inspired by the main computer on the famous television show *Star Trek: the Next Generation.*

SUMMARY:

Computers can be built inside many different devices. However, the main devices we think of as computers are desktop computers, laptop computers and mobile devices. Mobile devices usually can act as a cell phone as well as providing many of the functions you typically would use a laptop or desktop for: browsing the web, reading email, playing games, editing documents, etc. These mobile devices are a type of cell phone – a telephone device that uses communication towers organized into an overlapping network of areas where the devices can connect and send or receive electronic information. There are many types of mobile devices; they are all actually computers.

Now let's look at the components that allow devices and computers to display pictures, play sound, and other important functions.

CHAPTER 63:
CARDS

"Simplicity, carried to the extreme, becomes elegance."
-Jon Franklin (American writer, 1943-)

Cards are computer parts that perform specific functions. They look like this:

"Card' is short for "expansion card." Often, certain types of cards come built into your computer, but you can also purchase better cards to upgrade them, or different types of cards than what your computer comes with.

There are cards for a wide range of computer functions, like sound and video. You could even buy a card that allows you to hook up cable TV to your computer.

Most cards actually are like a type of "mini-computer," because they have a CPU on it that is built for a specific purpose. This CPU does not replace the main CPU for the computer itself; in fact, the main CPU runs the CPU on the card. You can think of the card as a tiny computer that the main computer can use to perform certain specialized tasks. This improves the overall performance of the main computer.

Graphics are pictures created on a computer. These can be 2D or 3D images and videos. They can be used for many kinds of displays, including computer screens, televisions and movie screens.

A "graphics card" helps to control the output on a monitor. A "network card," on the other hand, enables computers to connect to and operate on a network.

Cards are different than "Secure Digital cards" (SD cards). An SD card is a portable memory storage device. It is a small card that has electronics inside it. You can record electronic information on the card; the information can be accessed by computers.

They look like this (the ruler is provided to give a sense of their size):

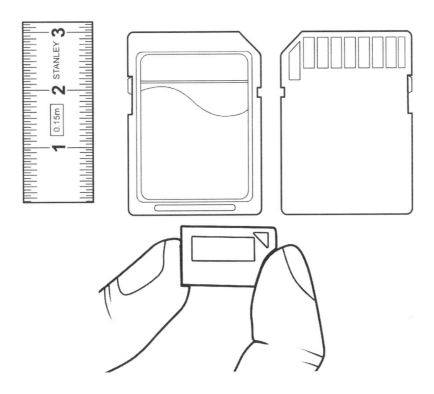

A very common use of SD cards is to save videos and photos taken with a digital camera.

SUMMARY:

You may want to add more functions to a computer than those built into it at the factory. Most computers allow for the installation of various "cards" (electronic devices that add functions to the computer). Common functions enabled by these cards are increased graphics capability and connection to networks of computers. Your computer comes with various cards already built in.

Now let's discuss a development that brought computers into peoples' homes.

CHAPTER 64:
PERSONAL COMPUTERS

"The good news about computers is that they do what you tell them to do.
The bad news is that they do what you tell them to do."
-Ted Nelson (American philosopher, 1937-)

If you were born in the 1980s or later, you most likely were surrounded by computers and computer devices. Most modern children utilize computer devices (such as smartphones or tablets) on a day-to-day basis. Prior to the 1970s, computers were massive machines that were mainly utilized by the government and large companies, and the idea of having a computer in one's home was almost unthinkable due to what they were previously used for, as well as their high cost and their large size.

But in the 1970s, a major step forward occurred with computers: microcomputers. Micro means "small."

Microcomputers are also referred to as "personal computers" (PCs). When you think of a computer, what you're most likely envisioning is a PC. Nowadays, PCs/microcomputers are simply called "computers."

The 1970s saw the arrival of many personal computers. For the first time ever, computers could be used at home and in small businesses.

Here are some pictures of a couple of the original personal computers:

These original PCs had basic functions and components, including: memory, keyboard, card reader, card recorder (data could be stored from the computer on magnetic tape or magnetic card) and processor.

These personal computers could be used to do mathematical calculations, play games, write documents, create basic programs and more.

In 1978, a major development in personal computers was the electronic spreadsheet. A spreadsheet is a type of computer program that allows you to organize, modify and analyze tabular (organized in a table) data. The data is stored in individual containers called cells; these cells are organized into rows and columns. A set of rows and columns is called a table. This type of computer program was developed based on existing accounting (having to do with managing financial matters and bank accounts) worksheets, where businesses would record important data on paper in a similar fashion.

Here is an example of a spreadsheet:

	A	B	C	D	
1	Country	Sales			▲
2	United States	7583			
3	United Kingdom	4359			
4	France	45995			
5	Germany	3933			
6	Spain	8738			
7	Italy	5239			
8	Greece	38282			
9					
10					▼

|◄ ◄ ► ►| Sheet1 / Sheet2 / Sheet3 / ◄ ►

With the development of electronic spreadsheets, people could now perform needed financial calculations much faster than they could do with a paper-based system. The popularity of spreadsheet programs helped drive up sales of these smaller "personal computers" – first to businesses, and then to individual users.

The 1980s saw huge developments in the personal computer industry, with Apple, Microsoft and IBM dominating the market.

With each new release, computers became faster, could store more data and perform more functions.

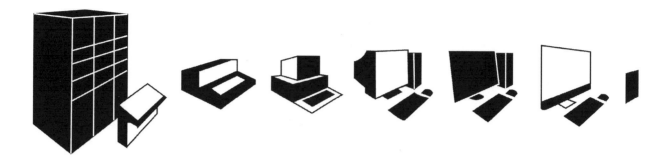

As a note: a whole book could be written on computer advancement in the 1970s and 1980s.

Computers began moving away from being intimidating and complex to being usable by the average person. This is referred to as "user friendly" – a computer program or device that is easy to operate. User-friendly means "designed from the user's perspective to give them a smooth and comfortable experience."

Mice, spreadsheets and other more user-friendly hardware and software became the norm in the 1980s. Remember, before this, data was in text form (no pictures) and accessed with a keyboard.

In 1981, the first laptop was made publicly available. It was called the Osborne 1 and was created by Adam Osborne (Thailand-born, British-American author). It looked like this:

One of the components that made personal computers possible was the microprocessor.

The microprocessor is the circuit containing the CPU, millions of transistors, sound card, network card and more. It basically puts the most important electronic parts of a computer all in one place. It looks like this:

The ability to place so many important components so close together and to make them all so small, greatly increased the speed of computers and reduced their size and cost.

SUMMARY:

Prior to the late 1970s and early 1980s, computers were large, expensive and were only affordable by government, educational institutions and big companies. The idea of a computer for one person to use at their desk, or their home, was far-fetched. Advances in the manufacture of the most important parts of a computer led to the creation of the microprocessor, which made all of those parts smaller and less expensive. The popularity of these small, personal computers (PCs) increased dramatically with the creation of a type of computer program called a spreadsheet; it let small businesses perform complex data organization and processing for a comparatively low price. As PCs became used even in the home, they were utilized for casual gaming, productivity work (like document writing) and other uses.

So, we know that computers run programs. What's the most important program on all computers?

CHAPTER 65:
SYSTEMS

"I was around computers from birth...
I don't think I have any particular technical skills – I just got a really large head start."
-Aaron Swartz (American computer scientist, 1986-2013)

An operating system is a special-purpose (made for exact applications and reasons) computer program that supports the computer's basic functions, such as scheduling tasks, running other computer programs, and controlling peripherals (external devices such as keyboards, mice and displays).

Most computer programs will require that an operating system already be installed on a computer before they can function on that computer.

As we covered earlier, "install" means to put something inside a computer that the computer can then use. This often applies to computer programs. You would obtain the program and move it onto the computer via a connection of some sort. You would then have that program on the computer and you could use it when you wanted.

Installing also applies to hardware. You could, for instance, install a new storage device in your computer that could hold more electronic information.

Nearly all computers available today come with an operating system already installed when they are purchased. Computer manufacturers install the operating system before they sell a computer.

Some operating systems are free, while others require payment.

One of the most well-known and popular operating systems in the world is called Windows. It is created and sold by Microsoft.

The operating system used by Apple desktop computers and devices is actually a "family" of operating systems. This is called the "Macintosh" family of operating systems. A Macintosh is a variety of apple, and the name "Macintosh" has been used by the company Apple for decades to name various devices and programs.

This family contains operating systems for the many popular devices sold by

Apple, and each operating system has a different name based on the type of device it is used on:

- MacOS for desktops and laptops,

- iOS for cell phones,

- iPadOS for tablets,

- watchOS for smartwatches, and

- tvOS for devices that help you manage the content you watch on your television.

Apple has changed the naming system for its operating systems several times.

Linux is a family of free operating systems that is used on desktop computers and laptops.

Android (which is owned by Google) is the operating system used on Google mobile devices.

Before operating systems, computers were turned on and did nothing until programs were fed into them through punched cards, magnetic tape or paper tape. Operating systems were a major step forward for computers.

(logos [left to right]: Apple, iOS, Linux, Android and Windows)

SUMMARY:

Early computers could run programs, but the instructions for the program had to be entered into the computer each time it was turned on. The development of digital storage devices allowed programs to be permanently stored for use by the computer. It was found that there were certain basic functions that nearly every computer would need, so specialized programs called "operating systems" were developed. They handled functions like scheduling certain common tasks, handling input and output (I/O) with the various peripheral devices connected to the computer, and facilitating the installation of other programs on the computer.

Operating systems are part of what makes up a computer "platform." So, what is a platform?

CHAPTER 66:
PLATFORMS

"Everyone's a nerd inside.
I don't care how cool you are."
-Channing Tatum (American actor, 1980-)

Platform is a term used to describe any one of several available combinations of hardware and operating system. When you speak of a platform, you are talking about what kind of hardware composes the computer and what operating system it uses.

There are many different types of platforms. Some common platforms are:

"Windows": Here, the hardware is a computer design called "IBM PC," based on a design from the technology company IBM that they created in the 1980s. The operating system is Windows, from the technology company Microsoft.

"Mac": Here, the hardware is a computer design from the technology company Apple. The operating system is macOS (one member of the Macintosh family of operating systems), also from Apple.

Usually, programs that are created for use on one platform will not work on other platforms. This is because the program, in order to be able to run on that platform, has to be written using instructions built into the exact CPU installed in the machine. The different CPUs used by the various popular platforms do not have the same instructions built into them.

If you buy a computer with the operating system Windows on it, the computer and all physical components and software (including the Windows program) is your platform. If you buy another program for your computer, you would need to make sure the program is compatible with (designed for and able to work with) the Windows platform.

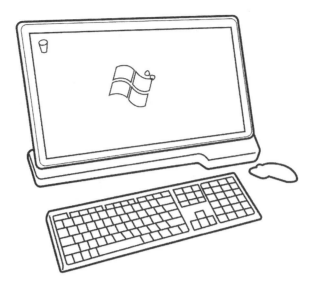

Cross-platform refers to a computer program that is developed so it can operate on multiple platforms.

Another term for "program" is "application."

In order to fully understand cross-platform applications, you need to understand the idea of a "native" application. Here, the term "platform" refers to the environment (the state of a computer, as determined by the combination of hardware, software, and running programs) in which a computer program runs. This applies not just to desktop and laptop computers, but to the environment on a particular mobile device – a "mobile device platform."

An example of this type of platform is the iPhone, a smartphone manufactured by the technology company Apple.

As a note on Apple mobile devices: they start with "i" – such as iPhone, iPad, etc. Steve Jobs defined this "i" as "internet" because of the fact that these devices connect to the internet. He went on to say that the "i" stood for "individual," "inspire," "inform" and "instruct."

Another example of a platform is Windows desktop and laptop computers. These are manufactured by many different companies, but they all use many things in common, regardless of who manufactured them.

There are a few key parts of the device platform:

1) The *physical hardware* of the device. This includes parts like the CPU, the

keyboard, the audio output devices (speakers), the microphone, etc. For mobile devices, it includes things like the camera, the motion sensors, and the physical controls for such things as power and sound volume. The physical hardware of an iPhone is not the same as that of an Android smartphone; nor is the physical hardware of a Windows computer the same as that of an Apple computer.

2) The *operating system* installed on the device. As was mentioned, the OS supports the computer's basic functions, such as scheduling tasks, running other computer programs, and controlling peripherals. iPhones have an operating system called iOS. iOS uses its own methods for performing those tasks; these methods are different than those used by Android, the operating system used on Android smartphones.

When creating a computer program for a computer (an "application"), programmers have two broad approaches:
1. They can write the application in such a way that it only works on a specific platform, or
2. They can write it in such a way that it can easily run on multiple platforms.

The first approach is called a "native" application; the latter is called a "cross-platform" application.

There are usually strong advantages to creating a native application – they generally perform faster than cross-platform applications, and they usually have greater access to the hardware features of the device (camera, motion sensors, buttons, etc.). This is because the computer programming language used to create those native applications was purpose-built for that exact platform.

When creating cross-platform applications, the goal is to use one computer programming language to create an application that can run on multiple platforms. This can greatly reduce the time and money needed to get an application into the market that can be used by multiple device platforms.

SUMMARY:

You will often see the word "platform" used in connection with computers. Usually, it refers to the idea of a unique combination of hardware and software. Specifically, it concerns the hardware of a device like a computer or a mobile device, as well as the operating system installed on the computer or device.

Some examples are the "Windows" platform, where the Windows operating system is installed on a computer design called an "IBM PC" (so named because the design was created and popularized in the 1980s by IBM), and the Android platform, where the Android operating system is installed on a mobile device called an Android device (so named because these devices are made to work specifically with that operating system).

In the past, a computer program (also called an application) had to be written with a specific platform in mind, and that program would not be able to be installed and run on other platforms. These are called "native" applications. New developments in computer hardware and software now allow for the creation of "cross-platform" applications that can be installed and run on multiple types of platforms.

One of the primary uses for mobile devices, such as the iPhone, are "apps." So, let's go over what those are exactly.

CHAPTER 67:
APPS

"There needs to be an app that edits what I say versus what I want to say."
-Blake Shelton (American country singer, 1976-)

"App" is short for "application." As covered in the last chapter, an app is just another term for a computer program.

Applications have exact purposes and are used by people to do certain things using a computer.

An application can also be something you use on the internet that performs exact functions and does things with and for you.

The word "app" typically refers to programs you use on a smartphone or handheld device, but technically means any program run on any type of computer.

Nowadays, phones come with several apps already installed. Examples of this are calculators, cameras and flashlight apps.

There are apps covering virtually any subject you can imagine – from games to entertainment to business tools.

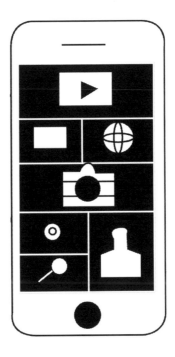

SUMMARY:

The phrase "there's an app for that" became popular as smartphones became popular. These mobile computers were more than just phones, they were computers in their own right. Computer programmers started creating programs specifically designed for these new devices, and the term "app" was used to describe them. However, this term is simply a shortened form of the word application, and it is just another program, able to be installed on a computer and run when the user desires.

Now that you have an understanding of programs, let's cover more data on how they interact with the internet.

CHAPTER 68:
REQUESTS

"Through our scientific and technological genius we've made of this world a neighborhood. And now through our moral and ethical commitment we must make of it a brotherhood."
-Martin Luther King Jr. (American civil rights leader, 1929-1968)

In this chapter, we will describe this picture:

Bob - Topeka, KS

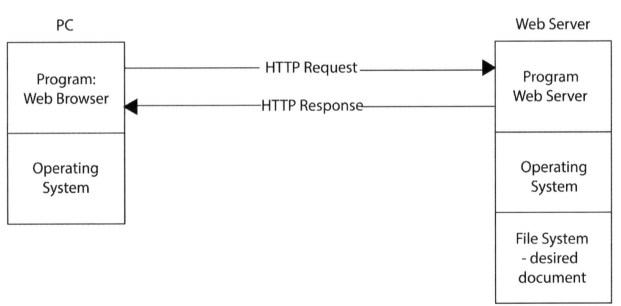

Let's take a look at this diagram, starting on the left.

Here we have Bob, in Topeka, Kansas. Bob has a computer, with an operating system and a web browser program installed on the computer. The browser lets Bob search for a document that is part of the web, bring a copy of that document to the browser program, and then create a visual display based on the contents of that web document.

As we covered earlier, the protocol we use is the "Hyper Text Transfer Protocol" – HTTP.

So, here's an example to show how it works: Let's say that Bob really likes Corgis – the dog breed.

Bob tells his browser he wants to see a specific webpage about Corgis – it's at a website called "pets.com," and the actual page is called "corgis."

He might type something like this into his browser:

http://www.pets.com/corgis

In plain language, this basically means he's telling the browser, "Using the HTTP protocol and the internet, locate the computer that has the website 'pets.com', ask that computer for the file 'corgis', retrieve a copy of that file, and use it to put cool pictures of Corgis on my computer screen."

Since Bob's computer is connected to the internet, the web browser on his computer can connect to the computer where the documents that make up the website "pets.com" are stored.

In the preceding picture, the computer on the right is the web server. Its purpose is to store webpages and give them to other computers who request them.

So our web server, on the right, has a special computer program on it called "web server software." This program listens for requests for webpages, finds the pages when asked, and sends them back to the computer that asked for them.

The whole sequence goes something like this:

1. The user's browser requests a specific webpage.

2. That request arrives at the web server computer.

3. The web server software tries to find the document for that webpage in its file system.

4. If the file is found, the web server sends it back as a response to the request.

5. The user's browser receives the file.

Now, the user's browser can scan through that file and use the code (computer instructions) in it to create a display on the screen.

That whole sequence is called the "HTTP Request/Response Cycle."

SUMMARY:

As covered earlier, the internet is a huge network of computers around the world, along with several protocols (formal agreements) that describe how specific types of data can be exchanged between those computers. The web is different – it's a huge collection of linked electronic documents, called webpages.

The protocol describing how these webpages can be exchanged between the computers of the internet is called HTTP (Hypertext Transfer Protocol).

The basic way this works is that a user's computer has a program on it called a web browser. The web browser sends a request out over the internet for a specific webpage. The computer where that page is stored receives the request, finds the webpage (it's just an electronic document, with text like letters and numbers in it) and sends the page back to the browser on the original computer. That browser reads the file, which has instructions that describe how the webpage should look, and makes the page appear on the computer display. This whole process is called the "HTTP Request/Response Cycle."

Now, let's return to popular computer uses.

CHAPTER 69:
WRITING

"If at first you don't succeed; call it version 1.0."
-Unknown

Just as a note on the word "version" used in the above quote, this refers to a particular "model" of software. Each version is the same basic software, except that newer versions are upgraded and modernized. This is usually written as: Version 1.0, Version 2.0, Version 3.0, etc. Sometimes there's: Version 1.1, 1.2, 1.3, etc. or even more detailed like: Version 9.45, 9.46, 9.47, etc. The higher the number, the newer the version.

Now, a major step forward in the development of computers was the development of word processors.

A word processor is a program on a computer that allows you to create, format (design the style and layout), modify, and print documents.

The actions you perform with word processors are referred to as "word processing."

Before word processors, people wrote by hand or typed on typewriters. Microsoft Word is a popular word processor and, as is implied, it processes words by creating them, editing them, deleting them, etc.

Notepad is a basic word processor from Microsoft that saves plain (not fancy or enhanced) text. That means you can't do things like make the text **bold** or *italic*.

Pages is an Apple word processor used to create documents.

When word processors were added to computers, it made them much more appealing to small businesses and to personal users at home.

SUMMARY:

Early computers were often used for complex math operations in commercial companies and the military. The development of special computer programs called "word processors" helped to make computers more useful to small businesses and individual users. A word processor lets you create text documents using the screen and the keyboard. These documents can be changed, printed, and deleted.

Word processors save documents as files, so let's take a look at what those are exactly.

CHAPTER 70:
FILES AND FOLDERS

"I have files, I have computer files and, you know, files on paper.
But most of it is really in my head.
So God help me if anything ever happens to my head!"
-George R. R. Martin (American author, 1948-)

Data on computers are usually organized in files and folders.

Files are collections of data stored on a computer. The data in a file is organized in a specific manner, usually based on how that data is going to be used by the computer. Files each have their own name and contain their own data. They often have a related thing, which is a folder.

Folders are a way of organizing files on a computer. They are a sort of "container" where one or more files are stored and are usually given a descriptive name.

Let's say you want to write Christmas greetings to all of your relatives. You could save your letter to your grandma as "Grandma," within a folder called "Christmas Greetings." Other letters to relatives could be stored there as well, such as "Aunt Karla," "Father," etc.

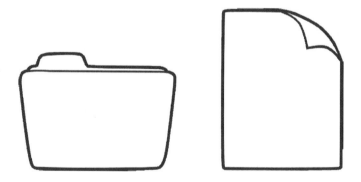

Files have various formats. A format is a specified structure for how to arrange, store, process or display data.

Written documents, pictures and videos are examples of different types of file formats. The data in these files is organized in a specific way, usually based on how the data will be used by various processes the computer does.

For example: The data in a file that is a written document will be organized in a very different way than the data in a file that is a video.

A common file format is "PDF." This stands for "Portable Document Format." This is a file format developed by the software company Adobe in the 1990s. This file format was developed to ensure consistent display of documents regardless of what computer they're being displayed on.

File formats are indicated by their extension. The extension is a code that states what the file format is (text, image, video, etc.). Extensions are tacked on at the end of the file's name.

Let's say you have a file entitled "Contract" and it's stored as a PDF. The file would be named "Contract.pdf" – .pdf is the extension.

Another common file format and extension is ".txt" (short for "text file"). This is a file type that utilizes pure, unformatted (no special design; plain) text. Microsoft Notepad saves and runs .txt files.

Or if you use Microsoft Word, the files are commonly saved with the extension ".doc" (short for "document").

SUMMARY:

We talked earlier about how computers contain instructions telling them what to do with data. They also contain the data to be operated on. This data is stored on the computer as electronic files. The data in these files is organized differently based on what type of information it represents. As long as a computer has a program in it telling it what to do with a certain type of file, the computer can use that type of file. To identify the type of data a file contains, an "extension," or special code, is added after the name of the file. Common extensions are "pdf" and "txt." These files are often organized into a collection item called a folder, to aid in organization.

So, what are all these files and folders stored in?

CHAPTER 71:
DRIVING

*"If you tell the truth,
you don't have to remember anything."*
-Mark Twain (1835-1910, American author)

Memory is stored in "drives."

A drive is a device that the computer can use to store data for later use. The creation of storage drives was a major breakthrough in the computer industry, as it allowed users to set up data in an organized fashion, store it on a device that the computer could access, and then have the computer use that data as needed – even if the computer had been turned off and turned back on again before needing to use the data.

Before this, users would have to manually enter data for the computer to use – if the computer was turned off, the data was gone, and it would have to be entered again when the computer was turned on again.

Drives are often referred to as "disk drives" because the first designs make use of one or more metal disks that are used to store computer data. The surface of these disks is magnetic, and can be modified so that it stores data for use in computers. When the computer needs to access data on the disk drive, the disk spins around quickly. As the disk spins, the data on the magnetic surface is read by the computer.

Here's a picture of drives:

The drive on the left contains disks, and the drive on the right is composed of chips and transistors.

The most important drive is the hard drive. The "hard drive" is a device used to store information that can be used by your computer. They're typically only slightly larger than your hand, yet can hold a massive amount of data.

The data in a hard drive is stored on one or more disks that are mounted, in a stack, inside a solid case. A small "reader" is positioned over the disks so it can access the data stored on them. These disks spin extremely fast so that data can be accessed nearly immediately from anywhere on the drive. The data stored on the hard drive stays on the drive even after the power supply is turned off.

When you wipe (erase) a hard drive, you are taking all the stored information off the drive.

Another term for this is "hard disk drive," so named because the disks were made of a rigid material. You'll sometimes see this abbreviated as "HDD."

The first ever HDD was created by IBM in 1956. The hard drive weighed about one ton and stored about .01% of the memory that your average computer can store today. It looked like this:

On the surface of the hard drive disks is a layer of magnetic material.

The way it works is that small pieces of the magnetic material can be changed so that some might point in one direction, while others point in another.

One direction means a "one," and the other direction means a "zero."

If you spin the disk and move the arm, you can reach any point on the disk. The tip of the arm can change the data at any place on the disk, or read the data at any place on the disk.

You've now managed to store electronic data that a computer can use.

A drive will have an identifier (a "name") so users will know where to go to get stored data. Computers can have multiple drives installed. Drives are sometimes assigned letters as names (like A, B, C, etc.) For many computers around the world, the "C drive" is often the place on a computer where important data is stored – but other naming systems are used as well.

The hard disk drive is differentiated from a similar type of storage device called a floppy disk. In a floppy disk, there is only one disk, and it is made of a flexible magnetic material. These floppy disks were popular in the past and used for portable data storage.

A floppy disk was contained in a hard plastic case. In order to be used by a computer, that computer must have a special component installed that can hold the floppy disk. This component is called a floppy disk drive. Once the floppy disk is inserted into the drive, the drive can spin the disk as needed in order for the computer to retrieve information from or add information to the disk.

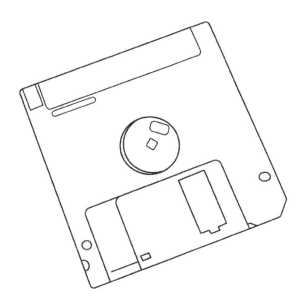

Note the difference here: a hard drive contains the motor and arm used to rotate the disk and read or write to the disk. A floppy disk, on the other hand, only contained the storage disk; the floppy drive installed on the computer contained the motor and arm needed.

Floppy disks are nearly obsolete. There are newer storage technologies that can hold much larger amounts of information and that can operate at much higher rates of data transfer.

Years ago, if you were to purchase a computer game, it might come on several floppy disks. In order to install the game on your computer, you would have to put the disks into the drive, one after the other, until all the program information was loaded into the computer.

The floppy disk was developed at IBM by a man named Alan Shugart in 1967. As you can see, IBM has been involved in many major computer developments.

Computers used to have a floppy disk drive, usually called the F drive. These drives were used to read, store and delete data on floppy disks. In the image below, the floppy disk is beneath the floppy disk drive:

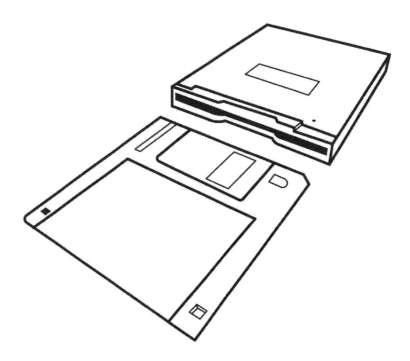

It is now very common for drives to have no moving parts – the data is stored in a solid piece of material that can hold millions of individual pieces of data. These are called "solid state drives" (SSD), but the older term "disk drive" is often used when talking about these newer drives. Whereas HDDs have arms with a needle that reads the data (kind of like a record player), SSDs pass the data along various paths without any components that move.

Here is a HDD (left) next to an SSD (right):

One primary factor of importance regarding drives is their capacity – that is, how much information can be stored on them. Current drives can hold millions of times as much information as those of just a few decades ago.

SUMMARY:

The ability to store electronic data in a computer for later use, even if the computer was turned off and on, was a big step in the development of the modern computer. A common technology used to solve this is a disk drive. These use thin rotating disks coated with magnetic material; the magnetic material can be modified to store data. Various types of disks have been used, from flexible plastic disks (floppy disks) to metal disks (hard disks). There are now "disk drives" that contain no disks and no moving parts; these are called solid state drives and they use solid electronic devices that can permanently store electronic information.

Now, have you ever had a computer shut down and you lost your work? Why is that?

CHAPTER 72:
RANDOM

*"After growing wildly for years,
the field of computing appears to be reaching its infancy."*
-John Pierce (American engineer, 1910-2002)

"Memory" is a physical device used to store information on a computer. It holds recorded electronic data that can be accessed by the CPU in the future.

A hierarchy refers to arranging things according to rank or status. It refers to arranging items according to their relative importance or characteristics.

A common example of hierarchy would be how most companies are arranged: there are bosses and functions are compartmented. For example: there's a Chief Executive Officer (CEO; boss) over the company, and a Chief Financial Officer (CFO) that oversees the accounting department.

Storage hierarchy refers to a system where various data storage devices are given a hierarchical importance ranking as far as how they are used by the CPU. The primary factor influencing a given device's ranking is its response time – how long the device takes to return a requested piece of stored data when the CPU requests the data. Faster response times are ranked higher.

Memory storage devices are either volatile or persistent. Volatile devices lose their data when they are not powered on; persistent devices maintain their data even when they are not powered. The hard drives we discussed in the previous chapter are persistent memory devices.

The most common type of volatile memory is called Random Access Memory (abbreviated RAM). Due to having very fast response times, RAM is typically at the top of a computer's storage hierarchy. RAM is ideal for meeting the CPU's need to rapidly manipulate data during computer operation.

Random Access Memory is called "random access" because any particular piece of data stored in the memory can be retrieved just as quickly as any other piece of data in the memory – that is, if you choose a piece of data at random that you wish to retrieve, it can be accessed just as quickly as any other piece of data.

The development of Random Access Memory was a big step forward in the speed of computer operations. The reason for this is that previous forms of volatile memory were NOT random access – that is, if you were to choose any piece of data at random that you wished to retrieve from memory, it would take a longer or shorter time to retrieve that piece of data than to retrieve any other piece of data. This is because previous forms of volatile memory were based on a physical design that wouldn't allow access to individual points of data with the same length of time between "request" and "response."

As an example, a common type of volatile memory was magnetic tape. These were basically very large versions of the common cassette tapes that are used to store pre-recorded music. The data on magnetic tapes like these was stored on a strip of magnetic material that was wound around two wheels.

To get to a specific piece of data on the tape, a motor had to turn the wheels until the exact point on the tape was reached that contained that exact piece of data.

You can see, then, that any particular piece of data on the tape would be reached in a length of time that was different from that needed to reach any other piece of data on the tape – therefore, any two randomly-selected pieces of data would have different access time, so this was not "random access" memory.

In a computer, RAM is typically stored on a stick that looks like this:

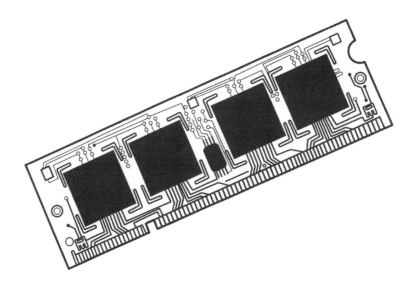

A RAM socket is a slot inside the computer that you plug RAM into. RAM sockets are housed inside your computer. They often have clips that prevent the RAM stick from accidentally coming out of them.

RAM was invented by an American inventor named Robert Dennard in 1968.

ROM, or "Read Only Memory" could be considered the opposite of RAM.

ROM is a physical component in a computer that is used to store data that can't be modified once it is first installed on the device – it's literally *memory* that can *only* be *read*. This data remains stored in the component even if the computer is turned off, and is available to the computer once the computer is turned on again.

One use for ROM is this: the instructions on exactly what the computer should do from the point it is turned on, until it is ready for user input, are stored in ROM.

Here is what it looks like:

The various types of memory all have one thing in common: they have many small locations that can be set up in one of only two available states. One state means it's storing a "one," and the other state means it's storing a "zero."

The CPU connects to memory through wires and, as a result, the CPU can store data, retrieve it later when it needs it, and change it as needed. And remember, that's the basic job of all computers.

SUMMARY:

Memory storage devices are used by computers to store data for use while it is operating. There are two types of memory devices:

1. **Volatile (meaning the data in it is lost when the computer is turned off), and**

2. **Non-volatile (meaning the data is preserved even when the computer is turned off).**

Most volatile memory is a type called RAM (Random Access Memory). The data in this memory can be changed as the computer operates. But remember, that data is lost when the computer is turned off. The purpose of RAM is to provide quicker access to memory, which it does by allowing random access to memory.

A common type of non-volatile memory is called ROM (Read Only Memory). It's used to store data and instruction that will not change at all – typically, this is data the computer always needs.

Now, let's look into what happens when a computer is turned on.

CHAPTER 73:
BOOTS

"If we knew what it was we were doing, it would not be called research, would it?"
-Albert Einstein (German scientist, 1879-1955)

Boot means to start up a computer. This is also called "booting up."

Booting up a computer means that you turned it on and now it is preparing to operate. It is actually short for "bootstrapping," which means "starting a self-sustaining process that is supposed to proceed without external input."

The term "bootstrap" started in America in the early 1800's through use of the phrase "pull oneself up over a fence by one's bootstraps." A strap is a tab, loop or handle of cloth or leather. Boots often have straps near the top of the boot that the wearer can use to help pull the boots on without the help of others. The phrase "pull oneself up by one's bootstraps" came to mean "perform a difficult task without external help."

The computer industry adopted this term to describe the process of getting a computer running because they needed to create a way for a computer to make itself ready for use after it was turned on, without any need for the user to take action.

During the "boot" process, a computer is doing several things that are needed before the computer can be used for its routine tasks. These are things like: connecting to peripherals (such as a monitor, keyboard or mouse), installing all required instructions into the computer's temporary data storage for use as the computer is operated, and turning on any specific computer programs that the user has said must be turned on when the computer starts.

You usually press the power button to boot up a computer.

One of the programs that handle the booting process is BIOS, which stands for Basic Input/Output System.

This is a special computer program that is built into a computer. It is the first computer program that is executed when a computer is turned on, and it is executed every time the computer is turned on. It provides access to the fundamental input and output systems on the computer.

If a computer did not have an operating system installed yet, such as Windows, when you turned it on, you would see a screen that presented the BIOS. You would be able to perform certain very basic functions of the computer from here.

The BIOS is mainly used by whatever operating system gets installed on the computer, so users rarely have to interact with it. There are times that is needed, though, and it looks like this:

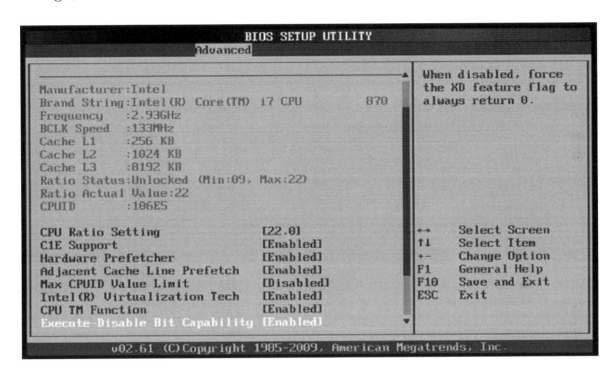

Think about this: A computer, when it is first manufactured, is just a potential tool. The CPU on it has several instructions that can be performed, but there's nothing to tell the computer to do any of those instructions – so the computer has the potential to do work. It needs a program, or a set of instructions, in order to do anything. That's why the BIOS is the first program installed on the computer.

Let's look over some of the terms you may come across while booting a computer. You've probably seen this while using a computer:

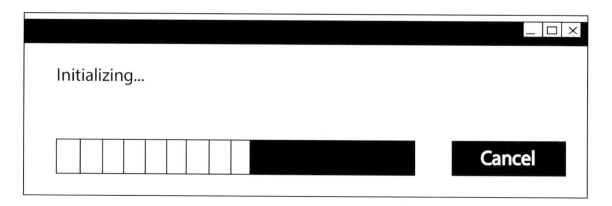

Initializing refers to preparing something for use for the first time. It means to put something in the proper format or condition for operation.

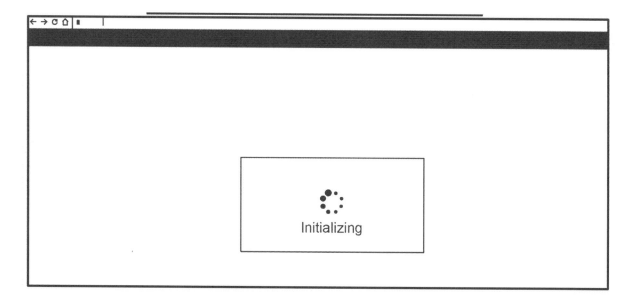

You've probably also seen this:

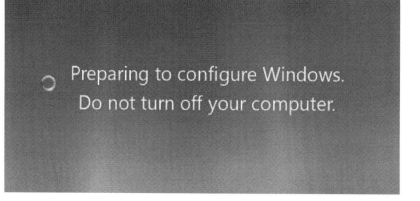

Configuring means to set up a machine to be used in a particular way. When there is a function that the computer does, and you make that function behave in a certain way, you are configuring that function.

If you bought a new computer game, you might have to configure some of its functions relating to how it displays things so that the image quality would align with what your monitor is able to do, or that brightness is adjusted correctly. Some monitors would have a lower quality display than others, for example, and you might individually configure the best possible picture for that monitor.

Now, has anyone ever asked you, "Have you tried turning it off and on again?"

There are several reasons that turning a computer off and on again works:

1. First off, when you power down your machine, it clears the RAM. Remember, RAM is volatile memory (memory that only retains data while the device is on). Sometimes there can be so much going on in your computer that giving the RAM a fresh slate can fix the problem and speed things up.

As a note: Some machines contain a capacitor. This is a component that stores small amounts of electricity in case of temporary power loss. For example: routers contain capacitors. The electricity comes in from the electrical outlet and travels through the power cord into the router. The router uses this electricity to operate and a tiny amount of electricity is stored within capacitors that look like this:

Some look like little batteries plugged into boards (thin, flat boards that contain complex electronic circuits). With some devices (like routers) you need to wait a few seconds after turning it off to ensure all the electricity is drained from the capacitors to make sure it is indeed off. Meaning, if you just click off and on, the device may not actually be fully off – give it a minute.

The point is: to ensure your computer is really off and that all electricity has been drained from the capacitors, wait for around a minute after turning the computer off or unplugging it before you turn it back on.

2. By turning a computer off, malfunctioning programs and processes (commands being executed) that are running are terminated (stopped). When you then turn the computer on again, those programs and processes are no longer running. For example, if you mistakenly opened a problematic webpage, restarting the computer will close it down.

3. Restarting the computer also allows the booting up process to run, which can initialize important computer programs and processes that may have stopped running for one reason or another. For example, you may have accidentally closed an important program, so restarting will ensure it turns back on.

Restarting computers is a great way to fix issues you're running into!

SUMMARY:

A computer can't do anything until it's told to, and so it needs certain programs installed onto it after manufacture. One of those programs is called BIOS (Basic Input/Output System). Without it, the computer won't do anything. With it, you can then install an operating system, and then other programs you want on the computer.

Restarting your computer when it isn't behaving correctly can often correct the problem, as the various programs in it have a chance to return to their original state.

Computers often are connected to hardware like printers, mice, displays, etc., and these need to be controlled and communicated with. The CPU can't do this unless it's told to, of course. So, what's the software that controls the hardware?

CHAPTER 74:
DRIVERS

"All of the biggest technological inventions created by man
– the airplane, the automobile, the computer – says little about his intelligence,
but speaks volumes about his laziness."
-Mark Kennedy (American businessman, 1957-)

Computers have permanently stored programs inside them called "firmware." The firmware is the software that controls the computer's hardware. An example of firmware is Basic Input/Output System (BIOS – covered in the previous chapter).

It is a combination of the words "firm" (unmoving; solid) and "software."

Firmware is also called "embedded software." Embed means to "firmly fix something inside another thing."

Another example of firmware is in printers. Printers have small computers inside them that control their operation. These computers don't have storage drives that you can install programs on; they come with firmware built in.

Firmware is stored in ROM (Read Only Memory – permanent memory, as opposed to RAM).

Another type of software that you may have heard of is a "driver." A driver is a special computer program that helps that particular model of computer work with certain devices. The driver acts as a "translator" between the computer and the device so they can understand each other and work together. A driver is software that coordinates the functions of the hardware.

Back to our printer example: In order to use a printer with your computer, it is usually necessary to install a driver so your computer understands how to control that exact printer model. These drivers are usually created by the printer manufacturer. The manufacturer needs to get the technical data about how that particular computer communicates with devices that get connected to it, and then make a computer program that aligns how their printer is controlled with how that particular computer works.

The term "driver" came about in the 1960s to refer to the software that "drives" (controls; operates) the hardware.

Firmware and drivers are software that have the purpose of ensuring hardware operates correctly.

SUMMARY:

Often, we need to permanently store a program into a computer in a way that it can't be changed. Usually these programs control very basic things about how the computer operates. This is called "firmware," since it's software that can't change.

A related concept is a special program called a driver. These are programs that help a specific type of computer control a hardware device, such as a printer.

We talked about how computers store memory. Now let's talk about some *devices* used to store memory.

CHAPTER 75:
STORAGE DEVICES

"If we have data, let's look at data.
If all we have are opinions, let's go with mine."
-Jim Barksdale (1943-, American businessman)

A CD (compact disc) is a flat plastic disk that you can store information on for later use by computers. Information on CDs can be accessed by computers and other specialized machines. Here is a CD:

Though they didn't come into wide use until the 1980s and 1990s, CDs were conceived in the 1960s by a man named James T. Russell. CDs are read from inside to outside edge – the opposite of records.

Another drive found in some computers is the CD-ROM Drive. This is short for "Compact Disc – Read-Only Memory Drive." As covered earlier, ROM refers to permanent, unalterable memory.

A CD-ROM is a CD that has some information stored on it at some point in time, and from that point forward, that information can't be changed.

The device in a computer that can access the data on these discs and deliver that information to the computer is called a CD-ROM drive. Typically, it has a thin, flat tray that can move outward from the computer, allowing a CD-ROM to be inserted or removed from the computer.

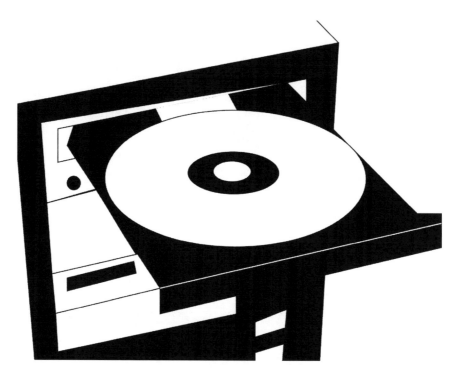

Many computer games come on a CD-ROM.

There is a persistent urban legend that some novice computer users have mistaken this tray for a coffee holder.

Another popular storage device is USB drives. They look like this:

USB stands for "Universal Serial Bus." "Universal" means "able to be applied by all; consistent use everywhere." "Serial" means "one at a time, in a sequence." Serial data is information transferred one piece at a time, as opposed to several parts at once.

A bus is a physical part of a computer that allows for the transfer of electronic information from one point to another. It is usually a set of wires connecting two or more parts. Electronic signals travel back and forth on these wires as the computer does its job.

Here is a picture of a type of bus:

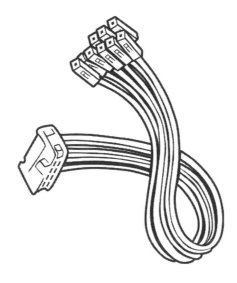

In terms of transferring data from one location to another, the computer sends bits as electronic signals on a physical piece of metal wiring. Here, a 1 bit is represented by the presence of electricity on the wire, and a 0 bit is represented by the absence of electricity on the wire.

In a system like this, you can set it up so that when you're sending a set of data, there is only one wire available for use. In that case, the data is broken up into small pieces, and each piece is sent one after the other. In other words, there is a series of pieces of data. This is serial data transfer.

You can also set it up so that you use multiple wires to transfer the data. In this case, the data is broken up such that each wire is only used to transfer part of the whole data and all the wires are used at once. This way the whole set of data is moved much faster. This is called parallel data transfer.

The Universal Serial Bus is a concept that all computer manufacturers agreed to use. It uses a standard physical port (something that can be plugged into) on the computer that can be used to send and receive information. The USB port looks like this:

Most charging cords for cell phones can plug into the USB port on a computer and use the electronic signal from the computer to charge the phone.

A USB drive is a portable data storage device. It is also called a thumb drive. It can be used to store electronic documents, images, songs, videos, etc. This is often useful for transferring information from one computer to another, using the USB port on the computer.

A thumb drive is about the size of a person's thumb, and that's how it got the name. Thumb drives are also called: USB drive, USB flash drive, USB stick, flash drive, disk-on-key, jump drive, pen drive and memory stick.

USB technology was released in 1996 and was invented by Ajay Bhatt (an Indian-American computer scientist).

SUMMARY:

As you've seen, there are many different types of devices used to store data for use in computers. We've discussed several so far. Now we come to CD-ROM (Compact Disc - Read Only Memory) drives and USB drives.

CD-ROM drives use a plastic disk to store permanent data – once the data is written on the disk, it can't be changed.

USB drives use a small stick containing electronic memory devices to store data and you can change this data if desired.

Let's discuss how data is organized on computers.

CHAPTER 76:
ORGANIZING FILES

"The only difference between a mob and a trained army is organization."
-Calvin Coolidge (1872-1933, American president)

A "hierarchical file system" refers to how files are organized and displayed.

It is how drives, folders and files are organized and displayed on a computer. In a hierarchical file system, the drives, folders, and files are shown in groups, which allows the user to see only the files they want to.

Here is a hierarchical file system diagrammed out:

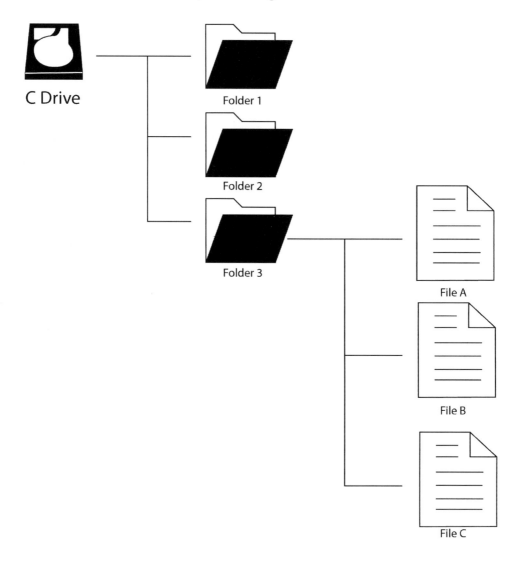

Inside hierarchical file systems are directories. A directory is a location for storing files on your computer.

Directory is another word for "folder" – the terms are interchangeable.

The route to a file is called a "file path." The "file path" is the address of a file and specifies the exact location of a file. It provides a "path" to the file.

File paths say things like, "You can find the file named 'Winter' inside the folder named 'Poems', which is inside the C drive."

The various components of a path are separated by a text character that is unlikely to be used in the name of a directory or a file. Usually this character is a slash, backslash or colon ("/," "\" or ":" respectively).

The "\" (backslash) symbol separates the different parts of a collection of electronic documents in computers and it has been used for a long time. It was created as an aid to organizing and finding the various files you might store on a computer.

In a file path, backslashes are used to show that one item is below another (in terms of hierarchy). The item on the left is above the one on the right. Our earlier example a file path would be written as:

C:\Poems\Winter

SUMMARY:

Computers can store lots of files, and it's valuable to have a standard way to organize those files. Nearly all computers use a hierarchical system of folders (also called directories) and files to organize files. Any individual file can be found using a "path," which is a standard way to specify the storage drive and folders leading to the file. An example is "C:\recipes\lunch\hamburger.txt," which says "The file called hamburger.txt is in the directory called lunch, which is in the directory called recipes, which is on the drive called C."

Let's take a look at some ways file paths are accessed.

CHAPTER 77:
COMMAND

"Technology is a useful servant but a dangerous master."
-Christian Lous Lange (Norwegian historian, 1869-1938)

An interface is a common point or boundary between two things. It provides a way for two things to interact smoothly and communicate with each other.

In computers, an interface is a device or program that enables one thing to communicate with another thing. Typically, the types of things involved are people, programs and computers, and so an interface might allow a user to communicate with a computer, or enable one program to communicate with another program.

A user interface (UI) is something that someone using a computer can view and interact with that makes the interaction with the computer easier or smoother. In early computers, user interfaces used buttons, lights and switches, and looked something like this:

One of the earliest types of user interfaces from the 1960s that is still in use today is the "command-line interface" (CLI). This is a method of operating a computer that uses a visual prompt (a symbol that tells the user that the computer is ready to receive an instruction) and accepts typed instructions.

Here are some examples of prompts:

>

>>

:

$

The user types instructions for the computer immediately after the prompt. When they press the Enter key, those instructions are given to the computer for execution.

The command line allows users to perform many actions, including: moving files, deleting things, copying files, etc. In the early days of computers, a CLI was the primary method for running a computer.

An example of how this could work is typing:

>copy activestudents\nancydrew graduates

This would mean to copy the file "nancydrew", which is in the "activestudents" folder, over to the "graduates" folder.

Note that you would not type the ">" character – that character represents the command line prompt that appears on the screen to let you know the computer is ready to receive instructions.

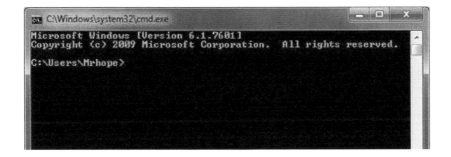

SUMMARY:

Often, we need to define a standard way for communication and control to happen between people, computers and computer programs. The device or program that allows this is called an interface.

The interface used to let users control early computers is called a command line interface (CLI), and it let users type in text instructions for the computer. CLIs still exist on most computers today for those who wish to use them.

A shift was eventually made from command lines over to another type of interface.

CHAPTER 78:
GOOEY

"A picture is worth a thousand words. An interface is worth a thousand pictures."
-Ben Shneiderman (American professor, 1947-)

Nowadays, most computers are operated by interacting with graphical representations (pictures) of the things on the computer. Here, "graphical" means "having to do with images created on a computer screen."

Most computers, however, can still be operated from a CLI if the user wants to do so.

The interface that most people are used to is the "Graphical User Interface." Abbreviated as GUI and pronounced "gooey."

As covered earlier, when computers were first being developed, the interface between user and computer was entirely text-based – all input and output was typed out. To access a file or program on the computer, the user would enter instructions, in text, that found that file or program and then opened the file or started the program. This was a challenging interface to use, as the user had to create a picture in their head of the arrangement of files and programs on the computer. The development of a GUI was a major event in the history of computers.

A GUI is a representation of the various objects in a computer – files, programs, etc. – in a graphical form. That is, it presents the user with pictures and diagrams that communicate what things are on the computer, and their arrangement. The pictures are not the things themselves; they are a graphical representation of the things.

It is much easier for a new user to move a file from one location to another by dragging the picture of a file with the mouse than by having to remember and type commands to accomplish the same task.

Here is a GUI (on the left) next to a text-based interface:

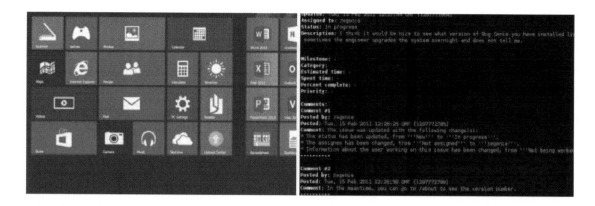

If you have an image of a folder on your computer, and an image of files inside that folder, that is actually a graphical representation of the file path.

The Alto personal computer, developed by the company Xerox in 1973, was the first computer with a GUI. It looked like this:

SUMMARY:

Early computers used a text-based system to allow users to interact with the computer. This was not very user-friendly. With the development of graphical user interfaces (GUI), computers became much easier for non-technical people to use.

GUIs use graphical representations of the objects stored on the computer. This makes it much easier to see what you're interacting with.

As you can tell, data is essential in computers. What actions can be taken to ensure it's safe?

CHAPTER 79:
BACKING UP

"Back up my hard drive?
How do I put it in reverse?"
-Unknown

A "backup" is a copy of information created as an alternate in case the original information is lost or becomes unusable. It is used to store information for safekeeping.

You could, for example, back up important files that are on your computer by saving the copies of those files on a thumb drive.

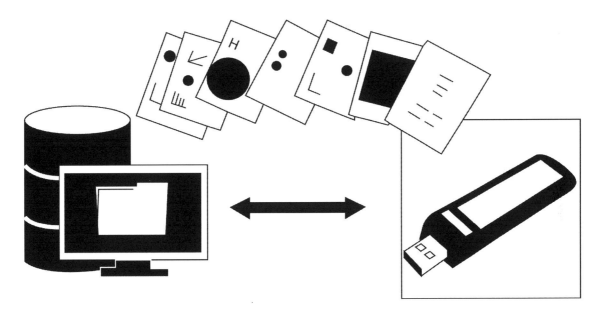

Many different systems, devices and services exist to facilitate backing up electronic data. Losing vital electronic records can have a damaging effect, so it is recommended that you back up data often.

SUMMARY:

Often, computers are used to process important data. It is smart to save a copy of that data in case you lose the original data. This copy is called a backup, and there are many different ways to make and store backups.

Now let's talk about databases.

CHAPTER 80:
DATABASE

"Database: the information you lose when your memory crashes."
-Dave Barry (American author, 1947-)

A database is an organized collection of related data, typically for use on a computer. Computers might connect to a database that is stored on another computer in order to access the data in the database.

This is the symbol for a database:

The symbol represents disks in a hard drive stacked on top of each other like this:

Usually, the data in a database is organized into tables. Tables are a data structure made up of rows and columns. Each column would represent a type of data that could be stored in the table; each row would represent one entry into the table.

For example, if you had a table that was meant to hold data about students, the columns might be:

Last Name
First Name
Date of Birth
Grade Point Average
Teacher

A row in that table might have the values (assigned characteristics or amounts):

Smith, John, 5/24/1969, 3.52, Mrs. Huber

A table often has many rows of data in it.

A large collection of data containing all the names of a company's customers, along with data about their addresses and ages, organized in a logical way, would be an example of a database.

FIRST NAME	LAST NAME	ADDRESS	CITY	AGE
Mickey	Mouse	123 Fantasy Way	Anaheim	73
Bat	Man	321 Cavern Ave	Gotham	54
Wonder	Woman	987 Truth Way	Paradise	39
Donald	Duck	555 Quack Street	Mallard	65
Bugs	Bunny	567 Carrot Street	Rascal	58
Wiley	Coyote	999 Acme Way	Canyon	61
Cat	Woman	234 Purrfect Street	Hairball	32
Tweety	Bird	543	Itotitaw	28

When a database is organized into collections of tables, it is called a "relational database." It is called this because the data in one table can have some sort of relationship to data in other tables.

"RDBMS" stands for Relational Database Management System. An RDBMS is a type of computer program that lets you manage relational databases. It is not the databases themselves; it just helps you run the databases.

There is also the term "middleware." This is software that connects the operating system to applications. It can also connect databases to programs and applications. Some refer to middleware as "software glue." An example of middleware would be software that allowed communication into a database (such as putting data in, extracting data, etc.).

One type of computer used to store databases is a mainframe. A mainframe is a large central computer that can maintain and process a lot of information and is very secure. Mainframes hold massive bodies of information and provide information to other computers. They can support hundreds to thousands of computers and are very powerful. These came before the smaller "personal computers" that we are all used to working with today.

The word actually comes from the early days of the telephone industry. There were places where many telephone wires could all come together, so that phone calls could be connected to various places around the country. These were called telephone exchanges. The wires and equipment for a telephone exchange would all be contained in a large metal frame. These came to be called mainframes. When the computer industry formed, the terminology started being used to describe the large frames that contained the parts of a large computer.

Here is a mainframe computer:

SUMMARY:

Computers, as we've covered, are used to take in data, process it, and output it. One of the more valuable developments in computer technology is the database, which is an organized collection of electronic data. Usually, this data is organized into various tables, each of which contains data that has something in common. The various tables in this system often relate to each other in some way, and the software used to manage these databases is called a Relational Database Management System (RDBMS).

Middleware is the software that connects operating systems to programs, and that can connect databases to programs.

A mainframe is a massive central computer used to securely maintain and process data.

Considering one of the primary uses of computers is accessing the internet, let's discuss this further.

CHAPTER 81:
SEARCHING

"A world where everyone creates content gets confusing pretty quickly without a good search engine."
-Ethan Zuckerman (American professor, 1973-)

A search engine is a special program that can access an index (a list of the various webpages in a website or the web as a whole) containing data about many of the webpages from websites around the world. Using a search engine, you can enter descriptive search terms and get back a list of all the webpages that contain those search terms. This is valuable because there are now billions of webpages available on the web.

Search engines are very popular tools used by nearly every user of the web. In fact, the most popular website in the world is google.com, the search engine owned by the U.S. technology company Google (company founded in 1998 by American computer scientists Larry Page and Sergey Brin).

Other popular search engines include:

• Bing: A search engine created by Microsoft.

- Yahoo! search engine.

There are other search engines, but Google, Bing and Yahoo! dominate over 95% of the market (meaning, over 95% of people use one of these three search engines).

A search engine is different than a web browser.

A browser is a program you use to view items on the internet. A search engine is used to find those items.

The most common activity people use browsers for is to view websites.

The most popular browsers are:

- Google Chrome (browser created by Google).

- Mozilla Firefox (commonly just called "Firefox" – a browser created by the company Mozilla Foundation).

- Microsoft Edge (previously known as Internet Explorer – this is a browser developed by Microsoft).

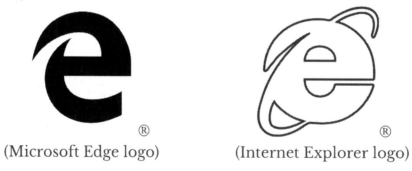

(Microsoft Edge logo)   (Internet Explorer logo)

- Safari (a browser developed by Apple).

®

- Opera (a web browser created by Opera Software).

®

The difference between a browser and a search engine is: a browser is used to visit and display websites, while a search engine is used to search for websites. For example: You could use the browser Google Chrome to search using Yahoo's search engine. In this case, you would use the Chrome browser to view the websites that were found by the Yahoo search engine. It would look like this:

Additionally, you could use the Google search engine inside the Safari browser and it would look like this:

Frankly, the most typical use is to run the Google search engine inside the Google Chrome browser.

A "window" is a framed area on a screen where data can be viewed. The previous pictures are windows.

A "tab" is a visual representation on a computer display that identifies an element on the screen. It is similar to the tabs that are placed on file folders in a physical organizing system (the part sticking up on the top left):

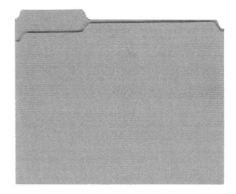

Tabs can be used in the case where a computer program allows multiple versions of a similar display element, so that each element can be identified and controlled.

Let's say you are using a computer program to work on three different written documents at once. On the screen, the program could present three small tabs near the top of the screen, with the name of each document on the tab. You could use these tabs to switch between the documents as you work.

Tabs are often used in browsers when you have more than one webpage open.

SUMMARY:

Special programs called web browsers are used to retrieve and display webpages. Other programs called search engines are used to find webpages you can retrieve and view. Common web browsers are: Google Chrome, Mozilla Firefox, Microsoft Edge, Safari and Opera. Common search engines are: Google Search, Yahoo! Search Engine and Bing.

Now let's go over *where* websites are stored.

CHAPTER 82:
SERVICE

"I did not have textual relations with that server."
-Unknown

A server is a computer that is used as the source of data and/or services by one or more other computers. In this case, the computers are connected into a network, and are equipped with specialized computer programs that allow them to communicate with each other over that network.

A common design for a computer network is to designate one or more of the computers in the network as a "server," and all the other computers as "clients."

The "client" is the computer that is requesting service from another computer (i.e. server), where the two computers are connected to each other in some way.

The servers will contain important data and computer programs needed by the client computers. Using those specialized computer programs, clients will request data or services from the servers. The servers will get the needed data from their storage devices and send it to the requesting client computer.

There are many different types of servers, depending on the need of the computer users. Let's look at how this applies to the web.

The electronic files that make up a website are stored on specialized computers called web servers. These computers accept requests from other, remote computers for specific webpages, and deliver those files needed to make the webpage display on the remote computer. The type of program you would use to view webpages is called a web browser. It is this program that would make the requests to the web server for the website files. In this example, the "web browser" is the "specialized computer program" referred to in the paragraph before last.

Google has over 1,000,000 servers, located at various places around the world.

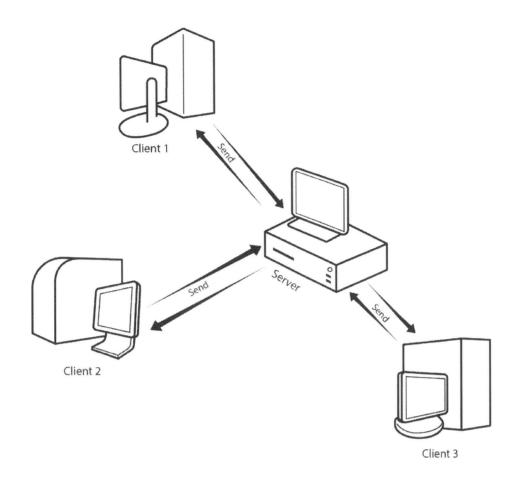

A host is a company that manages web servers. Using a host means you are basically renting someone else's computer(s) – as a server – to store your website in so that your site is kept safe and they can deal with all the work it takes to send your webpages to each person's computer that requests seeing them. Hosting is usually pretty inexpensive and allows you to set up a website with its own name and location on the web. The word comes from "host" which means to help and take care of someone.

With hosting, you can design a website and then pay a company a fee; they will save your website files somewhere on a server and when people want to check out your website, the person's computer communicates back and forth to the host computer (server). You still have full control over your website and what happens with it. Here are some servers used for hosting:

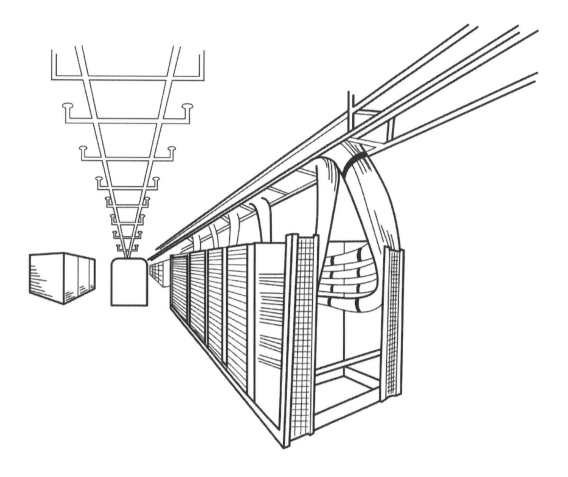

A hosting company is different than an internet service provider (ISP). ISPs are companies that provide people with access to the internet. Typically, they set up your router(s) and you pay them a monthly fee for an internet connection – such as wifi. The company Comcast is an example of an ISP.

SUMMARY:

Pretty much since the first time two computers were connected together in a network, people started designating certain computers in the network as "servers" – meaning, they contained resources that many other computers might want to use. Many of the computers on the internet perform a special function as "web servers." These computers store the files that make up the web – a collection of linked electronic documents. Often, companies will own many of these "web server" computers, and allow people to store the webpages of their website on the servers so people can access the pages. This is called "hosting" the website. An ISP (Internet Service Provider) is a company that provides customers with access to the internet – like Comcast.

Nowadays, many websites are also programs – let's look into this.

CHAPTER 83:
PROGRAMS ON THE WEB

*"The ultimate promise of technology is to make us master of a world
that we command by the push of a button."*
-Volker Grassmuck (German researcher, 1961-)

Programs on the web are called web applications. A web application is a computer program that uses both the browser and the web server to accomplish its functions. Part of the program is in the browser, and part of it is on web server.

The browser handles the display of information to the user and gives the user a place to enter instructions for the program. The web server handles various data processing actions based on the user instructions.

Note that this differs from the way many computer programs work, where the entire program resides on one computer.

Many websites nowadays are actually web applications.

For example, Dropbox is a famous web application that allows users to store and share files and folders online.

SUMMARY:

A website can be relatively simple, only containing pages that present data. However, you can design websites that provide complex functionality to users. These are called web applications, and they are programs that use both the web server and the browser to perform data processing actions.

These web apps are written in code, so let's discuss more about what code is exactly.

CHAPTER 84:
CODE

"Just because something doesn't do what you planned it to do doesn't mean it's useless."
-Thomas Edison (American inventor, 1847-1931)

As mentioned throughout this book, "code" is the written instructions you type into a computer to make programs.

Code is written in specialized computer languages.

As a verb, "coding" means typing out instructions (using a particular computer language) to create a program that will make the computer perform certain actions. Another word for these programs is "software."

Code can also mean: A system where you use a symbol to represent another thing. For example: Airports are often referred to by three-letter codes – the Portland International Airport in Portland, Oregon, USA, has the three-letter code PDX. So here, "PDX" is a code that represents the Portland International Airport.

Coding is another word for computer programming (the act of creating computer programs).

Coding also refers to the creation of websites.

The terms "coding" and "development" mean the same thing as programming. A software developer is a computer programmer; so is a coder.

Programming is a spectacular subject because it is one of the few skills that applies to virtually all industries. Yes, companies that create software definitely utilize coding the most, but if you think about it, most industries utilize technology (software, websites, databases, etc.). And so, coders are valuable assets for companies in any industry, including: construction, food service, retail (selling goods), transportation, etc.

There are many, many programming languages, and technology is ever-changing. The whole subject can be quite overwhelming, but there are basics that apply across the vast landscape of technology.

In general, the instructions in computer programs are executed in order, from the top down.

So this is how you create a program: You take the available instructions for the CPU, create a list of what you want the computer to do in order, and then have the CPU go through the list, doing each one in order.

As mentioned earlier, these instructions built into the CPU are called "machine language" (1s and 0s), since they are actually the only directions the machine can "understand."

Also covered earlier, writing code in machine language is how people had to program computers in the early years, but it's really hard to do.

In the first place, machine language instructions don't "mean" anything at first glance – they're just a series of ones and zeroes. So when you look at them, you probably can't tell what they do without looking them up.

Secondly, it's pretty easy to make a mistake in entering machine language. If you put a "one" when you mean to have a "zero," the program won't work correctly.

So now we come to one of the more important developments in the history of computers.

What happened is that early programmers saw that they were entering the same exact instructions many times in a program.

For example, if you wanted to add some numbers, the series of machine language instructions to do it might have seven instructions, one after the other. You would likely use the exact same seven instructions every time your program needed to add numbers. This is repetitive and error-prone (likely to contain mistakes).

Instead, a new way was developed: a little tool where programmers could type in something like "ADD," and the tool would be able to spit out those exact seven instructions into their program. It acted as a "lookup" tool – in our example, the word (code) "ADD" is used to look up a list of those seven instructions. Basically, it was a computer program that helped you make computer programs – something that's now really common in the industry.

This was SUPER helpful for two reasons:

First, the code you typed in "meant" something – the code "ADD" was easily understood, where the corresponding pattern of seven machine language instructions wouldn't be easy to understand.

Second, you wouldn't have any mistakes in that part of the program – the programmer won't accidentally put a one where a zero is supposed to be, for example.

Similar symbols were created for the other common actions programmers were entering into the computer – code like "MOV," for moving data to a place in the computer, or "SUB," for subtracting numbers.

Pretty soon, they had a collection of these coding words. The words and symbols used in a programming language, and how to use them, is referred to as "syntax." In normal English, syntax refers to the proper way to organize words. It's the same thing for a programming language – a programming language's syntax is how to write the code (instructions) in that language. A violation of syntax would result in errors in your code and so it wouldn't run properly.

The collection of coding words mentioned earlier (such as "MOV," "ADD" and "SUB") is called "assembly language" or "assembler," because you are using this tool to "assemble" (put together) your actual computer program.

Computer programming languages have become more advanced over time, but they all work in a similar way – the data you type in may look like real words, but that data is translated into machine language because that's actually the only language the computer can operate with. And, as you know, this machine language then results in various transistors in the computer being set to on or off.

SUMMARY:

Early computer programs were written in "machine language" – the instructions that were built into the CPU. This was not easy, since the instructions were unique patterns of 1s and 0s. Eventually, tools were created that let you use a code that represented an exact sequence of commonly-used machine language instructions. These codes were sort of like English (they might be "ADD" or "MOV"). This made computer programming much easier.

If we want to divide software into two sections, we can do so by categorizing elements as front or back. What does this mean?

CHAPTER 85:
FRONT AND BACK

"The internet is not a luxury,
it is a necessity."
-Barack Obama (Former U.S. President, 1961-)

Computer programs and web applications typically have two "sides," the "front end" and the "back end."

The term "front end" has to do with how programs are presented and interacted with.

It is the part of a website or program that a user directly interacts with and sees, as opposed to the back end, which are aspects behind the scenes that users don't typically deal with directly.

This is used most often when talking about web applications.

The front end is handled by the web browser. It encompasses things like preparing the requested website files for display, formatting the text and images that appear on the screen, handling user interaction with the webpage (clicking on text and images, etc.), and sending data back to the web server (like requests for further webpage data that were made on the webpage).

When you look at a website and you see the text and pictures, that is all the "front end." The back-end is all the functions that happen on the web server for that site.

The back end is the part of a website or software program that performs vital computing functions, but is not typically seen by the user of the site or program. This includes elements like a database (an organized collection of stored data used by the site or program), as well as the parts of the program that handle information that arrives to the web server after a user inputs them on a webpage.

Typically, back end developers are those skilled in the technology required to create and organize the back end, whereas front end developers are focused on making the website or application aesthetic (beautiful; physically appealing) and user-friendly.

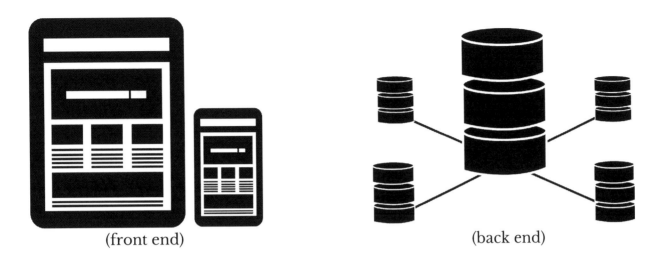

(front end)   (back end)

In a software program that allows a warehouse manager to monitor and manage the contents of the warehouse, the back end would be the collection of data about the warehouse contents. The front end would be the screens they use to view and change that data. If there were a screen where the manager could enter new inventory into the warehouse, once the manager filled out the form on the screen and submitted it, the back end would handle receiving the data from the form and modifying the database so that it reflected the new inventory that had been added.

SUMMARY:

Most computer programs, including web applications, have two main parts: the "front end" and the "back end." The front end is the interface the user sees and interacts with, and the back end is the data stored by the program and the instructions controlling what is done with that data.

Now, you've probably heard about data being stored in "the cloud." So, what is the cloud?

CHAPTER 86:
THE CLOUD

"There is no such thing as the cloud – there's just someone else's computer."
-Unknown

For many years, people and businesses would use computers that were located at their home or place of business to store data on or to run special computer programs on. At some point in the early part of the 21st century, new businesses started appearing that offered customers the use of large computers (servers) owned by these new businesses. These servers could be used by the customers to store data and programs on. The customers could connect to these servers from wherever they lived or worked, using the internet, and access the data or use the programs. This is the "cloud." The cloud actually looks like this:

Since the actual physical computers were no longer located in the home or office of the customer, they started being described as being "in the cloud," as in, "Well, they're somewhere up there in the clouds; I don't know exactly where..." The cloud is other people running computers on your behalf that you can reach over the internet.

For an example: You could take several pictures with your camera and then use a program to get the pictures off your camera and store them in the "cloud." Later on you could access those pictures using your phone or a computer.

Again, the photos "in the cloud" were actually just sent to servers via the internet. If you were connected to wifi when sending photos to the cloud, what actually happened in the physical universe was: your phone passed the data to a router through radio waves. Then the router passed data through a wire to a server. While there may be several vias (points that are passed through) in this process – it all comes down to 1s and 0s passed between machines that instruct computers which physical elements (transistors) should be on or off.

SUMMARY:

As computers became more advanced and less expensive, companies started offering a service where individual users and companies could rent the use of their computers (servers) for various purposes. These computers were accessed over the internet and this system became known as the "cloud."

What is it called when data is moved up or down from the cloud?

CHAPTER 87:
IT'S *IN* THE COMPUTER

"If computers get too powerful, we can organize them into committees.
That'll do them in."
-Unknown

Import means to bring something into something else. For example: You can import pictures by moving them in from one location to another. Importing refers to taking computer information from one location and placing it in another location. You can also import things onto a computer from a device (such as a camera or video camera).

On the other hand, export means to take some data that is used by a computer program and send it somewhere else, usually so that the data can be used by another computer program.

As an example, if you had a program that kept track of all the customers at your bicycle manufacturing company, you might export all the data about your customers so it could be used by a computer program that prints customized holiday greeting cards.

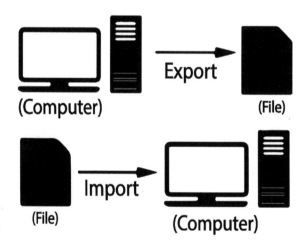

"Uploading" means to put certain electronic files from your computer onto a web server. This process of sending a file from your computer to a web server is referred to as uploading.

This term "uploading" assisted in the development of the term "cloud" because the data was "being sent up into the sky." Again, in truth, the data passes through radio waves and wires and ends up on servers.

As an example of "uploading," you could create a video and upload it to YouTube. It would then be on YouTube's web servers, and other people could go to YouTube and watch that video.

The opposite of uploading is downloading. Downloading means getting an electronic file from a web server and putting a copy of that file onto your computer. If you download a video, you are having your computer pull the electronic file that is the video over the internet from another computer and store that file on your computer so you can watch it later.

The process would work like this: the webpage would have a link (some text or image that, when clicked, will connect to another electronic file). Clicking on the link would make the browser request that file from the web server. The web server would send that file back to the browser; the browser would save the file on the user's computer.

There is also the factor of how powerful the computer is that holds the requested file. If 100 computers are downloading a song from the same web server at once, the song would download slower than if 50 computers were downloading it. This is because the web server that has the song on it has to coordinate giving a copy of that song to 100 computers at once, instead of 50.

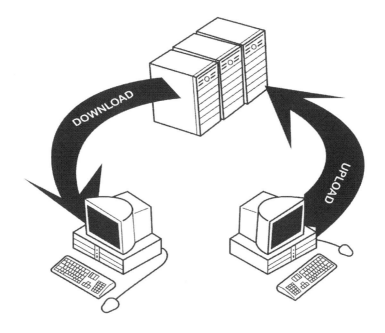

Another popular way to transmit data is "streaming." Streaming is a method of sending information from one computer to another where the information is used on the destination computer as it arrives to that computer, rather than being used only after all of the information has arrived.

This is used most often to describe a method of consuming (watching; listening; studying) video and audio media (something communicated). In this situation, it means that a company that provides the media content has the media files (the digital information that makes up the media) on its own computers.

When a remote computer connects and wants to consume that media, the company's computer starts sending the media one part at a time. As the parts arrive at the destination computer, they are processed and presented to the user right away. The media information is not usually preserved (stored) on the destination computer in this case.

In this situation, the source computer is said to be "streaming" the media to the destination computer. Usually, many destination computers can connect to the source computer at once. Each one will be receiving its own "stream" of information.

Netflix is used for streaming videos and is referred to as a streaming service. With Netflix, when you select a movie, the service then starts sending the electronic data for the movie to your television. You start watching the movie right away, without waiting for all the movie's data to arrive first.

SUMMARY:

Often we want to send information over the internet to another computer, or to get information from another computer over the internet. There are special terms for these operations. "Import" refers to moving data *in* to a computer, while "export" means the opposite. When you retrieve information from another computer (i.e. a server) and store it on your computer, it is called "downloading." When you send information from your computer to another computer (i.e. a server), it is called "uploading." You can also retrieve information from another computer in a stream – that is, the information is sent as a series of small pieces, and each piece is immediately used on your computer, rather than retrieving all of the information at once and then using it. This is called "streaming" and is a popular way to listen to music or watch video content.

Now that you have a good understanding of the internet, let's return to computer hardware.

CHAPTER 88:
MOTHER

"Why are computers so smart?
Because they listen to their motherboard.
-Unknown

As we covered earlier, a circuit is a path that electricity flows along from beginning to end. In that path, there might be certain components that perform work, control the flow of the electricity, etc.

A circuit board is a thin, flat board that contains complex electronic circuits. They are also called "printed circuit boards."

Printed refers to the fact that someone initially designs the circuits for the board and then the metal tracks that comprise the circuits are printed by a machine onto the board – similar to how you could type a document and then print it out using a printer.

If you opened up a printer at your office, somewhere inside you would find a printed circuit board that contained the important electronic circuits that controlled the printer's operation.

Printed circuit boards look like this:

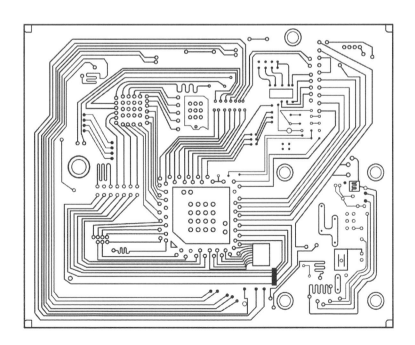

The motherboard is the largest board in a computer. It contains the most important electronic parts in the computer. Lots of components are placed on top of and as part of the motherboard.

Every part of the computer is connected in some way to the motherboard. It can be considered the "glue" that holds all sections of the computer together. It looks like this:

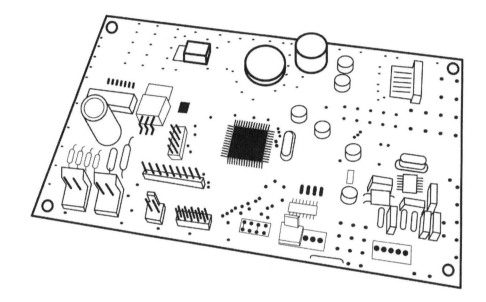

Here, "mother" is used to refer to something that protects or cares for other things.

More individual parts of the computer are stored on the motherboard than any other part of the computer.

The components normally included on the motherboard are:

- The microprocessor (which includes the CPU, various cards [parts that perform specialized functions] and more).

- The BIOS (Basic Input/Output System – the program that runs every time you start your computer).

- RAM (Random Access Memory).

    And more.

Now remember, the basic functions of a computer are: take in data, process that data and then output data.

We use external devices, called peripherals, to get data in and receive the data the computer sends out.

You can see the connections where you plug in peripherals (like a mouse or keyboard) on the back of computers:

These connection points that you plug into are called "ports." Most attach directly into the motherboard, as you can see here:

Since the motherboard is where most of the computer work is done, it helps to have the peripherals connect right to it.

Another component in the motherboard is the heat sink. This is a heat exchanger (a device that can move heat from one place to another) in a computer that helps prevent overheating of certain electronic components.

As you know, computers use electricity. When they are doing lots of work, they use more electricity. When electricity flows, it generates heat. This means there are parts of a computer that can get hot when the computer is operating. A heat sink is something installed on those parts in a computer to keep them cool.

They are usually made of metal, and have a large surface area to facilitate heat dissipation (spreading; causing to disappear). They look something like this:

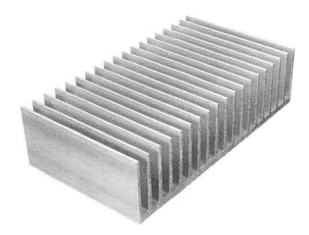

A fan can also be used to help make the heat sink even more effective at removing heat from the computer. The fan would blow air across the heat sink so that heat would be carried away in the air more quickly. Fans inside the computer look like this:

In this picture, the fan is mounted on top of a heat sink on a printed circuit board. You can also see a computer fan on the top right of the tower pictured earlier in this chapter. Sometimes you can hear a whirring sound inside your computer; that's the fan blades spinning.

Occasionally you hear a clicking sound inside your computer. One of the reasons for that sound is due to the reader arm inside your hard drive moving around. You can see the hard drive reader arm circled in the image below:

SUMMARY:

The most important piece of hardware in a computer is the "motherboard" – a thin, flat board that has many electronic circuits and devices on it. On it is the CPU, which controls the operation of the entire computer, as well as other vital parts. The connections that allow you to attach various peripheral devices connect to the motherboard so that the CPU can communicate with them.

We've talked about the concept of "digital" a little already, but let's go over it further.

CHAPTER 89:
DIGITAL

"When something is important enough, you do it even if the odds are not in your favor."
-Elon Musk (South African technology leader, 1971-)

As we covered earlier, photography film is a smooth, continuous preparation of chemicals applied to a piece of clear plastic. Whatever light is allowed to hit the film creates an image on the film. The film isn't divided up into many small squares like a computer screen. The quality of the image depends on the quality of the chemical preparation.

In a digital camera, light is allowed to hit a "sensor." The sensor has lots of individual locations, and each location registers a certain brightness and color of light. That information has to be somehow translated into digits (actual numbers) that the computer can store. The quality of the image then depends on how many of those locations the sensor has, and how well each location can produce a number that accurately represents the light that landed on it.

While digital cameras were available for purchase as early as 1990, film cameras had better image quality than digital cameras well into the early 2000s. Once digital cameras were good enough, the general shift to digital cameras happened. This wasn't really because the pictures were better, it was because digital is cheaper and easier to work with. Taking digital pictures costs nothing, whereas film is not free and cannot be reused. Of course digital image quality continues to improve to this day and in most every application is now superior to film.

Cassette tapes were purely analog. When they were first sold in 1962, the tape itself had a layer that could be magnetized. The varying wave of sound from the physical universe was duplicated and translated into a varying wave of magnetism laid down on the tape. But since the tape would always have some stray (leftover) magnetism on it, this would be picked up as a "hiss" and could not be avoided.

One of the first truly popular mediums (ways to do something) for storing digital information was Compact Discs (CDs). Computer processing power was sufficient to make CDs possible in 1982. In the process of recording sound on a CD, the sound wave is sampled (read) about 40,000 times per second, and digital information representing the sound at each instant in time is recorded on the disc as numbers. Each of these recordings (up to 40,000 distinct sound instances a second) is recorded as one point of data.

Few people use CDs anymore because we can transfer this same digital information through the internet or store it on our computers. Up until the mid-1990s, a single CD held more data than the full capacity of most computers. Now, however, 15 minutes of high-quality video recording is often more data than can be placed on one of these.

Like cassette tapes, video tapes were also analog at first.

Like pictures and music, though, eventually technology improved to the point that all the data on a video tape could be chopped up into numbers and stored and processed by a computer. Considering that you need to see 24 images per second for smooth motion, and you have to record sound about 40,000 times per second for quality audio, you can see that the computer must be able to record and play back a lot of data rapidly to show you a video!

The data in this chapter so far gives you some idea of analog and digital in our consumer (purchaser; user) media world, but let's get back to the topic at hand: computing.

There's very little "computing" that can be done in an analog fashion – outside of the human mind. If you are deciding whether you want a ham and cheese sandwich or a peanut butter and jelly sandwich at home, you might mentally weigh the taste, health impacts, and cost of each in some sort of "sliding scale" (amounts that vary in accordance with an established standard), continuous fashion. That's an analog thought process, and it's very simple and rapid. You most likely would NOT assign number values (digits) to each sandwich in each category and determine a scoring plan with a point total for each – but if you DID, this would be a digital approach to solving this snack time dilemma!

As we've covered, digital computers actually only work with 2 digits: 0 and 1. This is because our digital technology – all the little circuits and devices – are just looking for electricity being either "on" or "off." There aren't any analog "circular dial" switches or even digital "Off / Low / Medium / High" switches in a computer. Any time it *seems* like there are – such as the sound volume of your computer or brightness adjustment on your screen – the adjustments are, in fact, made up of *only on and off switches*. What's actually happening is that the volume or brightness is being changed from one level to another, in tiny increments – it just sounds (or looks) like it's a smooth change.

There are thoughts of someday having analog computers which think more like we do, but given the limitations of our current technology and the fact that all modern devices were designed on the binary number system, digital is our only option at this time.

SUMMARY:

Early technologies used for recording data like sound, still images and video were analog – meaning, the copy of the data stored on the device was very much like the original data. The way it was similar was that the data in the copy could change smoothly from one state to another, just like the original data changed. For example, if a sound smoothly increased in volume, the copy of it would do so as well. The analog versions were copies of the physical universe.

When we started recording data using digital devices like computers, this changed. Because digital devices can only store data made up of exact, distinct parts, they could not perfectly reproduce a smooth transition from one state to another. Instead, they have to get as close to the original sound as they could, occasionally losing the data that was in between one digit and another.

With modern computers having tremendous ability to store and process large amounts of data, we can usually reproduce things like audio and video so that they are indistinguishable from the original thing.

You now have enough of a foundation in place where we can explain to you how computers count. While it has been touched upon, we are now going to take a deeper dive.

CHAPTER 90:
HOW COMPUTERS COUNT

"On two occasions I have been asked, 'If you put into the machine wrong figures,
will the right answers come out?'
I am not able rightly to apprehend the kind of confusion of ideas
that could provoke such a question."
-Charles Babbage (English mathematician, 1791-1871)

To recap, a bit is a binary digit. Binary is the number system used by computers and is made up of only 0s and 1s (off and on respectively), and a byte is a series of eight bits, like: 1100 0011

So, let's say you want to store an amount on your computer. The basic process goes like this:

1. The user types a number (such as 9).

2. The computer translates the number to binary (0000 1001).

3. 8 transistors (a byte) inside your computer are switched to a state of on or off based on the above binary. In this case (moving from right to left), the first transistor would be on, the second and third off, the fourth on, and the fifth through eighth off.

The "number 9" is literally stored in a physical form on your computer, like this:

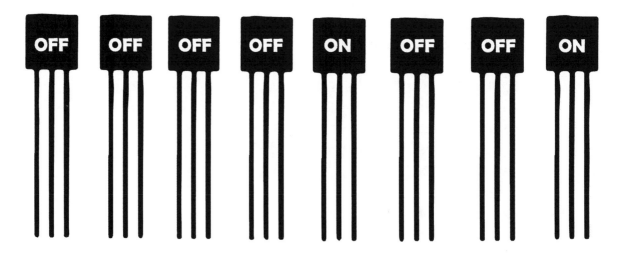

Computers come pre-programmed to "understand" that certain combinations of bits, as represented in binary, mean exact things. These instructions are programmed into the instruction set in the CPU. An instruction set is made up of all instructions in machine code that can be recognized and executed by the CPU.

The CPU instruction set provides commands to the CPU, such as: ADD (combine two numbers), COMPARE (determine sameness/differences in numbers), LOAD (move information from RAM into the CPU), and more.

To perform math inside your computer, various transistors are set to combinations of on and off to store the amounts, and then the proper instruction (for example: ADD – which may be written as 0100) is performed.

The point of this chapter is to ensure you understand that all of the functions your computer does and everything it displays is a representation of a *physical* action inside your computer in terms of transistors being on or off. These transistors are microscopic, combined billions to trillions of times, and can be manipulated extremely quickly. It all comes down to 1s and 0s.

Though some of this has been covered already, it bore repeating.

SUMMARY:

We talked earlier about the number system called binary. It is used in computers to represent the data the computer operates on, and the instructions for what to do with that data. These 1s and 0s of the binary system, as they are used in the computer, actually represent physical changes in real objects. The billions-trillions of tiny transistors in the computer either pass electricity (1), or they don't (0).

Now let's go back to computers and the internet.

CHAPTER 91:
CHANGING SIGNALS

"Fame means when your computer modem is broken,
the repair guy comes out to your house a little faster."
-Sandra Bullock (American actress, 1964-)

The word "modem" comes from these two terms: "modulate/demodulate." To modulate a thing means to change it. To demodulate means to reverse that change.

Modem is short for "modulator-demodulator."

In computers, this means you take a constant electrical signal and add to it (modulate it) so that it now carries information along with the constant signal.

As an example, you could have a machine that puts caps on soda bottles at a soda plant. The machine could output a continuous sound, with a constant volume, when no bottles are being capped.

When the machine starts to operate and put caps on bottles, you could then cause that sound to spike up in volume for a split second every time a bottle was capped. You have now modulated (changed) the output signal so that it carries information along with it – in this case, the information it carries is the rate at which bottles are being capped.

A visual representation of the signal, over time, might look like this:

Here, the "_" character represents the constant-volume, steady sound emitted by the machine, and the "|" character represents the spike in volume of that sound whenever a bottle is capped.

Since it would be easy to lose track of the count if you were listening to the changing sound, it would be good to have another piece of equipment that could just keep track of the spikes in the sound signal. That would be a demodulator.

The demodulator, knowing what the constant-volume, steady sound was like could look for the variations in that sound and determine when a bottle was being capped.

A common type of modem is one that converts data from a computer into a signal that can be transmitted over telephone lines, or vice versa. Most computers have a modem installed inside them. External modems look like this:

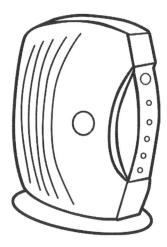

The modem does two things, depending on whether it is receiving information or sending information:

1) When a computer has information it wants to send to another computer, it gives that information to the modem. The modem takes that information and uses it to modulate a constant signal that can be sent over phone lines.

2) When the destination computer is receiving the information, its modem extracts the information carried on that constant telephone signal and turns it into computer information. Here is what it might look like:

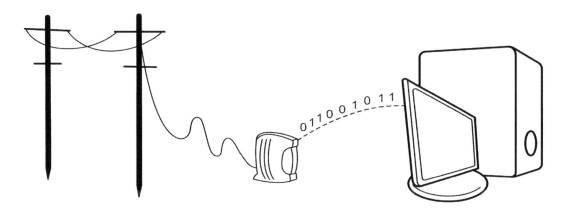

On some modems, you can plug your phone line directly into it for internet access. In fact, an internet connection is the primary use of a modem. But wait, isn't that a router? Well, nowadays, most routers have modems built in them. The modems within routers perform the functions covered in this chapter for the router. The router, as covered earlier, handles the work of connecting various computers and managing the traffic between them.

In 1962, the first modem was released to the public. It was called the "Bell 103" and was created by the telephone company AT&T. It looked like this:

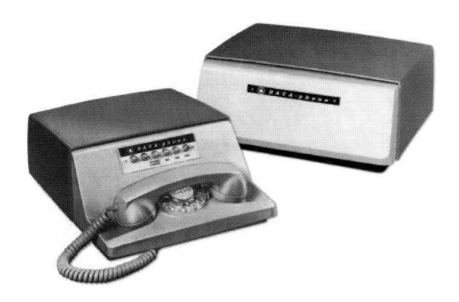

SUMMARY:

As we've covered before, computers can be connected together so data can be sent back and forth between them for various purposes. Special equipment was needed in order to send and receive the data. One important device for this purpose is a modem – a "modulator/demodulator." These devices modulate (change) a stable signal to reflect the data to be sent, and demodulate (extract the changes from) the modified signal in order to get the data in it. Modems are commonly built into (contained inside) routers and computers.

The essence of the internet is "data transfer." Let's look at how data can be altered so as to make the transfer smoother.

CHAPTER 92:
ZIP

"A picture is worth a thousand words but it takes 3,000 times the disk space."
-Unknown

"Compress" means "to make something smaller." Literally, compression means that a file is changed so that it utilizes fewer bits (on and off transistors) inside the computer.

In computers, compressing is the changing of data in such a way that it can be stored in a computer using less storage device space than if it were stored in its original form. Compression programs are special computer programs that convert electronic files to a smaller format so that they take up less room, making it easier and/or faster to send those files to other locations. This can also free up available storage space in a computer, as the files don't use as much space.

If you have a large document that uses the phrase "This page intentionally left blank" over and over, a compression program might assign that exact phrase a code like "#blnk123#" and replace every point in the document that had the text "This page intentionally left blank" with the code "#blnk123#." This will make the document smaller, since there are fewer characters in the code than there are in the text it replaces. Later, when the user wants to view that document, that same compression program can reverse the process, restoring the actual text in the file wherever it finds the code "#blnk123#."

When you compress a file, this is referred to as "zipping." I.e. when you zip a file, you are compressing it to save size.

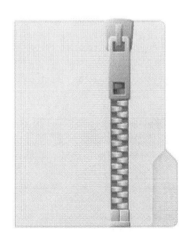

329

Unzipping the file restores it to its original size.

If you tried to view a zipped text document without unzipping it first, it would look like gibberish. Unzipping files converts them to their original form. In addition to saving space on one's computer, zipping files can make it easier to send files over the internet because it takes less time to transfer the entire file. Also, emails have a limit on the size of attachments, so a zipped file can sometimes be an option to keep attachments under the required size limits.

SUMMARY:

Continual improvements have been made in how to rapidly transfer data between computers. One important development involved "compressing" the file to be sent. In basic terms, this means to make the file smaller by replacing common items in the file with a shorter code that represents the common item. The file now is smaller and it takes less time to send the whole file to another computer. When the compressed file arrives at the destination computer, it also comes with instructions on how to decompress it – in other words, it is told what codes were used to replace longer content in the file. By replacing those codes with the actual content, the original file is restored.

Now, let's change gears and go over one of the most popular uses of the internet.

CHAPTER 93:
SOCIAL

*"It seems to me, Golan, that the advance of civilization is nothing
but an exercise in the limiting of privacy."*
-*Foundation's Edge*, written by Isaac Asimov (American author, 1920-1992)

A social network is a website that allows people to communicate to one another socially through messages, commenting on their page, posting pictures, etc.

Social networking is interaction over the web between people – using websites, email and other communication methods – so they can get to know each other better. "Networking" refers to meeting new people and making connections. Social networking allows people to communicate to one another socially through messages, commenting on information they have put on a website, posting pictures, etc.

Social media (posts, pictures, videos, etc.) is the content you put on social networks.

The terms "social media" and "social network" are sometimes used interchangeably, but they're technically different. The social network refers to the website, and social media is what's on the website.

Facebook is the most popular social network and social media company and is referred to as both. It was founded in 2004 by American computer scientist Mark Zuckerberg.

Referring to Facebook as a "social networking website" would be correct, and so would calling it "social media"!

Other popular social networking and social media sites include:

- Instagram (a website, owned by Facebook, used for sharing videos and photographs),

- Twitter (a website that allows people to write short messages [no longer than 280 characters] called "tweets" that can be viewed by other users of Twitter),

- LinkedIn (a website owned by Microsoft that focuses on business and employment services – it's mainly used for professional networking).

There are others and will be more in the future!

SUMMARY:

Now that we have a huge network of computers around the world (the internet), and now that many people around the world have computers, devices and smartphones that connect to this network, we have a system where people can quickly communicate and share content with others. This has led to the development of "social networks" (groups of people with similar interests connected together through various websites) and social media (the content people share over those websites). The biggest website in this area is Facebook.

Let's return to computer hardware to cover some more common wired connections you've probably come across.

CHAPTER 94:
PLUGGING IN

"It doesn't stop being magic just because you know how it works."
-Sir Terry Pratchett (English author, 1948-2015)

You may have heard the term "HDMI." It stands for "High-Definition Multimedia Interface." "Definition" refers to how clear something is. The definition of an image is how sharp and clearly defined the image is. High-definition (HD) refers to extremely clear images. "Multimedia" means "including video and audio (sound)." As covered earlier, an interface is something used to communicate with a computer.

HDMI is a specification (a standardized method of construction and operation) for equipment used in transferring high definition audio and video signals. It was created in the early 2000s. It is usually applied to cables that connect computers to televisions and other display devices.

HDMI cables can be used to connect computers with certain televisions. HDMI cables were created in the early 2000s by a group of major technology companies and they look like this:

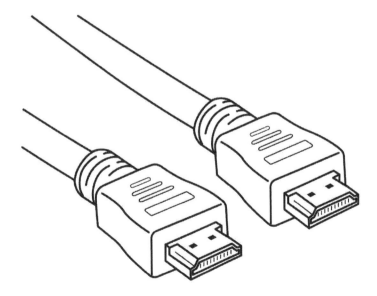

HDMI ports exist on most televisions, laptops and computers, and look like this:

VGA stands for "Video Graphics Array." "Graphics" refer to "images" and an "array" is a "wide range."

A VGA cable is used to connect a video source to a display device (monitor). They look like this:

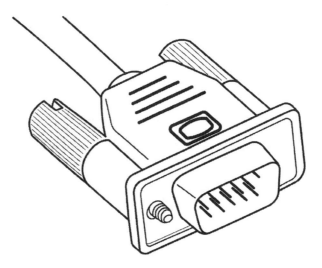

VGA came out in the 1980s and most laptops and computers have VGA ports used to connect a monitor:

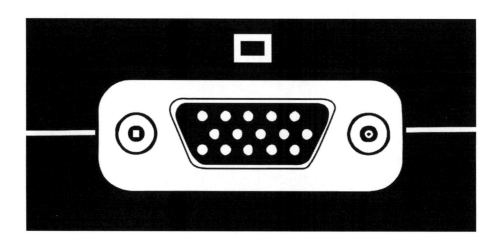

DVI stands for "Digital Video Interface" and is a type of connector that is used to connect a video source to a display device. They look like this:

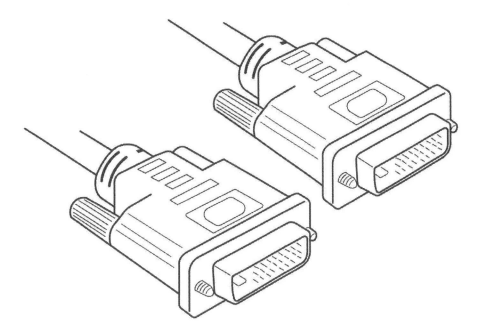

DVI cables were developed in the 1990s and allow higher quality video displays than VGA. You plug them in to ports like this:

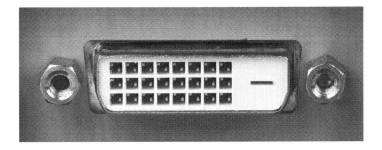

There are several different types of connectors that relate to passing video and audio signals. This is because manufacturers of audio and video equipment have continued to improve the performance of their equipment over the years, and this means that often earlier connectors can't take advantage of the newer, better features of that equipment – so new connectors had to be designed.

SUMMARY:

Various technologies have been developed over the years to enable display of video and audio content using computers. Each technology has its own type of connection to hook up a source of video and audio content (usually a computer)

to a device that can display video and audio (a monitor). Common technologies like this are VGA, DVI and HDMI.

Now, we've talked about how data is stored on computers, but let's take a look at how bits relate to file size.

CHAPTER 95:
BITS AND PIECES

"The human mind is our fundamental resource."
-John F. Kennedy (American president, 1917-1963)

As we discussed earlier in this book, a bit is short for "binary digit." A binary digit is a 0 or 1 – 0 representing the transistor being off and 1 representing on.

You can also use the term bit to describe the size of electronic files. A picture, a document, a movie, etc. are saved on a computer as electronic files. These files are all composed of a certain number of bits. The bigger the file, the more bits the file is.

A small file might utilize 25,000 (twenty-five thousand) bits. A large file might use 50,000,000 (fifty million) bits.

You may have noticed that sizes of files affect how fast a computer operates. For example, a movie file might have billions of bits, whereas a photograph might be made up of millions of bits. If you were to download both of these files, the photograph would arrive on your computer faster because there are fewer bits that need to be transferred.

As we mentioned earlier, when a group of 8 bits are put together for certain purposes, this group is given a special name: a byte.

Computers are often characterized by the size of the instructions and data that they can process at once. This measurement is given in bits. This would mean that an 8-bit computer could only handle an instruction that was made up of 8 binary digits (a byte), whereas a 64-bit computer could handle an instruction that was made up of 64 binary digits (8 bytes). This means that the 64-bit computer could process information much faster than the 8-bit computer, since each instruction could contain much more data.

Computers are typically either 32-bit or 64-bit. Technically the "bit size" of a computer refers to how much memory at one time the computer is able to access. The largest number able to be represented in 32 binary digits (bits) is:

1111 1111 1111 1111 1111 1111 1111 1111

This is 4,294,967,295 in decimal (the number system most people use to count). And so, a 32-bit computer can access up to that many different points in a computer's memory and process commands up to that size.

The largest number able to be represented in 64 binary digits (bits) is:

1111 1111 1111 1111 1111 1111 1111 1111 1111 1111 1111 1111 1111 1111 1111 1111

That's 18,446,744,073,709,551,615 in decimal. That's far more capability than current computers need, so 64-bit computers will continue far into the future.

Why does all this matter? There are three main reasons:

1. You may have already come across this subject, so now you should have a better understanding of it. If you haven't run across this yet, it's likely you will in the future.

2. Sometimes when you download and install software, it asks whether you want a 32-bit or 64-bit version of the program. To find out what type of computer you have (32 or 64 bit), Google something like "how to find out how many bits my ___ computer is" and follow the instructions (you will need to include the type of computer you have).

3. If you ever have a choice between a 32-bit computer and 64-bit, you now know which to choose.

SUMMARY:

The data a computer uses is formed of various combinations of 1s and 0s – the two binary digits. The files that contain data can be measured by how many bits (binary digits) the file contains. When you group 8 bits together, they have a special name: a byte. Different computers can work with different amounts of data at any one time. Older computers could only work with data in pieces 8 bits in size (1 byte). Modern computers can work with data that is 64 bits (8 bytes) in size.

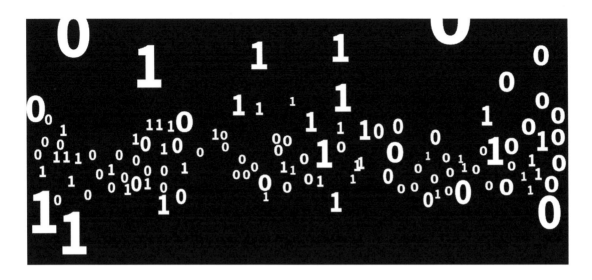

Now let's take a look at how accurately we can represent different types of data with a computer.

CHAPTER 96:
SPEED AND QUALITY

"Before you marry a person you should first make them use a computer with slow internet to see who they really are."
-Will Ferrell (American comedian, 1967-)

"Resolution" means how clear an image is. On a computer or TV, pictures are made up of many pixels (tiny little dots), arranged in a grid. A higher resolution means there are more of these little dots in a given area, so a higher level of image clarity will be present.

At low resolution, you can actually see these pixels (the dots are bigger) and the image would be relatively unclear. At high resolution, you can't identify the individual dots.

 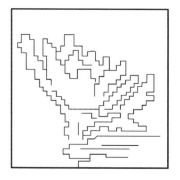

High-resolution   Low-resolution

Each pixel is represented by bits, so the more pixels, the more bits. Meaning, the higher the quality of an image, video, file, etc., the bigger the file is (i.e. the more bits it's made up of).

And then there's the matter of speed. Computers measure how fast data is transferred or saved in terms of "number of bits transferred per second."

Size and speed are measured in bits using prefixes telling what magnitude (size) of number they are in. These are taken from Greek words. They are:

- Kilo, meaning "thousand);
- Mega, meaning "million"; and
- Giga, meaning "billion".

"Kb" stands for "kilobit".

In computers, a kilobit means one of two things:

1. A kilobit is one thousand bits, or

2. More accurately, a kilobit is considered to be 1,024 bits. That's because computers commonly operate off of powers of two. "Power" refers to multiplying a number against itself – for example: 2 to the first power is 2; 2 to the second power is 4 (2 x 2); 2 to the third power is 8 (2x2x2), etc.

2 to the tenth power is 1,024. Since 1,024 is the closest "2 to the power of ___" can get to one thousand, the computer industry uses the term "kilo" to describe that number (1,024).

"Kbps" stands for "kilobits per second." This indicates that a network can transfer data at a rate of ___ thousand bits a second. E.g. 20 Kbps indicates a transfer speed of 20,480 bits in a second.

If an internet connection had an upload speed of "500 Kbps," it would take 10 seconds to upload a 5,000 Kb file from your computer to another computer on the internet.

A notepad document like this might be around 16 Kb in size (16,448 bits – i.e. it would place over 16,000 transistors in various states of on and off within your computer):

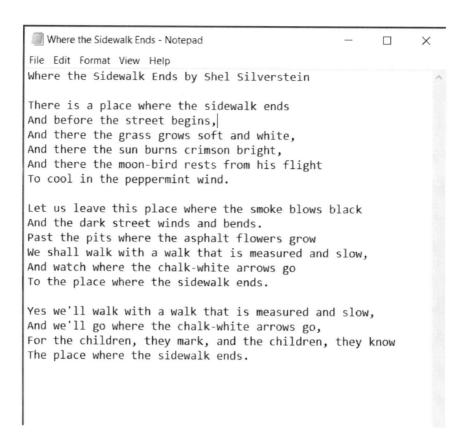

As a reminder, a "byte" is 8 bits. KB stands for "kilobyte." Notice the capital B. A lowercase b indicates "bit," whereas uppercase indicates "byte."

Like Kb, a KB is one of two amounts:

1. One thousand bytes (or 8,000 bits). E.g. 3.4 kilobytes is 3,400 bytes, or

2. More accurately, a kilobyte (KB) is 1,024 bytes (8,192 bits).

In the past, kilobytes were used to measure computer memory (how many bytes a computer can store). You saw computers promoting 16KB. That would mean the computer could hold 16,384 bytes of memory (or 131,072 bits).

For example, this 1981 IBM computer could store up to 256 KB of memory (very small by today's standards):

KBps indicates the transfer of digital information from one location to another at a speed of 1,024 bytes (8,192 bits) per second. Remember, the "K" actually stands for 1024, not 1000.

The other four common measurements of bit sizes and transfer speeds are:

1. Megabits – abbreviated as "Mb." Mega means "million," so a Mb is 1,048,576 bits (it's not exactly one million because, as we covered, computers operate off the power of two – in this case 2 to the 20th power).

2. Megabytes – abbreviated as "MB." A MB is 1,048,576 bytes (8,388,608 bits).

3. Gigabits – abbreviated as "Gb." Giga means "billion," so a Gb is 1,073,741,824 bits.

4. Gigabytes – abbreviated as "GB." A GB is 1,073,741,824 bytes (8,589,934,592 bits).

Just like "Kbps" and "KBps," "Mbps," "MBps," "Gbps" and "GBps" refer to how many bits/bytes are being transferred per second.

A Mb is a thousand times more bits than a Kb. A Gb is a million times more bits than a Kb and a thousand times more than a Mb.

To help give you an idea on sizes, a high-quality image would be around 2MB in size (2,097,152 bytes, or 16,777,216 bits). If your computer had a download speed of 1 MBps (quite slow by today's standards), it would take two seconds to download (move from the internet to your computer) the picture. This picture would utilize

16,777,216 bits of available memory in your hard drive:

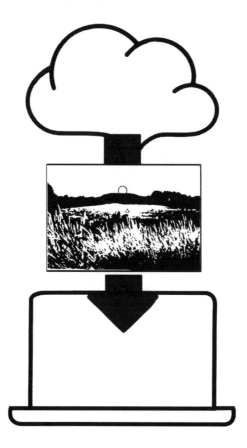

A high-definition movie that's about an hour and a half long would be around 4 GB in size (4,294,967,296 bytes, 34,359,738,368 bits or 32 Gb). Let's say the download speed of your internet was 1 Gbps (a good speed by today's standards). That means it would take 32 seconds to download. Notice that we said 1 Gbps, not GBps.

There are larger file sizes than KB, MB and GB. As you've probably noticed, for each order of magnitude, there is a new name. The next size above GB is terabyte (TB). "Tera" is a trillion. A TB is 1,099,511,627,776 bytes (8,796,093,022,208 bits). There are more.

As a reminder, we earlier discussed Hertz (a measurement of the frequency per second of a wave – frequency is the rate of vibration of a wave).

1GHz is 1,000,000,000 Hertz (one billion waves handled in a second). When you see a computer advertised as having an 8GHz processor, what that means is that the CPU can perform operations at a rate of 8,000,000,000 instructions per second.

Each of these instructions being processed is referred to as a "tick." And so, in an 8GHz processor, this would be eight billion ticks every second.

To sum up this chapter:

1. The size of a file directly affects how long the file takes to transfer,

2. For media files, the larger the file, the higher quality the file (image, video, song, etc.) is.

SUMMARY:

File sizes are written as MB, Gb, GB, etc. – the larger these files are, the more bits they contain. A lowercase "b" indicates "bit" – while an uppercase "B" means "byte" (8 bits). Since one of the most common uses for computers involves sending and receiving data, it's good to know something about how this is measured. Usually, we look at how many bits are transferred per second (bps), or how many bytes are transferred per second (Bps). Modern computers typically exchange data at rates of around 50-100 million bps (Mbps).

Due to the fact that there are many levels of screen resolution, each with their own name, we will now define these and talk a bit about how they are used.

CHAPTER 97:
LEVELS OF DEFINITION

"With high definition TV, everything looks bigger and wider.
Kind of like going to your 25th high school reunion."
-Jay Leno (American comedian, 1950-)

Here are the most common levels of screen resolution:

- 144 – this refers to 144 total pixels from top to bottom on a screen. This is considered very low definition – the image would be pixelated and blurry. Unless otherwise stated, from here forward on the list, the number written indicates how many vertical (up and down) pixels there are on a screen – i.e. the total number of pixels top to bottom.

- 240 – Though it's almost double the number of pixels contained in 144, 240 is also considered low definition.

- 360 – this is the next step up in resolution/definition and is also low definition.

- 480 – this is the first level of what is considered "standard definition" or "standard resolution."

- 720 – this is the first level of "high resolution" or "high definition." Again, like all numbers before, this simply refers to a total of 720 pixels running from the bottom of a screen to the top.

- 1080 – this is also high resolution/high definition. To differentiate it from 720, 1080 is sometimes referred to as "HD ready", "Full HD" or "standard HD."

- 4K – now we shift from vertical (up and down) to horizontal (left to right). 4K refers to about 4,000 pixels running left to right across a screen. 4K is also referred to as Ultra HD (UHD).

- 8K – this is currently the highest possible definition – like 4K, this refers to the total horizontal pixels, which in this case is about 8,000.

There will be higher resolutions and different types in the future, but these levels should give you a basic understanding about how displays are typically categorized.

To be clear, screens and monitors are designed to display up to a specific level of resolution; this usually means they are also capable of displaying the levels below the one they were designed for. There are Full HD screens, 4K screens, etc.

Separately, videos have their own level of resolution. The resolution is established when they're recorded, saved or uploaded. For example, a 4K video camera can record 4K videos and video editing software allows users to choose what level of resolution they'd like to save the file as.

Of course, a video is recorded so it can be watched later – so with video, we are concerned with resolution during both the recording process and the playback process (the point where the recorded video is later displayed on a screen of some sort).

The resolution/definition of a displayed video is established by two factors: the resolution level at which the video was recorded, and the resolution level of the screen the video is being displayed on – whichever is lower.

For an example: A UHD (4K) video would not display as 4K on a standard definition (480) screen – it would be displayed as 480.

Additionally, some video players allow users to choose the level of definition of the video during playback. This is also limited by the level of definition of the original video and the user's display (screen) – the lowest level wins.

Videos are transmitted in "frames" – each frame is a single image composing the video. "Frames per second" (fps) is how many of these individual pictures make up a video per second. 60 fps would mean there are sixty pictures being displayed in succession each second.

Sometimes you see a lowercase "p" next to the resolution number, like 1080p. The "p" stands for "progressive scanning." Progressive scanning is a way to display videos where each line of pixels of an image is displayed one at a time, in sequence. This is as opposed to interlaced scanning (indicated by "i" after the resolution number), where half of the lines are displayed before the second half (such as showing all the even lines of pixels, followed by the odd lines). We don't want to get too technical on this, but it's worth covering since you may come across things like 720p or 1080i in the future, if you haven't already.

As we covered earlier, the higher quality-level video or picture, the larger the file size – e.g. 8K videos are *much* larger than 1080 videos, and so take longer to download, stream and transfer, and they take up more memory storage.

SUMMARY:

Resolution and definition refer to the same idea: the level of visual clarity of an image. This is typically represented in the number of horizontal or vertical pixels contained in an image or able to be displayed horizontally or vertically across a screen. Resolution is limited by the definition of the original image or video file and the definition of one's screen – whichever is lower. The i following resolution numbers refers to images where the pixels are displayed 50% at a time (such as all pixels on an even numbered line, followed by all pixels on an odd numbered line). "p" follows resolution numbers where the pixel lines are displayed "progressively" - one at a time, in sequence. The higher the resolution number, the clearer the display.

You've most likely observed that as time goes on, more and more machines are able to access the internet. Let's discuss that.

CHAPTER 98:
THINGS

"And just like any company that blissfully ignored the internet at the turn of the century, the ones that dismiss the Internet of Things risk getting left behind."
-Jared Newman (technology journalist, unknown age)

One term that you may have heard and that will definitely be more common in the future is "Internet of Things" (also called "IoT").

IoT refers to connecting everyday objects to the internet. This allows control of and communication with all sorts of devices through the internet. IoT allows various machines to be controlled remotely (at a distance).

An example of IoT would be controlling the locks on your house using your phone, via the internet. Other objects and devices that can be embraced by IoT (i.e. hooked up to and controlled through the internet) are thermostats, security systems, cars, refrigerators, lights, alarm clocks and more.

The concept of IoT has been around for decades – the idea that you could control machines from a distance over a network. For example, Coca Cola did so in the 1980s. They connected to Coca Cola vending machines over a distance and were able to see if there were drinks available and if they were cold.

In addition to the increased efficiency, IoT has as a purpose – "data gathering." Meaning, as all of these machines are connected to the internet, the data they all pass along the internet can be collected and analyzed. For an example, a traffic light connected to the internet could automatically track how many cars pass by it every day. If this were expanded across the entire country, the data gathered by all of these traffic lights could be used to discover the most efficient traffic systems or rapidly isolate the most common causes of traffic accidents.

The term IoT was first used in 1999 by the British technologist (an expert in a particular tech field) Kevin Ashton during a presentation. He is the "inventor" of the term and had this to say about it during an interview in 2009:

"The fact that I was probably the first person to say 'Internet of Things' doesn't give me any right to control how others use the phrase. But what I meant, and still mean, is this: Today computers – and, therefore, the internet – are almost wholly dependent on human beings for information. Nearly all ... of data available on the internet were first captured and

created by human beings – by typing, pressing a record button, taking a digital picture or scanning a barcode. Conventional diagrams of the internet include servers and routers and so on, but they leave out the most numerous and important routers of all: people. The problem is, people have limited time, attention and accuracy – all of which means they are not very good at capturing data about things in the real world...

"If we had computers that knew everything there was to know about things – using data they gathered without any help from us – we would be able to track and count everything, and greatly reduce waste, loss and cost. We would know when things needed replacing, repairing or recalling, and whether they were fresh or past their best.

"We need to empower computers with their own means of gathering information, so they can see, hear and smell the world for themselves, in all its random glory."

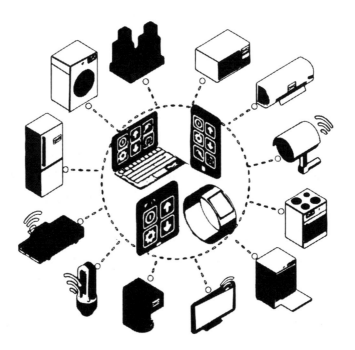

SUMMARY:

Now that most people around the world can connect to the internet, new uses are being found for this huge network. One active area involves adding computers in devices that wouldn't normally have them, and having those devices connect to the internet through that on-board (internal; installed inside) computer. This allows many things, including the control of that device remotely using a distant computer, such as a smartphone. This system is called the Internet of Things (IoT), and it is an area of heavy experimentation and rapid progress.

Let's take a look at one form of data gathered every time you visit a website.

CHAPTER 99:
COOKIES

"If I had 10 cookies and you took half, do you know what you would have?
That's right. A black eye and an injured hand."
-Unknown

A cookie is a set of data that a website causes to be stored on your computer for use now or later. Often, they are used during the session (a span of time in which a web browser maintains a connection to a particular web server) when they were created, but they can also be used when you connect to that web server at a later date.

These cookies are managed by your browser program. Cookies can be a tool to help make a particular website more quickly display the way you want it to, or to personalize your experience on that site.

In general, there are two types of cookies: temporary and persistent.

A temporary cookie expires when a web browser session ends – usually, this happens when the browser program is closed down. This is a session cookie. In this case, the cookie's data is not stored on your computer permanently.

The data in a persistent cookie is stored on your computer for a specified time period – hours, years, days, etc. These cookies always have expiration dates; the cookie is erased from your computer after the expiration date.

Not all websites make use of cookies. It is considered good practice for a website to inform you if it uses cookies.

An American computer programmer named Lou Montulli invented cookies in 1994. He states that the term was derived from "magic cookie," a phrase that meant "data passed between communicating programs."

The initial purpose of these cookies was to verify if users had visited a particular website before. They also began becoming useful when users purchased things online because the cookies could remember what you shopped for in the past. This led to the ability to display things like "continue shopping for ___," "pick up where you left off," "buy more ___s," etc. Cookies also affect some of the ads shown on your computer.

SUMMARY:

As the web became more popular, creators of websites realized it would be valuable to be able to store information related to a specific user, so that the user's experience with the website could be personalized. A common approach to this is to store a small file on the user's computer, called a cookie, that stores information unique to that person. This information can then be used to change the behavior of the website just for that person, based on that stored data.

Now let's discuss how search engines determine which websites come up at the top of search results.

CHAPTER 100:
IMPROVING SEARCH RESULTS

"The best place to hide a dead body is page two of Google."
-Unknown

To optimize something means to make it more optimum (ideal; close to a perfect state). So it is with computers – optimization means to make a certain aspect of the computer or something contained in the computer perform better and accomplish things more efficiently. Optimization is an attempt at doing something as near to perfect as possible.

The term "optimize" is used often in reference to making sure that the webpages on a website will operate well and have a pleasing appearance even when the device that is displaying the webpages is not a normal computer display. Specifically, there are many devices today capable of displaying webpages that are much smaller than a usual display. Since there is much less display space available, the designer of the webpage often sets the page up so that it displays differently on smaller screens. This process is called optimization.

If you looked at a website using your computer's regular display, and then looked at that same website using a smartphone, they would probably look different – possibly there might be a different arrangement of the elements on the page so that they were in one long stack, rather than being broken into two or three side-by-side columns. If so, the website has been optimized for mobile devices.

There is another common use of the word optimization in computers, related to how search engines work.

Search engine optimization (SEO) is the process of setting up a website so that it is more likely to appear near the top of search results for specific search terms. These search terms are written within a search bar that looks like this:

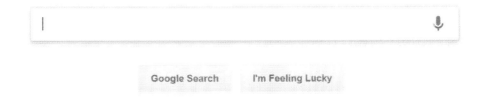

For a variety of reasons, operators of a website might want their site to appear near the top of the search results for a particular search. For example, if you have a website where you sell antique bicycles, you would want that website to appear at or near the top of a listing of websites when the term "antique bicycle sales" was entered into a search engine.

There are many factors involved in where a website might rank in a particular search result, and those factors change fairly often. The basic elements, though, are related to how much the website really aligns with a particular search term.

As an example, consider the website that sells antique bicycles. The content and images on the site probably relate to the sale of antique bicycles. Because of this, a search for "lawn mower repair" would probably not even have the antique bicycle website in the search results.

It is usually considered good practice to update the content of a website often, and to ensure that the new content accurately represents the purpose of the website. That action is one aspect of search engine optimization.

Organic search results are the results of searching the index of webpages available to the search engine, as opposed to paid promotion or advertisements provided by the search engine company based on the search terms entered by the user. When a search engine returns its search results, it usually gives you two types of data: organic and paid. Organic search results are simply the search results that most closely relate to your keywords (the search terms used – literally the words you write within a search bar).

When you search for something on Google, all the search results (except paid ads) are organic search results. Usually, the paid advertisements are clearly labeled as such. SEO only affects organic search results, not paid ads.

SUMMARY:

Optimization applies to two key areas of the modern technology world. First, it can mean the process of making a website or program work well on multiple types of devices. Second, it can refer to the various actions you could take to make your website be higher in the search results of a search engine, based on what terms were used in the search. This second area is called SEO, or Search Engine Optimization. This process is different than paying for ads.

Speaking of paid ads...

CHAPTER 101:
ADS

"The man who stops advertising to save money is the man who stops the clock to save time."
-Unknown

Impressions refer to how many times a certain thing is seen by the members of an intended audience.

This term is most often used in terms of advertising or content that people can view on their computers. Since you usually can't know with certainty that the content was actually read, you may need to rely simply on whether or not the content was on a display screen where a member of your audience could see it if they were looking. This is called a single "impression."

If your ad were displayed on the computers of 10,000 users, that would be 10,000 impressions.

As mentioned in the last chapter, the opposite of organic search results are paid ads. People can pay to have their website come up at the top of search results as an ad.

The ads which are displayed are chosen based on a variety of factors, including:

1. The search term entered by the user. On Google, the first 1-3 search results are usually actually ads. For example, if you search for "chimney repair company," ads will come up of companies that paid for their website to be listed.

2. The type of website a user is visiting. For example, a user on cats.com may see an ad about cat food.

3. The user's search history (based on cookies) – meaning that ads can be displayed based on past searches, purchases and website visits. For example, a user who buys a pair of shoes online may see ads for shoes later on.

4. Information users put on their online profiles (a summary of a user's personal information). For example, if a user lists "television" as an interest, they may see ads for television shows.

In the past, print ads (ads printed on paper – like in magazines and newspapers) were an extremely popular form of advertising. In modern times, the most effective form of advertising is on the internet. Factually, most companies can't succeed without an internet presence because that's where the vast majority of people go to find things.

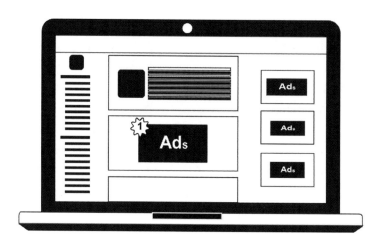

SUMMARY:

As the web has become more and more popular in terms of a place to find and purchase goods and services, companies have ramped up their efforts to be noticed and gain customers. The main way they do this is by putting ads on the various websites they think their potential customers might visit. Since lots of data is available about people using the internet, advertisers can be very precise about how to get their ads in front of potential customers.

With all these online purchases occurring, security is vital. Let's cover that.

CHAPTER 102:
SECURITY

"The only truly secure system is one that is powered off,
cast in a block of concrete and sealed in a lead-lined room with armed guards."
-Gene Spafford (American professor, 1956-)

Encrypt means to change data into a form that can't be understood by regular means, but can be converted back to its original form through certain actions.

If you have the password: "catsarefun" and then encrypted it, it might look like "4s(7_G^k" to anyone else viewing it. If you needed to send that password to another person but wanted to keep it safe, you would encrypt it, and tell the other person the method you used to encrypt it. Computers work the same way; there are several standard ways of encrypting data, and if the computer that is receiving encrypted information knows the way it was encrypted, it can restore it to its original form.

Encryption is used to keep personal information secure. Your bank will encrypt your personal data when its computers send that data to each other, so that if anyone intercepts the data, they won't be able to understand what they are seeing.

A secure password is a password that is hard for other people or computers to guess. "Password" is not a secure password, but "Z$7k!f_25@" could be.

A scary example of an unsecure password is the fact that the password for a computer controlling some of the nuclear missiles in the U.S was 00000000 for eight years.

"Hacking" means to break into a computer without authorization. It can also refer to stealing someone's data. It's basically a form of digital trespassing.

The word "hack" isn't always negative, however.

Some people also use the term to refer to coding (writing computer programs). In this case "hacking" is used to mean "the actions of a skilled computer expert." For example, computer programming competitions are sometimes called "hack-a-thons."

Computer security (keeping private information safe) is an important subject. Here are some tips:

1. Use secure passwords,

2. Use different passwords for different websites (don't reuse passwords),

3. Do not email any private data – don't send credit card numbers, passwords, social security numbers, etc.,

4. Do not send money to people you don't know, and only use secure payment systems on trustworthy sites for actual services and products,

5. Be careful about trusting people online – impersonation of others is too easy to pull off and happens often.

Unfortunately, there are dishonest people who will attempt to steal your identity and money. This is usually done through them asking you to send them private data. Sometimes they email, pretending to be your bank, or they'll send you a message telling you they want to pay you money but need your bank account data to send it.

There's even a popular television show called "Catfish," which is all about people faking their identity. These people steal pictures of another person, pretend to be someone they aren't, and attempt to develop friendships or romantic relationships with others. For an example, there was a case of a 55-year-old man who set up a fake profile with pictures of a female model and was speaking with other men. These other men thought they were talking to a beautiful woman the whole time.

"Catfish" means to lure someone into a relationship with a false online identity. The term comes from the act of catfish nipping at the tails and fins of other fish.

Let's go over another effect of nonsecure data.

There are several signs that can indicate a person is lying about their identity online, including: refusal to speak over the phone; they're not willing to meet in person; they can't video chat (won't show you their face); etc. Basically, the person is acting suspiciously. You can even take their picture and do a "reverse image search." A reverse image search is where you can search for an image on the web to see if it exists elsewhere. For an example, you could search a picture of a woman that's messaging you online to see if that picture is being used by anyone else. If so, one or more of those people online is not the actual person.

Legitimate people and companies will not ask you to send private data online. Only provide such information through secure websites you trust or in person.

The subject of computer security is commonly referred to as "cybersecurity." "Cyber" means "relating to computers and technology." The word comes from "cybernetics," which means "the science of communication in people and machines." Cybernetics has to do with automated control systems – ways to cause actions to occur automatically. It is derived from the Greek word *kubernan*, meaning "to steer."

Cybersecurity concerns keeping computers, networks, websites and software safe from digital attack. It is a field in its own right, with its own professionals.

SUMMARY:

Not everyone who uses the internet and browses the web is an honest person. It's important to try to keep your personal information secure when using the web. One technique used by computer programmers is to encrypt private data before sending it to another computer – this means to change the data so it can't be understood, using a complex system, before you send it. If the computer that receives the private data can use that same system, it can return the data to its original, readable form.

It is smart to use common sense when you're browsing the web and using a computer. For example, use passwords that no one else could guess, don't tell anyone your password and avoid suspicious people. Remember, if it's too good to be true, it probably is.

Let's discuss some of the various types of cyber-attacks.

CHAPTER 103:
VIRUSES

"Passwords are like underwear: you don't let people see it,
you should change it very often, and you shouldn't share it with strangers."
-Chris Pirillo (Television host, 1973-)

Malware is a category of computer programs created to perform certain harmful actions to computers. "Mal" means "improper" or "bad," and "ware" is a shortening of "software."

A virus is a specific type of malware. It is characterized by the fact that it is designed to modify other programs on the infected computer by inserting some of its own instructions into those programs. In this way, the virus replicates itself.

As an example, if someone wants to steal your credit card information, they could create a small computer program that can search your computer for that information and send it to their remote computers. They could disguise the computer program as a document called "surprise birthday party – driving directions" and send it to you. Not suspecting the document is dangerous, you open it. When it opens, it isn't a document after all – it's malware, and the action of opening it causes that small computer program to look for any financial programs you have on your computer and modify them so they steal the credit card data.

A worm is a specific type of malware. It is characterized by the fact that it is designed to copy itself onto a computer, find a way to get itself sent to another connected computer, and then install itself on that second computer – and so on.

A Trojan is another specific type of malware. It is characterized by the fact that it is designed to mislead users as to the actual intent of the program.

Trojan is malware that is installed on a computer with the intention of damaging the computer, stealing information, etc. The Trojan is created in such a way that the person who receives it is led to believe that it is harmless.

Trojans get their name from the ancient story of the Trojan horse. According to myth, there was a war about 3,000 years ago between the Greeks and the residents of the huge city of Troy (now known as Hisarlik in Turkey). The Greeks had been trying to conquer the city of Troy for 10 years. In an effort to trick the Trojans, the Greek army constructed a large wooden horse and hid a group of soldiers inside. They then pretended to sail away, as if they were retreating. The Trojans, believing they were now victorious in defending their city, went out and brought the wooden horse into the city as a victory trophy. That night, the soldiers inside the horse crept out and opened the city gates for the rest of the Greek army, which had returned in the darkness of the night. The Greek army was then able to enter the city and defeat the Trojans.

In similar fashion, a Trojan may be attached to a seemingly harmless message you receive on your computer. By opening the message, you might allow the Trojan to be installed on your computer, thereby allowing another person to connect to your computer and operate it without your knowledge.

Opening suspicious email attachments, downloading strange files and clicking weird links sent to you over email can all open up your computer to attacks and data theft.

Security software (programs that can protect your computer) can assist by finding and removing malware, blocking hackers and in other ways.

So, how do you know if something is secure? Well, one of the best tools you have is judgement. Some malware is pretty obvious, such as an email riddled with typos.

Also, secure websites (https) are typically secure since they've been certified as such.

In addition to the tips in the last chapter, we'd add:

• Only install software from legitimate companies, and

• Only interact with people and companies that you trust.

SUMMARY:

Computer programmers are not all honest. Some of them create computer programs that can harm computers or gather private information so it can be used for criminal purposes. There are various types of these programs, like viruses, worms or trojans, but they are all in a category called "malware," from "mal," meaning "bad," and "ware," a shortening of "software."

It is a good idea to use common sense when using the internet, including only putting files on your computer that are from sources you can trust.

In the next chapter, we will cover another important security tip.

CHAPTER 104:
UPDATES

"When we launch a product, we're already working on the next one.
And possibly even the next, next one."
-Tim Cook (Chief Executive Officer of Apple, 1960-)

An update is a process or an object that brings something up to its newest version. This happens often in the world of computers. Sometimes an update is done to fix any problems that might be happening with the computer or an update can be done to add something new to it.

For example, your smartphone might get an update that makes it faster or fixes a problem you have been having with it.

Nowadays most updates happen through the internet, wherein the update file is downloaded and installed on your computer or mobile device. Updates allow developers to fix issues and enhance software after the first version is released.

Updates play a role in security as well, because updating your computer, phone, software, etc. ensures that all the most up-to-date security protections are in place and makes it much harder for criminals to steal data. It is recommended to always accept updates of trustworthy software and operating systems.

SUMMARY:

Often, after a device or a computer program is first released, changes are needed over time to add new features, fix problems, etc. The process of getting these changes installed on your device or program is called "updating" or "installing an update." It is a good idea to install updates when you get them, as they often contain up-to-date protections against harmful software or other security problems.

One of the situations that can occur sometimes when using a computer is: the computer doesn't do what you want it to do! Let's go over some tips for when that happens.

CHAPTER 105:
FIXING ISSUES

"Never let a computer know you're in a hurry."
-Unknown

Troubleshooting means to locate the sources of errors and fix them. The term originated from the 1800's term "troubleshoot" – a person who works on telegraph (system for sending written messages over long distances by wire) or telephone lines. The original trouble-shooters would find issues behind transmission problems and fix them in the physical telegraph/telephone lines, or work around them.

Let's face it, computers can be frustrating. Sometimes they do odd things and won't follow instructions.

Here are some useful tips for getting your computer to do what you want it to do!

1. As covered earlier in this book, it never hurts to just turn it off and turn it back on again.

2. If your computer or device is running slowly, close all the programs and apps that you aren't currently using. This will free up computer memory and processing power.

3. The issue may be related to malware and security issues. The solution for this is security software. If you already have security software, perform a scan (this is where the security software looks through all the files on your computer to find and get rid of dangerous files). If you don't have security software, install a reputable (having a good reputation) one!

4. The problem could be an internet connectivity issue. Here are some tips for that: a) Restarting your router (unplugging it for at least 30 seconds and then plugging it back in again) is always worth a try. This whole process can take around 5 minutes, but usually works. b) You might be connected to the wrong wifi network. For an example, if you have separate wifi for downstairs and upstairs, and you're connected to the downstairs wifi while you're upstairs, that could be an issue. c) For phones, sometimes it's best to go off wifi all together (turn wifi off) and just use data (using your phone service to connect to the internet, as opposed to a router).

5. On some computers there is a program called "Task Manager." For example, in Windows it looks like this:

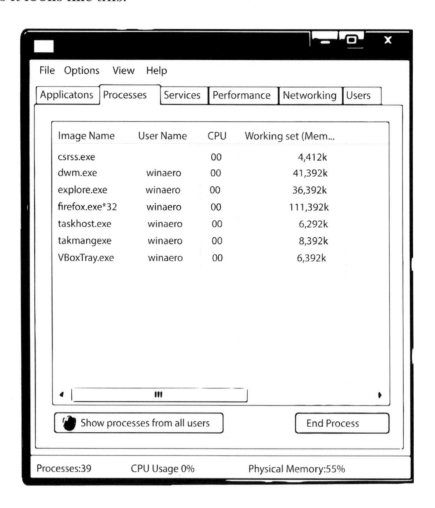

Task manager displays all the programs currently running on your computer. It is usually accessed by pressing the following keys all at the same time: "ctrl," "alt" and "delete." You can use Task Manager to close frozen programs by selecting the program and clicking "End Process."

6. Sometimes when things aren't running smoothly, certain programs and drivers need to be uninstalled and then reinstalled. There are various reasons behind this. Maybe an important part of the program was accidentally deleted. An example of this is printers. If it isn't printing properly, sometimes installing (or reinstalling) the printer driver can fix the issue and get it working again. Drivers can typically be found online and downloaded.

7. GOOGLE IS YOUR FRIEND. The answer to virtually any problem is at your fingertips. If your phone won't turn on, Google "My iPhone won't turn on." If your computer freezes, Google "How to fix my computer freezing." As a note on

this, the more specific your question, the better. For an example, include the type of computer or phone you have in your search terms.

8. Computers sometimes give error codes. For example: "File can't save. Error code: 15932." Error codes are used to identify exact issues. You can take these error codes and Google them to find the solution.

9. As mentioned earlier, you may need to update a program or your OS.

10. Ask a nerd. If you have a tech savvy friend, have them take a look. Our only advice on this point is try to have them teach you. Have them explain what the problem was and walk you through how to fix it. Who knows? You may become a nerd yourself someday.

11. Just like your car, sometimes you need to bring your computer or device into a repair shop.

12. The issue may be that you need a new computer or device. Like every machine, sometimes they just need to be replaced.

13. Educate yourself in technology. This can be achieved through taking tech classes in a university or school, enrolling in a coding boot camp (an intensive computer programming study program), or even through self study. The more you understand about technology, the better you can resolve issues.

Also, realize that sometimes it isn't your fault. Maybe the website you're trying to visit is not operating, or the computer program you're using is faulty. In such cases, there's nothing you can do until the owner fixes the issue.

Here is a helpful little "checklist" (list of actions completed in sequence) that can assist in computer troubleshooting.

a. Have a clear understanding of how the computer *should* be operating.

b. Determine what symptoms are being observed (computer won't shut down, can't find document, phone is extremely slow, etc.).

c. Make a mental list of all the potential causes.

d. Work out how to test each of these causes and do so. For an example, computer won't turn on – is it plugged in?

e. Through this process of elimination, isolate the exact cause of the issue. Once found, fix the problem.

And as covered earlier, if you don't know what problems to look for or how to solve them: Google it!

SUMMARY:

Computers can sometimes be difficult. There are many potential solutions when you run into difficulties that usually come down to isolating the issue and researching solutions.

Now, some of the most confusing elements of technology are the names. Let's talk about that!

CHAPTER 106:
NAMES

"I'm sorry, Dave. I'm afraid I can't do that."
-HAL 9000, fictional spaceship computer

One of the annoying traits of technology are the names! For example: Every new version of a phone has a different name, an internet service is promoted as "XG 5S Max Loopy-doopy Z-Factor service!", etc.

Keep in mind that most of these complicated names are just names. While there is sometimes significance behind their meaning, they're mainly named that way for marketing purposes and to sound advanced.

Think of cars. The "Jaguar XF" or the "Mazda CX-5." In the Jaguar example, XF is the model number (there's also an XE model, by the way). In the Mazda name, CX-5 is also a model number and the CX refers to "crossover" – a combination of a car and an SUV (sports utility vehicle, a powerful vehicle, often with four-wheel drive, that can drive over rough terrain). The 5 indicates the size and model type of a car (there's also a CX-3 and CX-7 for example, and for some reason they arbitrarily skipped by two in the names; 3, 5, etc.). Again, these names are meant to impress.

An example of this in tech are computer CPUs. They tend to have fancy-sounding names, like: i9 Core Processor. The "i" stands for Intel (the company that makes the processor). The 9 indicates the version, but here's where that gets confusing: like the Mazda, they skipped from i3, to i5, to i7! Core is another word for CPU and is used as part of the brand name.

The purpose of this chapter is to point out that technology names can be confusing and arbitrary. It would be useless to attempt defining all of the names of various products out there because new models come out every day and this chapter would soon become completely outdated.

Other examples of arbitraries associated with names are: Windows 10 and iPhone X.

The version of Windows that came before Windows 10 was Windows 8. When asked why they didn't named Windows 10 Windows 9, Microsoft responded something along the lines of, "Windows 10 is more than just a small upgrade – it's a major overhaul – so going directly to 10 'made sense'."

Apple jumped from iPhone 8 to iPhone X (Roman numeral for 10) because the iPhone X was released ten years after the original iPhone.

You don't have to understand why every tech product has a particular name because a lot of the time it was intentionally made to sound complex, as a marketing tactic.

The point? Don't place too much value on the names of various devices, and if you're curious why they were named that way, Google it.

SUMMARY:

You will notice lots of names for new technology products and services. Often, these names sound important or significant. Equally often, they are just cool-sounding names meant to create interest in the product or service. It isn't necessary to understand why various technologies have certain names.

Now, let's discuss some terms you've probably run across while using your smartphone.

CHAPTER 107:
THE Gs

"Technology is, of course, a double edged sword.
Fire can cook our food but also burn us."
-Jason Silva (Venezuelan television star, 1982-)

Have you ever noticed that cell phone internet connections are sometimes referred to as "3G," "4G," etc.? The "G" stands for "generation." "Generation" means "a level or stage of development of cell phone or device."

As of 2023, there are five generations (1G, 2G, 3G, 4G and 5G) available, with a sixth (6G) in development. Here is each generation defined:

1G: This refers to cell phones that could only make phone calls.

2G: Cell phones that had other functionalities on top of being able to make calls, such as text messaging.

3G: A major advance in cell phones and devices that allowed internet usage. This is when smartphones came out. 3G devices can email, browse the web, download videos, send pictures, etc.

3G devices transmit data at speeds up to around 10 Mbps (10,485,760 bits transferred each second).

4G: This refers to devices that can do all that 3G devices can do, but that are able to transmit data at a rate of up to 150 Mbps.

5G: Devices that perform all the functions that 4G devices do, with faster speeds that sit around 20 Gbps.

As a note on this: just because a device is 5G doesn't mean it operates at that speed because *it needs an internet connection that allows for that level of speed*. It doesn't matter how fast your phone can operate in accessing the internet if the connection to the internet is slow.

Your mobile devices can connect to the internet in two main ways:

1. Using wifi,

2. Via a cell tower (also referred to as a "cellular network").

When you use a cell tower to connect to the internet, this is referred to as a "data connection" or using your phone's data plan (a cell phone coverage plan that allows a certain amount of internet usage, in terms of total transmitted data). A data connection is not wifi. As a reminder, wifi connects you to the internet via a router. Again, a data connection occurs via cell towers.

Cell towers also have the same generations as cell phones. Meaning, a 2G cell tower only allows calls and texts (no internet access), whereas a 4G cell tower allows up to 150 Mbps internet connection.

Your data speed and mobile device capabilities are determined by: the generation of your mobile device *and* the generation of the nearest cell tower. Your connection is as fast as the *lowest* generation out of the mobile device and cell tower – meaning, you are limited by whichever is slowest.

For example, if you have a 5G smartphone, but are connected to a 3G internet connection, you will be connected to the internet at 3G speeds. No matter how good your device is, if you are out in a rural area with a 2G network, you won't be able to access the internet via your device without wifi, since 2G equipment doesn't access the internet!

As a note of interest, when 4G first came out, cell phone networks weren't all set up to accommodate. That has since been fixed. The same issue occurred with 5G.

"LTE" stands for "Long Term Evolution". You sometimes see this on your phone – for example: 4G LTE. This is actually a step between 3G and 4G – it's faster than 3G and slower than 4G.

Frequencies have various bands, which are different ranges of frequencies. You can see examples of wave frequencies pictured here:

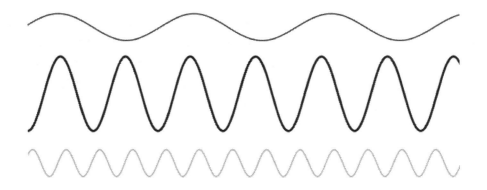

Remember, the wifi equipment and cell towers are passing digital information back and forth between the various computers and devices on a network. To do this, they are sending and receiving beams of energy. These beams are vibrating at a certain frequency, and they contain the actual information being sent back and forth.

As a reminder GigaHertz (GHz) is a wave containing a billion frequency cycles per second; see the earlier chapter entitled "Tick Tock" if you need more of a refresher.

In 5G, data is transmitted in the following bands:

A. Low-band: less than 1GHz (has a greater coverage area but lower speeds).

B. Mid-band: 1GHz–6GHz (mid-sized coverage and middle-level speeds).

C. High-band: 24GHz–40GHz (higher speeds but a smaller coverage area).

You will find other abbreviations used along with 5G, such as:

- 5G UW: "UW" stands for "Ultra-Wideband." It is a marketing term from Verizon Wireless to indicate you are connected to a high-band or mid-band network.

- 5G+ (plus): This is a marketing term from AT&T to indicate you are connected to a high-band or mid-band network.

- 5G UC: "UC" stands for "Ultra Capacity." This is a marketing term from T-Mobile that indicates you are connected to a high-band or mid-band network.

Usually, when your phone displays only "5G," you are connected to a low-band network. Mid- and high-band networks usually have additional letters or symbols after 5G. This may change in the future.

6G is currently under development and will be significantly faster than 5G and will support additional technology beyond mobile devices. It is currently estimated that 6G will operate at speeds ranging from 30GHz to 3,000GHz and data transmission of potentially over 100 Gbps. To be clear, the capabilities of 6G hadn't been fully established when this was written.

Please keep in mind that as new technology comes out, new abbreviations and symbols will be used. You can always define these terms online and we encourage you to do so.

Simply put: the higher the generation, the faster the speeds. But keep in mind that the speed of your device is limited by the generation of the network and the generation of the device. For an example, a 3G device will operate at 3G speeds, even if connected to a 4G network.

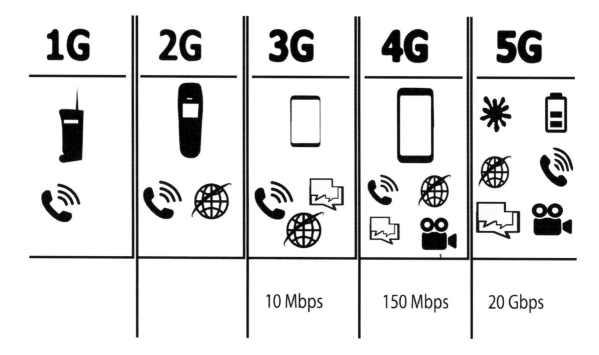

None of this is related to the "G" you sometimes see in wifi (i.e. 2.4G and 5G wifi networks). This G is actually short for GHz.

Most wifi equipment sends and receives signals that are either 2.4GHz in frequency or 5 GHz in frequency. Here are the primary differences between the two:

1. 2.4G wifi can support up to 450-600 Mbps in data transfer speeds,

2. 5G wifi can support up to 1,300 Mbps,

3. 5G has a shorter range than 2.4G wifi, and the signal has more difficulty passing through solid objects (like floors or walls). So, if you're close to the wifi router, 5G is the better choice. If you're further from the router, such as in a bedroom, 2.4G is a stronger/faster internet connection.

SUMMARY:

Cell phones, and the towers that they use to connect to each other, have evolved over time. Each time a stable point in their development is reached, a new "generation" is designated. Early cell phones, and the towers they used, were called "1G," or "first generation", and they only allowed the cell phone to make phone calls. Successive generations allowed access to the internet, and eventually the transfer of large files like movies. Your internet speed is limited by the cell tower your phone is connected to or the generation of your phone, whichever is slower. The current popular generation is 5G, with 6G currently under development. These are different than wifi network speeds – of which 2.4G and 5G are the most common. Whereas 5G wifi networks are technically faster, 2.4G is the better choice at longer distances and through barriers.

Now let's go over the factors that make a computer fast or slow.

CHAPTER 108:
WHAT DETERMINES COMPUTER SPEEDS

"The attention span of a computer is only as long as its power cord."
-Unknown

The speed of your computer depends on several factors, including:

1. Internet connection speed (i.e. bandwidth). The stronger and faster your internet connection is, the faster it will surf the web.

2. RAM storage capacity. A computer with 32GB RAM will run programs faster than one with 4GB because RAM allows your computer to use and display more volatile (impermanent) memory at once.

3. Hard drive (permanent memory) storage capacity. The closer your hard drive is to full, the longer it takes your computer to locate data. Having a large hard drive (such as 1TB – over eight trillion bits), will make for a faster computer than a 256GB hard drive.

4. Type of hard drive. In an earlier chapter we mentioned SSD (Solid-State Drive) – a type of hard drive with no moving parts (i.e. no moving disks). This type of drive loads data faster than the typical HDD (hard disk drive).

5. CPU. The two most popular processor manufacturers are Intel and AMD (Advanced Micro Devices). There are many different models of CPUs, but the safest bet if you want the best processor is to purchase the newest version.

   As a recap, the CPU is the part of a computer that processes data one command at a time. With each new CPU version, the number of tasks the CPU can process per second increases.

   As a note on CPUs: one type that you may have heard of is a "quad-core processor." Since "quad" means "four," this refers to four processors within the CPU, which means the CPU can perform *four* tasks at a time – as opposed to the typical one task.

6. Software. The quality and age of the software you're using is a factor. For example, some browsers are faster than others, and some word processors are faster than others. Using the newest versions of the best software can increase the speed of your computer.

7. Operating system. If you're using an old operating system, this can slow down your computer. The solution to this is updating your operating system or purchasing and installing a newer version.

8. The age of your computer. It's pretty safe to bet that the newer your computer, the faster it will operate. They'll typically have the newest software, hardware, operating system, CPU, etc.

Also, tech companies stop releasing updates and support for older software past a certain point. Meaning, if your computer is a little old, you may start finding that software on it is breaking down and there will be no help available because the software company has already moved on to newer versions of the software.

Having the best of all of the above means the fastest possible computer. And like most products, most of the time, the more expensive a computer is, the better it performs.

With all that said, any one of the above factors could drag down the speed of even the best computer. Here are some examples:

a. Let's say you have a top-of-the-line computer with an extremely slow internet connection (e.g. weak wifi in a coffee shop), your computer will still be very slow online.

b. If you have a computer with a great CPU and lots of RAM, but your hard drive is full, it might take long for things to load.

c. If you have a strong internet connection, good CPU, but weak RAM (such as only 2GB, instead of 8GB or more), your internet may seem slow. Especially if you have multiple programs open.

SUMMARY:

To recap, the factors that directly relate to the speed of your computer are: hard drive, RAM, CPU, internet connection speed, operating system, software and the age of your computer. They can each positively (or negatively) affect the speed of your computer.

Now, let's discuss the main tech hub (center of activity) on Earth – a place you've probably heard of and that's the birthplace of many major technical advances.

CHAPTER 109:
SILICON VALLEY

"The natives of Silicon Valley learned long ago that when you share your knowledge with someone else, one plus one usually equals three.
You both learn each other's ideas, and you come up with new ones."
-Vivek Wadhwa (American businessman)

Silicon Valley is a region in California that is thought of as the center of technology in the United States. Here is a picture of California; the highlighted section is Silicon Valley:

"Silicon" refers to the silicon chip (semiconductors – material whose ability to conduct electricity can be turned on and off) manufacturers located in the area when the term Silicon Valley was first used in 1971 by an American journalist named Don Hoefler. "Valley" refers to the fact that that section of California is located within a valley (land surrounded by mountains). The California cities San Jose, Palo Alto, Cupertino, Mountain View and more are included within Silicon Valley.

Many of the top tech companies on Earth are headquartered in Silicon Valley, including: Apple, Google, Facebook and Intel. Here are some characteristics that people associate with Silicon Valley:

- Startups (new businesses),

- Investors (people who give companies money in exchange for partial or full ownership) and investments (the money put into these companies),

- New inventions and cutting-edge technology,

- Demanding work schedules, like developers and business owners working 70+ hours a week with little sleep, and

- Extremely high cost of living (very expensive rent, food, properties, etc.).

Silicon Valley is one of the reasons that America is a leader in the technology industry.

SUMMARY:

The area in California just south of San Francisco is called "Silicon Valley." It is the largest center of computer technology and innovation in the U.S. It is called Silicon Valley because some of the original technology companies there made silicon chips, and because it is in a valley. Some of the biggest tech companies in the world, like Google, Apple, Intel and Facebook, are headquartered there.

One subject you may have heard about is "artificial intelligence." But if computers are inanimate, what does that mean?

CHAPTER 110:
ARTIFICIAL INTELLIGENCE

"The human spirit must prevail over technology."
–Albert Einstein (German scientist, 1879-1955)

A "robot" is a machine that resembles a human and can perform some similar movements to a human. You've probably seen these in movies:

A robot can also be used to refer to a machine that automates various functions. In this definition, robots don't particularly look anything like humans. Here are robots building a car:

Robot comes from the Czech word *robota* which means "forced labor" or "slave."

Even though that may sound dark, keep in mind that robots are simply machines – they aren't people and they have no soul. All machines, from your car to your phone, are technically slaves. One should feel no different towards using these than one would feel about using a pen or a hammer.

Artificial intelligence (commonly referred to as "AI") is a machine or a program that is built to "think" like humans think. It refers to a machine or a program that has been programmed to learn and to change its behavior based on its experiences. One of the purposes of AI is for computers to perform actions typically handled by people.

A robot that handled all housekeeping and cooking, and that could learn from its mistakes as well as come up with creative new food ideas, could be considered an AI.

AI can refer to robots that look like humans, but at its root, AI is software that is programmed to "observe and learn." An example of AI is voice recognition software (computer programs that attempt to process words that humans say). When you use "voice to text" on your phone (having text messages written out for you based on the words you say), this is AI.

Many science fiction TV shows and movies contain AI. Some even make the case for "AI rights" and argue that they should be treated as human. The folly in this is that everything that AI can do was predetermined by a human, and no matter how advanced they get, they're still just a machine and thereby only a distant "extension" of humans. One could program a computer to feel "pain" when a component is broken but this "pain" would only be a series of 1s and 0s contained within the software of the AI unit.

Only those who believe they are a computer (a machine made of plastic and metal into which commands are inputted and processed) would believe a computer to be human. This point is being stressed so that the reader understands that no matter how realistic AIs become, they are soulless machines. Humans and machines are not the same – they are very different.

In the future, some people may attempt to marry an AI or assert that they're forming an undeniable human connection with these advanced robots. But at the end of the day, the true connection is between them and the designers and programmers behind the AI. The true source of whatever affection one feels for the machine is its human creators.

"Machine learning" is sometimes used interchangeably with "AI" but there is a slight difference between the two terms.

Machine learning is using AI to allow computers to "learn" based on data. It is a subcategory of AI that specifically relates to computers using data to make predictions or decisions without having previously been specifically programmed to make those exact predictions or decisions.

An example of machine learning would be image recognition. You could program a computer to "recognize" which pictures contain cats. You wouldn't have to program every cat picture that ever existed into the computer but instead give exact parameters (instructions; boundaries that define the scope of a particular activity) that lay out what the computer is to look for when scanning images. Then a computer could recognize that an image it never saw before contains a cat!

SUMMARY:

One of the more interesting developments in the computer industry is AI (Artificial Intelligence). This is the use of machines or programs to perform actions that are like those of a human. Because computers are machines that can only ever act according to directions put into them by people, they will never have the same kind of intelligence that an actual person has – they don't have life or a soul in them. AI devices and software can provide valuable functions to people, though, especially in an age where so much data is available via the web and the internet. Machine learning is a subcategory of AI which refers to computers being programmed to be able to learn and, therefore, make predictions and decisions.

AI will continue to advance in the future. Let's take a look at some other future tech.

CHAPTER 111:
ADVANCED COMPUTERS

"The very fast computing power given by quantum computers
has the potential to disrupt traditional businesses..."
-Jeremy O'Brien (Australian physicist, 1975-)

"Quantum" is the Latin word for "amount" and, in modern understanding, means "the smallest possible discrete (individually separate and distinct) unit of any physical property, such as energy or matter."

You may have heard the word used in the phrase "quantum leap" – which means "a large increase; major advancement; a huge step forward."

A quantum computer is a theoretical machine that could perform calculations based on the behavior of particles at a subatomic level (below the size of an atom or occurring inside an atom). Atoms are the tiny building blocks of matter. They're so small that you'd have to place 100,000 atoms next to each other before you could see them with the human eye.

Due to its subatomic processing ability, a quantum computer would be capable of processing far more millions of instructions per second than any existing computer.

This advance in processing capability would be based on the fact that the data units in a quantum computer can exist in more than one state at a time. As you know, in computers today, the data units can only exist in one state – "on" or "off."

The field of quantum computing is still in its infancy and, as of the date this book was written, no actual quantum computers have been created. At this point, they only exist in science fiction.

Quantum computers are different than "supercomputers." "Supercomputer" refers to a computer that operates at the highest possible level of modern computers. Meaning, they're simply the best computers in existence today. Supercomputers exist and are in use by many of the top companies, whereas quantum computers don't.

Here are rows of supercomputers:

SUMMARY:

Computers have advanced rapidly, and new methods of creating them are being explored. One of the more interesting of these is the idea of a quantum computer, one that uses the smallest individual objects in the universe to store the data a computer would operate on and use as instructions. At present, this is only a theoretical idea; no quantum computers have been made. Whereas, supercomputers *do* exist and are computers that operate at the highest possible level of modern computers.

Now, let's go over another computer of the future.

CHAPTER 112:
TINY

"Real stupidity beats artificial intelligence every time."
-Sir Terry Pratchett (English author, 1948-2015)

The purposes of this and the preceding chapter are:

1. To define terms you may have heard, and

2. To prepare you for the future.

As we covered earlier in the book, "nano-" means one billionth. "Nanotechnology" is technology that utilizes objects of sizes ranging from about 1 nanometer (one billionth of a meter) to 100 nanometers (ten millionth of a meter). As a reminder, a human hair is about 75,000 nanometers in width.

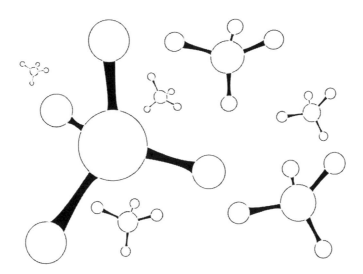

An atom is around .1-.3 nanometers (10%-30% of the size of a nanometer). We are getting really small here.

The point is that nanotechnology is basically "really small technology." Why does this matter?

Well, as you know, the smaller we can get technology, the faster it can operate (due to less space to travel across) and (usually) the cheaper we can make it for (due to less needed materials).

Nanotechnology refers to the ability to see and control atoms.

How does that relate to computers?

A "nanocomputer" would be a computer that utilizes nanotechnology. It is a microscopic computer. Like quantum computers, nanocomputers are theoretical and don't exist yet.

Nanocomputers would operate in the same way as existing computers, just on a much smaller level.

SUMMARY:

Another interesting area of research in computers is the use of nanotechnology to create computers. Nanotechnology just means "technology that uses extremely small objects." "Nano" is a term related to size; it means "one billionth" of a thing. Nanocomputers, like quantum computers, are theoretical at this point – no one has created one, yet.

With all this talk about the future, let's look at how various stages in computer development are categorized.

CHAPTER 113:
COMPUTER GENERATIONS

*"Each generation imagines itself to be more intelligent than
the one that went before it,
and wiser than the one that comes after it."*
-George Orwell (English author, 1903-1950)

It is generally accepted that there are six generations of computers. A "generation" refers to the technology utilized by a computer to operate – particularly the hardware and software. The history of computers that we covered earlier are actually broken down into these generations.

This is different than our earlier chapter regarding 2G, 3G, etc. which relates only to cellular data networks and cell phones.

1940-1956, First Generation:

The first generation refers to computers that used vacuum tubes (tubes with all air removed) for their circuitry (electric circuits) and magnetic drums (memory stored on large metal cylinders that can be read and written on). These computers were enormous and took up entire rooms. They were also extremely expensive to operate.

Programmers working on first generation computers used machine language (code written in as direct 1s and 0s) which was typically input with punched cards and tape.

1956-1963, Second Generation:

Computers utilized transistors instead of vacuum tubes. Even though transistors were invented before 1956, they weren't widely used until the late 1950s. Transistors were more efficient and cheaper to operate than vacuum tubes.

Programmers working on second generation computers began utilizing assembly language (a language that replaced the numbers used in machine language with easily-remembered English words and phrases that people can understand).

The second generation moved away from drum memory to magnetic core memory (wires run around a magnetic ring used to store data).

1964-1971, Third Generation:

Computers started utilizing silicon chips (semiconductors – inexpensive material that through a small application of electricity can turn "on" and "off"). This led to a major increase in speed and reduction of cost.

The third generation also saw the arrival of using keyboards and monitors as interfaces, and started to move away from punch cards and printouts. Computers in this generation were smaller and cheaper than their predecessors, and could run multiple programs at once.

1972-2010: Fourth Generation:

The microprocessor arrives, allowing CPU, memory, input/output (I/O) controls (the component that controls peripheral devices, like the keyboard) and other components to exist on one chip. This further reduced the size of computers and increased their speed.

You could now have the abilities of a computer that in the past would have filled an entire room, but in a device so small you could hold it in your hands. At the beginning of the fourth generation, chips contained thousands of integrated circuits (circuits formed by tiny semiconductors made of silicon).

The fourth generation saw the arrival of the GUI (Graphical User Interface), mice, consoles (electronic devices for playing video games), laptops and hand-held devices.

2010 forward: Fifth Generation:

This is the generation of artificial intelligence, a topic we covered in a previous chapter. AI (such as facial or voice recognition) exists in many modern computers.

While there is no sixth generation yet, the aforementioned quantum computers and nanocomputers could fit in that category.

SUMMARY:

As computer technology has advanced, there are five generally recognized "generations" of technology. These begin in the 1950s with the first generation, and move forward to today with the fifth generation. With each generation, computers became smaller, more powerful and less expensive. Future generations will likely continue this trend.

One technology term you may have heard is "cryptocurrency." What does this mean?

CHAPTER 114:
DIGITAL MONEY

"There are three eras of currency:
Commodity based, politically based, and now, math based."
-Chris Dixon (American businessman, 1972-)

Cryptocurrency is digital money. "Crypto" means "secret" or "hidden."

Cryptocurrency allows individuals to stay anonymous (not reveal their identity) and it operates independently of a central bank.

Users can store their cryptocurrency online and use it to make purchases.

The most popular form of cryptocurrency is bitcoin. It is a combination of the word "bit" (binary digit) and "coin." This is the bitcoin logo:

A secure record of all bitcoin transactions is stored online. New bitcoin is released slowly over time. In a little over 100 years from now, there will be no further bitcoin released.

Bitcoin has a cash value that fluctuates often. You can sell your bitcoin for cash or other cryptocurrency. You can purchase things with it as well.

Cryptocurrency utilizes the blockchain. Blockchain is a record of all cryptocurrency transactions that is maintained across a network of several computers.

A "block" is a record of a new transaction, and when a block occurs, it is added to the "chain" (items linked together).

Blockchain allows cryptocurrency to be distributed but not copied – meaning, each individual piece of data can only have one owner at a time.

A popular website about blockchain called "Blockgeeks.com" gives a good example of blockchain: *"Picture a spreadsheet that is duplicated thousands of times across a network of computers. Then imagine that this network is designed to regularly update this spreadsheet and you have a basic understanding of the blockchain."*

Verifying cryptocurrency transactions is referred to as "mining." It is called this due to its similarities in mining valuable minerals (like gold) – it takes hard work and persistence.

Every time a bitcoin transaction occurs, a "miner" (one engaging in mining) is responsible for verifying the authenticity (accuracy and honesty) of the transaction. The mining is accomplished with specific hardware and automated software. "Miners" are rewarded with occasional cryptocurrency in exchange for their work.

Satoshi Nakamoto is the fictitious name of the unknown person or group that invented bitcoin. Their true identity is hidden. They released bitcoin (the first cryptocurrency) in 2009 and there are now over 1,000 other types of cryptocurrencies.

As an interesting note on digital money, not just cryptocurrency: only about 10% of the world's currency is physical money, the rest only exists on computers.

SUMMARY:

The huge network that is the internet has made the development of a new form of currency possible. This is called "cryptocurrency." Basically, it is money, tracked entirely online using computers and software. The technology behind it involves keeping a continuous record of every piece of this digital currency, and what has happened to it, on multiple computers simultaneously. That way the accuracy of the currency and its history can be verified at any time, so people can trust its use. It also allows people to remain anonymous.

Have you noticed how tech seems to almost double in speed every couple of years? There's actually a name for this.

CHAPTER 115:
DOUBLING

"The computer is really a useful gadget for consuming time."
-Gordon Moore (American businessman, 1929-)

Gordon E. Moore is the co-founder of Intel (the world's largest manufacturer of computer chips).

In 1965 he made statements that eventually became known as "Moore's law."

Moore's law is the observation that over the history of computers, the number of transistors (devices that can alter the flow of electricity) in a computer chip doubles approximately every two years.

In the decades since Moore's law, the statement has proven pretty accurate! It is unknown exactly how long into the future Moore's law will hold but it's impressive that his prediction was so spot on in the first place.

This doubling of transistors is one of the factors behind the continual increase in speed and power of computers.

SUMMARY:

Gordon Moore, the co-founder of the huge computer chip manufacturer Intel, said many years ago that the number of transistors used on computer chips would double every two years. This has held true for the most part, and it illustrates how rapid the advance in computer capabilities has been in a relatively short period of time.

Now let's discuss a relatively new and up-and-coming tech subject.

CHAPTER 116:
DATA SCIENCE

"Never theorize before you have data.
Invariably, you end up twisting facts to suit theories,
instead of theories to suit facts."
-Sir Arthur Conan Doyle (English Author, 1859-1930)

Data science embraces a wide range of scientific methods, systems and processes to extract knowledge and insights from data.

The term was first used by an American computer scientist named William S. Cleveland in his article "Data Science: An Action Plan for Expanding the Technical Areas of the Field of Statistics."

The purpose of data science is basically to make decisions based on data.

Data science includes such topics as:

- Data visualization – Representing information in pictorial form (like graphs or pie charts).

- Statistical analysis – Identifying trends in different data sources.

- Data analysis – Evaluating data to discover useful information and assist in decision making.

- Artificial intelligence – As covered earlier, programming a machine to perform human-like actions, such as facial recognition or voice recognition.

- Machine learning – A subcategory of AI that deals with a computer's ability to "learn" – meaning, the ability to perform certain actions based on past experience without explicit instructions.

Data science is a field in and of itself. Those trained in the subject are referred to as data scientists.

There are also specialists in several of the bullet points listed above. For example: There are statistical analysts, data analysts, people who specialize in AI, etc. A data scientist is trained in one or more of the subjects listed. It's a broad subject.

This next subject is considered a part of data science by some, and thought of as a different subject by others. The subject is "big data."

Big data describes the storage, maintenance and use of a very large amount of electronic data, often from multiple sources – so much data that a special database (an organized collection of electronic data) and/or special software must be used to store, maintain and use the data. It can also refer to the business or technology impact of having access to, or responsibility for, such collections of data.

Data science and big data help predict future trends, solve issues and can be used to identify the key reasons behind success and failure.

There are even programs that allow one to observe 3D data. This is usually done through use of virtual reality.

The main English definition of the word "virtual" is hundreds of years old, and means "nearly as described, but not according to strict definition." For instance, let's say you got a secret spy message on paper and you were told to read it, then remove it from existence. So, you burned the piece of paper, put the ashes in muffin mix, cooked the muffins and fed the muffins to your dog. You have virtually removed the original piece of paper from existence. A scientist would say the original paper still exists in altered form so it's not "removed from existence according to strict definition," but it's pretty clear that no one could read it at this point.

Nowadays, "virtual" is used to describe something that seems to exist in the physical world, but instead is generated by a computer.

In "virtual reality" (abbreviated VR) you wear a helmet that shows an image to each eye and blocks all other vision. It changes what you see as you move your head. If you look down and it shows your feet on the ledge of a skyscraper, and the image quality is good, you might experience a real fear of heights! It feels like reality, but of course you are not really on the ledge of a skyscraper, nor in any danger. Here is an example of a VR headset:

SUMMARY:

Some of the more fascinating areas of development in the computer industry are data science, big data and virtual reality.

Data science involves the collection, formatting and analysis of data so that the data is valuable to people.

Big data is two things: huge collections of data for calculation and analysis, and also the business or technology impact of having access to data like that.

Virtual reality is the representation of objects in a computer-generated environment in such a way that they appear to be real.

With all of the freedom that comes with technology, there are associated responsibilities that we all share. Let's look into this further.

CHAPTER 117:
COMPUTER ETHICS

"The time is always right to do what is right."
-Martin Luther King Jr. (American civil rights leader, 1929-1968)

Like any tool, computers can be used for good or bad.

"Ethics" refers to the actions that affect one's quality of survival. Abusing illegal substances would be an example of poor ethics because of the adverse effects it has on one's life – including the potentiality of an early death. Good ethics would be eating vegetables or exercising as these enhance one's quality of life.

Computer ethics refers to intelligent and responsible use of computers. It includes not using them to harm others.

While ethics can be an arbitrary (based off opinion) subject (i.e. not everyone agrees on what is good or bad behavior), there are some guidelines we'd like to provide here that we consider good practice:

1) Always remember that anything you place on the internet is permanent. Statements you write can be used against you later. There are examples of comments over 20 years old coming up again and harming people later. Photos and videos that you post now will last forever. *Even if you place data online that you immediately take down, chances are that a record will exist or be able to be found later.* Therefore, when putting any sort of content online, always keep in mind that it is everlasting.

2) Email and online messaging aren't secure. Communication you send through those mediums can be seen by people other than who you sent it to. For example, an email you send to a significant other might get out if you break up later, or a message you send to a friend may be "leaked." Keep in mind that this also includes photos and videos – don't send any that you aren't comfortable with everyone seeing. There are far too many examples of communication going public that was only intended for one person to see – whether due to hacking, accidents, broken relationships, or other reasons.

3) Respect the privacy of others. For example, do not spread other people's personal information without their permission, or if you ever end up building a website

or app, don't utilize user data without their express permission. A major software company was recently sued for tracking the location of users without their okay.

4) When using another's computer (a friend, one loaned from school, a work machine, etc.), follow the rules. Don't use the computer in such a way that will violate agreements.

5) While this is obvious, avoid illegal activities. Just like you wouldn't go into a store and steal boxes of software, don't steal software online without paying for it. Following the law is advised because illegal actions are punished just the same whether committed online or offline.

6) It is recommended that you never say something to a person or company online that you wouldn't say to their face. While this point is simply an opinion, there are far too many examples of individuals saying inappropriate things to others that they would never dare say in person. If you need examples, just read the comments on some social media websites or some negative online reviews – most people would never talk that way in "real life." Before you say something you regret later (because remember, it's permanent) it's always safe to only type statements you're comfortable telling another in person. Keep in mind that you might even run into that person in the future!

To summarize these points: the Golden Rule (the principle of treating others as you want to be treated) applies to computers and technology.

Even though computers and the internet can seem like "another world," they are very much a part of the real world. The actions you take therein will definitely affect your real life.

To further clarify computer ethics, in 1992, the Computer Ethics Institute (a nonprofit organization primarily concerned with computer ethics) created the following Ten Commandments of Computer Ethics:

1. *Thou shalt not use a computer to harm other people.*

2. *Thou shalt not interfere with other people's computer work.*

3. *Thou shalt not snoop around in other people's computer files.*

4. *Thou shalt not use a computer to steal.*

5. *Thou shalt not use a computer to bear false witness.*

6. *Thou shalt not copy or use proprietary software for which you have not paid (without permission).*

7. *Thou shalt not use other people's computer resources without authorization or proper compensation.*

8. *Thou shalt not appropriate other people's intellectual output.*

9. *Thou shalt think about the social consequences of the program you are writing or the system you are designing.*

10. *Thou shalt always use a computer in ways that ensure consideration and respect for other humans.*

SUMMARY:

Never say or do anything on a computer or on the internet that you wouldn't do in the real world.

There's another related idea: Don't believe everything you find on the internet.

CHAPTER 118:
MISINFORMATION ONLINE

"I invented the internet."
-Facebook post from George Washington

An important fact to keep in mind is that data on the internet was put there by people or by computer programs that were created by people. And the truth is, people can make mistakes and people can lie.

An obvious example of this are reviews of companies. These can be dishonestly written by competitors of that company, ex-employees that were terminated for gross misconduct or even people *paid* to smear (damage the reputation of) the company.

The examples are endless. Anything you find on the internet can be fabricated, including but not limited to: studies, articles, blog (short for web log – a website about a particular subject) posts, quotes, pictures and videos. There is even technology that can replace faces and voices in pictures and videos.

Though there are regulations, anyone can edit Wikipedia articles. It is all too easy for misinformation to spread.

The point is: just because something is found online, does not make it fact.

Technically, this is true of other forms of communication, such as newspapers and television, but since the internet is the most popular communication medium in existence, it warrants (deserves) this chapter.

Another factor to keep your eye out for are allegations versus proven guilt. Far too often, you'll find an interview or article on the internet that accuses a person of committing a crime or performing a heinous (wicked) act. There may even be "proof," but presumption of innocence *must* be applied.

The presumption of innocence is the legal principle that people are considered innocent until proven guilty. In many areas of the world, presumption of innocence is a legal right.

It is actually an international human right under the United Nation's Universal Declaration of Human Rights, Article 11.

Imagine this: someone posts a video online that shows you stealing Christmas presents meant for children at a hospital. But it never happened! It isn't you. You would never do that. Regardless, the media picks it up and suddenly you're viral (refers to images, videos, data, etc. that spread rapidly across the internet and typically reaches millions of people).

You have people barraging you with negative comments and messages, you even start receiving threats, and you haven't even had a chance to tell your side of the story. You find out the video was made by an enemy that you had slighted (offended; insulted) somehow. Even if at the end of it all you were able to clear your name, you thereafter will always be known as the "person who stole Christmas gifts from children."

It is best to get a person's side of the story and to let the judicial process play out before jumping to judgements. Also, *reacting* to situations in a negative fashion, as opposed to utilizing calm logic and evaluation, can result in miscalculations and mistakes. Use logic, not emotion.

The best weapon against false information online is judgement. Does the person stating the information have a vested interest against the subject? Are they being paid to attack that person or company? Has the accuser done a full investigation and is the evidence valid? What does the accused have to say about it all? Get both sides of the story and keep an open mind. Get all the data before you decide you're outraged.

Logic, intelligence, common sense and, again, judgement are the best ways to protect against misinformation.

And frankly, it's probably best to avoid inflammatory news and drama online and, instead, spend one's time on productive and positive pursuits.

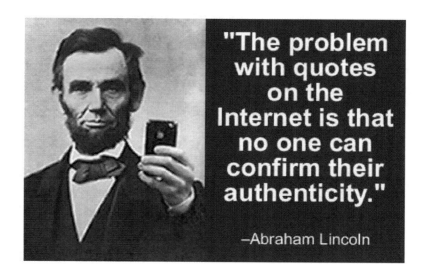

"The problem with quotes on the Internet is that no one can confirm their authenticity."

—Abraham Lincoln

SUMMARY:

Don't believe everything you see on the internet, get both sides of the story and think for yourself before reacting.

We've spoken about computers "solving problems." Let's delve into how that works exactly.

CHAPTER 119:
SOLVING PROBLEMS

*"The art challenges the technology,
and the technology inspires the art."*
John Lasseter (American filmmaker, 1957-)

"Algorithm" is a mathematical term that means a plan for solving a problem. It consists of a sequence of steps to solve a problem or perform an action.

Computers use algorithms. An algorithm is a set of instructions that is used to get something done.

For example, an algorithm for selecting the right kind of shirt might have the following steps:

1. Pick a shirt from your closet.

2. Put the shirt on.

3. Look at yourself in the mirror.

4. If you like it, go to step 6.

5. If you don't like it, return to step 1.

6. End of procedure.

Computers perform functions by processing algorithms. You can create algorithms for computers to follow that other people can then use in the future without having to write out the entire list of steps again.

For example: When your computer prints something, there are many massive algorithms it uses to figure out which type of printer you have, how to convey the document to the printer in a way it understands, etc. This is all taken care of in the background so that all you need to do is click "print." These algorithms were written by others to get the computer and printer to comply with your wishes.

Another example of an algorithm could be a simple recipe, such as:

1. Crack three eggs and pour their contents into a small bowl – attempt to avoid

getting eggshell in the bowl.

2. In the case of eggshells, remove any eggshells from the bowl.

3. Beat the 3 eggs for 90 seconds in the small bowl.

4. Put a small frying pan on the stove and turn the burner on to medium temperature.

5. Pour the eggs in a small frying pan and cook until very little to no wetness remains.

6. Serve the eggs.

While there are similarities, computers and people do not use algorithms in the same way; there are similar features between real life algorithms and computer algorithms, but they are not identical. Computers can't think – they operate in a completely literal manner – so when writing an algorithm for computers, there are certain characteristics that must be present for a computer to use the algorithm. People can deduce things and extrapolate data; people have imagination. Computers can only do what they've been told to do.

To fully understand what an algorithm is for computers, some terms and concepts must be cleared up first. Algorithms are composed of five separate characteristics:

1) Result: The outcome of something.

In computers, a response could be considered the result. You type in: "Tell me the date," the computer replies: "Jan 3, 2022." "Jan 3, 2022" would be the result. Answers to problems are also considered a result.

Algorithms always have a result. If there is no result, it cannot be considered a valid algorithm.

EXAMPLE: Print the number "2," Result: 2.

2) Finite amount of time: This is an exact amount of time for something.

Algorithms should have a finite number of operations included in them and should execute these operations in a set period of time. Algorithms should never be open-ended or infinite. Since each step of an algorithm takes a certain amount of time to be completed, this would mean the algorithm would be completed in a finite amount of time.

An incorrect algorithm would be:

1. Start at an amount of 1
2. Add 1 to that amount
3. Go to step 2

The computer would then count 0, 1, 2, 3, 4, etc. forever.

EXAMPLE: "Count from 1 to 10, then print a message that says, 'I counted from 1-10'," would be a correct algorithm because it contains a finite amount of steps.

3)   Well-ordered: If something is well-ordered, it means it is listed out in the correct sequence and in an organized fashion. Computers can only execute an algorithm if it is well-ordered. If it is put out of sequence or no sequence is specified, etc., the computer cannot process the algorithm.

EXAMPLE: This is an incorrect algorithm because it is not well-ordered:

1. Close the program
2. Print "I am here" inside the program.
3. Save your work in the program
4. Open the program

4)   Effectively computable operations: This refers to a command that can be processed successfully by a computer. The phrase literally means an operation that can be computed in an effective way.

In algorithms, all of the parts of the algorithm must be possible to execute.

EXAMPLE: A non-effectively computable operation could be: "multiply green by red" – the computer can't process this because it isn't computable. Operations contained in algorithms must be effectively computable operations, such as, "2 + 2 =."

5)   Unambiguous: Ambiguous means unclear, confusing, not specified. Un = not. Something that is unambiguous means that it is clear and defined.

In computers, your algorithms must be unambiguous. You have to be extremely specific about each step/part of an algorithm or the algorithms cannot be processed by the computer.

EXAMPLE: If you have an algorithm that is processing a list of ten numbers, then a step of your algorithm is "delete the number," the computer cannot process this because you did not clearly specify which number you wanted deleted.

Now that you know the above terms and concepts, we have the full definition of "algorithm" as defined in the book "Invitation to Computer Science" by American authors Schneider and Gersting:

Algorithm: *A well-ordered collection of unambiguous and effectively computable operations that when executed produces a result and halts in a finite amount of time.*

Sorting means to put items in an exact sequence or order. Computers sort items often. On your computer, you can sort files by when they were created, their name, etc. Algorithms can be used by computers to organize data.

For example: You can sort files on your computer by name or date. This is done by a sorting algorithm within the computer. There are several different ways algorithms can be written to sort data.

In learning how to program, you would write algorithms to perform various functions. Computers have many algorithms programmed into them already that cause them to do a lot of the actions you use computers for. For example, your computer performs many complicated steps to save a document on your computer. These steps are taken care of because programmers entered in algorithms to handle it for you.

SUMMARY:

Programmers create computer programs. One of the fundamental parts of a computer program is an algorithm. An algorithm is a set of exact steps that a computer can understand and perform. It is designed to perform a certain action or actions, and it is also designed not to go on forever. While you may not code, it is helpful to understand that computers have to be told exactly what to do, and algorithms are one of the main things programmers use to do this.

Whether or not you ever learn to write code, it is helpful to know the elements that make up a program, which we will now cover.

CHAPTER 120:
FIVE ELEMENTS TO A PROGRAM

"You might not think that programmers are artists,
but programming is an extremely creative profession."
-John Romero (American video game developer, 1967-)

You are approaching the end of our book, and to assist you in your overall understanding of computers and technology, we are going to more thoroughly explain computer programs. Bear with us. This chapter is the longest in the book, but well worth it.

There are five key elements to any computer program:

1. Entrance
2. Control/Branching (decision points within a program)
3. Variables
4. Subprograms (programs within programs)
5. Exit

Let's go over each of these in detail.

ENTRANCE

A computer is a simple machine when you get down to it. It can only do one thing at a time, and it performs a computer program's instructions in the exact order in which the computer programmer puts them. It can only execute (perform or run) an instruction if it is directed to.

This means that any computer program has to have a clearly marked "first instruction." This is the first task that the computer will perform when the computer program is started. From that point forward, each instruction in the program will direct the computer what instruction to perform next after it performs the current instruction.

There are different ways to specify the entrance point, depending on which computer programming language is being used, but every computer program has a defined entrance point.

CONTROL/BRANCHING

Computers are often used to automate actions that would otherwise be performed by people. One of the most common things a person will be asked to do in performing a job is to assess the condition of a thing and, based on the condition of that thing, choose between two or more possible courses of action. In other words, they will have to make a decision. An example would be the activity of "a teacher grading a stack of papers":

1. Take the next student paper from the top of the stack.
2. Grade the paper.
3. Write the grade on the paper.
4. If the grade is 70% or higher, put the paper in a "Passed" stack.
5. If the grade is below 70%, put the paper in a "Failed" stack.

You can see that there are two possible "paths" here. A path is "a possible course of action arising from a decision." Think of it as what happens when you come to a fork in the road. You have to decide on a course of action – which road do you take? This is also called a branch.

All but the simplest of computer programs will need to do the same thing. That is, they will have to check the condition of a piece of data, and based on the condition of that data, they will have to execute different sets of computer instructions.

In order to do this, the program will make use of special computer instructions called "control" instructions. These are just instructions that tell the computer what to look at in making a decision, and then tell the computer what to do for each possible decision. The most fundamental control statement for a computer is "if." It is used like this:

IF [condition to check] THEN [branch of computer instructions to execute]

Here, the "IF" is the control statement; the "THEN" is the branching instruction that points to the path of the program to execute if the control statement is true.

VARIABLES

We covered variables earlier and they are a key part of programs.

As a recap, a variable is a piece of data that a computer program uses to keep track of values that can change as the program is executed. This might be something like "the grade of the student paper that was just graded" or "the color of paint to use for the next car on the assembly line."

Variables are a vital part of any computer program because they make it so a computer program can be used for more than a single, predetermined set of values. You can imagine that if "the color of paint to use for the next car on the assembly line" was only ever able to be "blue," the computer program using that data wouldn't be very useful. It would make a lot more sense to make it so the computer program could change that value for each car that was going to be painted.

410

When you are writing variables in a computer program, they usually are written in a manner like this:

```
[name of the variable] = [value of the variable]
```

For example, you might have something like this:

```
color = "red"
```

Here, the variable is named "color," and the value of that variable has been set to "red." In other words, the variable named "color" is now "equal" to the word "red."

Let's look at the example of "a teacher grading a stack of papers." Here, we could have a variable called "Paper Grade" that changed each time the teacher graded a paper. You could also have variables for the total number of questions on the paper ("Total Questions") for both the number of questions the student answered correctly ("Correct Questions") and for the grade of the paper.

The written description from above:

```
1. Take the next student paper from the top of the "To Be Graded" stack.
2. Grade the paper.
3. Write the grade on the paper.
4. If the grade is 70% or higher, put the paper in a "Passed" stack.
5. If the grade is below 70%, put the paper in a "Failed" stack.
```

In computer language, the procedure might look something like this:

```
1. Retrieve Next Paper
2. Set Total Questions = [total questions in current Paper]
3. Grade Paper
4. Set Correct Questions = [number of questions answered correctly]
5. Set Paper Grade = [Correct Questions/Total Questions]
6. If (Paper Grade >= 70%) then Paper Status = "passed"
7. (Paper Grade < 70%) then Paper Status = "failed"
```

This is a simple computer program.

As a note, the >= (greater-than sign followed by equal sign) is a symbol used to show that a comparison should be made. Specifically, this "greater-than or equal" symbol is an instruction to check whether the data on the left side of the symbol is more than or equal in amount or quantity to the data on the right side. The answer to this comparison is an answer of "true" or "false."

For example: 5 >= 4

411

This means "check whether 5 is greater than or equal to 4." Since five is in fact greater than four, the answer is "true."

Another example: 3 >= 6

This means "check whether 3 is greater than or equal to 6." The answer is "false."

As a final example: 6 >= 6

This means "check whether 6 is greater than or equal to 6." The answer is "true."

The reverse (opposite) symbol of >= is <=, which checks for whether the data on the left side of the symbol is *lesser/fewer* or *equal* to the data on the right side.

Each time the computer runs the seven-step procedure listed earlier, it could have different values for each of the variables in the program, depending on how many questions the paper being graded has and how many of those questions the student answered correctly.

For example, let's say the paper has 100 questions, and the student answers 82 of them correctly. After the program is run, the result would be the following:

```
Total Questions:        100
Correct Questions:      82
Paper Grade:            82%
Paper Status:           Passed
```

As another example, let's say the paper has 50 questions, and the student answers 30 of them correctly. After the program is run, the result would be the following:

```
Total Questions:        50
Correct Questions:      30
Paper Grade:            60%
Paper Status:           Failed
```

To clarify the need for variables: Let's say that at the time this computer program was being created, all papers at the school had 100 questions, and the teachers told the programmer to make it so that the number of questions was always assumed to be 100. In that case, the programmer wouldn't use a variable called "Total Questions."

Instead, they could make the program look like this:

```
1. Retrieve Next Paper
2. Grade Paper
3. Set Correct Questions = [number of questions answered correctly]
4. Set Paper Grade = [Correct Questions/100]
5. If (Paper Grade >= 70%) then Paper Status = "passed"
6. If (Paper Grade < 70%) then Paper Status = "failed"
```

Notice that on line 4 of the program, the programmer set the number of questions to 100.

Now, let's say that the school introduces the concept of "quizzes," which are smaller papers with only 20 questions. If the paper being handled by the computer program is a quiz, the grade will no longer be accurate – even if a student got all 20 questions correct, they would only get a grade of 20% (20/100).

A good programmer will analyze the need that the program is meant to resolve, then build the program so that it can handle changing aspects of that need over time.

Another valuable control statement is a loop. This is where part of the program is executed over and over until a certain condition is met.

In real-world terms, an example might be "grade papers one at a time until all the papers have been graded" or "make five copies of this document."

In a computer program, a loop would look something like this:

- [start loop]
  o Perform action
  o If [end condition has been met] then [exit the loop]
  o If [end condition has not been met] then [repeat the loop]
- [end loop]

The program we looked at that grades papers could be set up as a loop. The instructions would be laid out like this:

- [start loop]
  o Take the next student paper from the top of the "To Be Graded" stack.
  o Grade the paper.
  o Write the grade on the paper.
  o If the grade is 70% or higher, put the paper in a "Passed" stack.
  o If the grade is below 70%, put the paper in a "Failed" stack.
  o If there are no more papers in the "To Be Graded" stack, exit the loop.
  o If there are more papers in the "To Be Graded" stack, repeat the loop.
- [end loop]

Often loops make use of a special variable called a "counter." The counter keeps track of how many times the loop has been executed. This can be used to make sure the loop is only executed when needed.

Let's add a counter to the grading program we're looking at as well as two new variables: "Total Papers" will be used to hold the value "how many papers need to be graded," while "Counter" will be used to hold the value "how many times the loop has been executed."

```
1.      Set Total Papers = [total papers to be graded]

2.      Set Counter = 0

3.      If (Counter < Total Papers):
        a.      Retrieve next Paper
        b.      Set Total Questions = [total questions in current Paper]
        c.      Grade paper
        d.      Set Correct Questions = [number of questions answered correctly]
        e.      Set Paper Grade = [Correct Questions/Total Questions]
        f.      If (Paper Grade >= 70%) then Paper Status = "passed"
        g.      If (Paper Grade < 70%) then Paper Status = "failed"
        h.      Counter = Counter + 1
        i.      Go to step 3

4.      [Continue on with the rest of the program]
```

Here, the loop is found in step 3.

Let's break down what each step is doing here:

Step 1:   Count how many papers are in the "to be graded" stack and set the value of the "Total Papers" variable to that number.

Step 2:   Create a variable called "Counter" and set it to the value zero. This variable will be used to keep track of how many papers are graded.

Step 3:   Use the control statement "if" to see if we should execute a loop.

Step 3a–3g: Grade the paper; this has been covered above.

Step 3h: Since we have now graded a paper, add one to our Counter variable.

Step 3i: Go to the top of the loop, where we check to see if we need to execute the loop all over again.

Let's see what would happen if we used this program to grade two papers. Let's say that the papers look like this:

```
Paper 1:
Total questions on the paper: 100
Total questions that were answered correctly: 95

Paper 2:
Total questions on the paper: 20
Total questions that were answered correctly: 10
```

If we analyze what happens when the program is executed by the computer, it would look like this:

```
Total Papers = 2
Counter = 0
0 is less than 2, so loop will be executed
Paper 1 Retrieved
Total Questions = 100
Paper 1 Graded
Correct Questions = 95
Paper Grade = 95%
Paper Status = "passed"
Counter = 1
1 is less than 2, so loop will be executed
Paper 2 Retrieved
Total Questions = 20
Paper 1 Graded
Correct Questions = 10
Paper Grade = 50%
Paper Status = "failed"
Counter = 2
2 is not less than 2, so loop will not be executed
[Continue on with the rest of the program]
```

SUBPROGRAMS

As covered earlier, computer programs are generally executed in order, from the start point to the end point. This is called the "path of execution."

The main series of instructions in a program is called the "main program."

It is sometimes valuable to create another program that can be used by the main program as needed. This is called a subprogram. It is no different from any other program – it is made up of the same elements (entrance point, variables, control and branching statements, and exit point). However, a subprogram isn't used all by itself. Instead, the main program can execute the subprogram as needed. Here, the main program stops executing, and the subprogram starts executing. When the subprogram is done executing, the main program continues on where it left off.

This is referred to as "calling" the subprogram – that is, the main program calls the subprogram, the subprogram starts and stops, and the main program continues on where it left off before calling the subprogram.

This is useful in creating programs because the computer programmer doesn't have to enter the instructions of the subprogram over and over. You only type them in once, and then when you need that subprogram to be called by the main program, you only have to type in one instruction – the instruction to call the subprogram. This lets you reuse the instructions you entered in for the subprogram rather than rewriting them.

EXIT

Every program must have an instruction that tells the computer that the program is no longer running. Much like the Entrance, the exact instruction for this varies based on the computer language used, but all computer languages will have this type of instruction.

SUMMARY

The fundamental elements of any computer program are:

1. An entrance point – the first instruction to be performed.

2. Control and branching statements – to control what is done and in what order.

3. Variables – changeable items, held in computer memory, for the program to use as it operates.

4. Subprograms – repeatable sets of computer instructions that act like mini-programs. The main program can use them as needed.

5. An exit point – the last instruction to be completed, so the computer knows the program isn't operating anymore.

Now, as we have mentioned, there are various languages used to write programs. Let's talk about some of these.

CHAPTER 121:
LANGUAGES

"Technology is the campfire around which we tell our stories."
-Laurie Anderson (American artist, 1947-)

As we covered earlier in this book, programming languages are organized systems of words, phrases and symbols that let you create programs. They're also called computer languages.

There are many different types of programming languages, each of which was created to fill a specific purpose. Usually a language is created in order to make the creation of certain types of computer programs easier.

Some programming languages are specifically made to create websites, while others are solely for making apps. In this chapter we are going to cover some of the most well-known programming languages. But first, there are a couple of terms to cover in relation to programming languages. The first is "markup."

"Markup" is the action of adding instructions to a document to control the format, style and appearance of the content of the document. This applies to physical printed documents, as well as to electronic documents that are displayed on a computer screen (like websites).

A markup language is a type of programming language that is used to specify markup instructions for the data in a document. In other words, markup instructions aren't the data in the document; they are data *about* the data in the document.

There are several types of markup languages. Usually they were created for commonly-used types of documents which have exact specifications as far as their structure. Often, these specifications as to document structure are well-known around the world and available to anyone who wants to create documents of that type.

A script is a list of commands the computer performs automatically without your involvement. A scripting language is a computer language used to make scripts.

Often the tasks these scripts accomplish are valuable to automate, so that the task steps don't have to be entered into the computer again every time you want to do those tasks.

The origin of the term is similar to its meaning in "a movie script tells actors what to do"; a scripting language controls the operation of a computer, giving it a sequence of work to do all in one batch.

As an example, if you wanted to make it so that every night at midnight, a list of all the people who signed up for your school classes was printed, you could use a scripting language to make a script that did this work.

As of 2020, the most popular programming and markup languages (in no particular order) are:

1. Python: A popular programming language created in the late 1980s by Dutch computer programmer Guido van Rossum. Born in 1956, van Rossum worked for Google from 2005 to 2012, where he spent half of his time developing the Python language. In the Python community, Van Rossum is known as the "Benevolent Dictator For Life" (BDFL). BDFL refers to the fact that he continues to oversee the Python development process, making decisions where necessary. Due to the fact that Python resembles common English words and speech, it is considered by many to be one of the easiest languages to learn. Python can be used to create apps, websites, games, and many other things. It is a very versatile language with many uses. Python was named after the famous British TV show *Monty Python*, which aired from 1969–1974. Python is used to build many popular web applications, including Dropbox. It was even put to use in developing the search engines of YouTube, Yahoo, and Google.

2. C#: A programming language that was developed in 1999 by the technology company Microsoft. It has many uses and can be used to create several types of programs. It is one of the most commonly used programming languages. C# is well-suited to make large software programs that enable companies to manage business processes. As an example of its use, C# was used in the development of the Windows operating system.

3. HTML: HyperText Markup Language is the markup language that makes up the webpages on the World Wide Web. It was created by Tim Berners-Lee (the inventor of the web) in 1990. Hypertext is a system for linking electronic documents. In an HTML document, hypertext is words, images, videos, etc. that link to other HTML documents. When a user selects the hypertext, the linked document is retrieved and displayed on the computer screen. HTML is used to create webpages. A computer programmer uses HTML to put markup instructions before and after the content of a webpage. These markup instructions give the computer data *about* the elements of the document – text, images, video, etc. When the document is actually displayed on a screen, those markup instructions aren't displayed on the screen – instead, they are used to control *how* the actual content of the document is displayed. As of 2020, HTML5 was the newest version of HTML. Here is an example of an HTML website from the 1990s:

4. CSS: Cascading Style Sheets was created in 1996 and is used to control the appearance of the text, images, video, etc., on those webpages. A style sheet is a tool used to design the format of a webpage. Style sheets are a central place to

store data about how that page will appear and how it will behave. They can be used to store information about how to display colors, pictures, text, etc. A style sheet is a sheet that handles the style of the website. Styling is not concerned with the content of a page; rather, it is concerned with the appearance of that content. Cascading is a term that comes from the idea of water dropping down a series of drops in height. Think of it as a series of small waterfalls. Information can cascade, meaning it can be stored at one central, most important location and then can be applied to other locations that are considered to be lower than, or derived from, that more important central location. For web pages, that means you can set style information in one high-level web page, and that same styling information can "cascade" to other, lower pages without any further work. CSS is usually used in conjunction with HTML to upgrade the appearance and functionality of HTML websites. As of 2020, CSS3 was the newest version of CSS.

5. Java: A programming language created in 1995 by a team of developers. Java has similarities to other languages, but was simplified to eliminate common errors people were making with other languages. Java is able to run on most computers and is a general-purpose language with a number of features that make it useful for use in making programs for business. Many people and companies use Java. As an example of its use: the popular free word-processing program OpenOffice was created in Java.

6. JavaScript: Not to be confused with "Java," JavaScript is a computer language that is able to work on most computers. It was created in 1995 by an American named Brendan Eich and is particularly useful in making websites. JavaScript is used mainly to make websites more dynamic (describing websites that have content that changes based on user action or other factors, rather than being static in appearance and content). There are many other uses for JavaScript; it is used in the creation of many different types of computer programs. JavaScript can make programs and websites more interactive, such as making it so videos start to play as soon as a user moves their mouse over them.

7. SQL: Stands for Structured Query Language (pronounced "SEE-kwull" or "S-Q-L"). A query is a specific instruction to a computer to search through a database and collect all data that matches a certain set of criteria. An example of a query could be: Say you had a database that stored sales data for a bicycle manufacturer. If you were trying to analyze sales trends for the company, you might want to create a query that searched the database and gave you "all sales since the beginning of the year where the retail price was above $400 and the bicycle color was red." You would create a query to perform that search. You would need a special computer language in order to create that query. Structured Query Language is one such language. SQL is a language invented by IBM in the early 1970s that is used to monitor and handle databases. It can edit, change, modify, delete, etc. data in a database. An example of a command in SQL might be this:

```
SELECT Price, ItemName FROM Products WHERE Price < 10.00
```

This would look in a database and find all the products in the table "Products" that cost less than $10.00. It would then make a list that had the price and name of each of those products.

8. PHP: Originally, PHP stood for "Personal Home Page." Currently it is short for "PHP: Hypertext Preprocessor." PHP is a scripting language invented in 1994 by Rasmus Lerdorf that was designed for web development. This means that you could have an HTML page, and you could put a script inside it that performed some function; this script would be executed by the computer that was hosting the webpage files (the server). The script could be written in PHP. The code written in PHP is stored on a web server, with the HTML pages it's meant to work with. PHP can also be used as a general-purpose programming language, not just for adding functionality to webpages. The main use of PHP is to create interactive websites and web applications. As an example of its popularity: PHP is one of the languages utilized by Facebook.

9. Objective-C and Swift: These are the two main programming languages used to develop programs for use on Apple computers and devices. Objective-C was developed in the 1980s. Development of Swift began in 2010. As an example of its use: the LinkedIn app was created in Swift.

10. C++ is a programming language that was created in the beginning of the 1980s. It is based on one of the most popular computer programming languages, C. C++ has many uses and can be used to create many types of programs. Many computers contain something on them that was created using C++. As an example of its use: many computer games have been made using C++.

SUMMARY:

There are many different computer programming languages. Each one has certain features that make it better for certain types of computer programming activities. At the end of the day, though, programs written in any of these languages will need to be converted to machine language, since that is the actual language the CPU can use.

We've gone over a lot of milestones in this book, in and out of sequence. As promised at the beginning of this book, in the next chapter we will lay out all of the major computer developments covered in this book, in sequence.

CHAPTER 122:
<u>HISTORICAL RECAP</u>

"Without memory, there is no culture.
Without memory, there would be no civilization, no society, no future."
-Elie Wiesel (Author, 1928-2016)

    While most of the technological historical milestones covered in this book were listed in chronological order, we did jump around a bit. This was necessary in order to ensure data was presented in the proper sequence. For example, we had to ensure you understood what computer memory was before explaining RAM.

    So, to give you all of these landmarks in sequence and as a recap, here are the dates of major technological advances that relate to computers:

2000 BC: The abacus (tool made up of rods and beads that can be used for calculating) is invented in ancient Egypt.

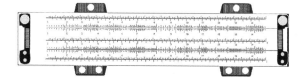

1622: William Oughtred invents the slide rule (a ruler with a strip that slides that can be used to make rapid calculations).

1801: Joseph Marie Jacquard develops the Jacquard loom (a loom that used punch cards to automatically weave fabric designs).

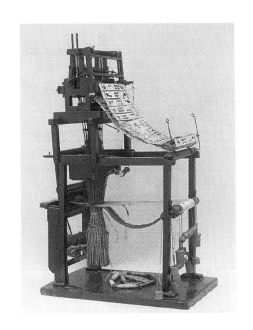

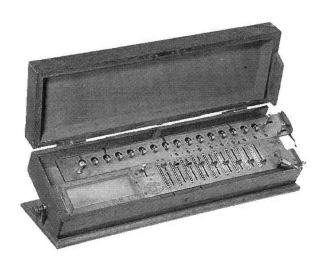

1820: Charles Xavier Thomas invents the arithmometer (first digital mechanical calculator to be used on a wide scale).

1821: Michael Faraday constructs the first operational electric motor.

1835: In the same year, two different inventors separately develop the relay (a switch controlled by electricity).

1836: Charles Babbage writes the first computer programs (which were later found to contain some errors). Around this time he also develops the designs of the first computers, which later proved to operate correctly.

1840s: George Boole develops Boolean logic (a form of logical analysis in which the only possible results of a decision are "true" and "false").

1842: Ada Lovelace writes the first flawless computer program.

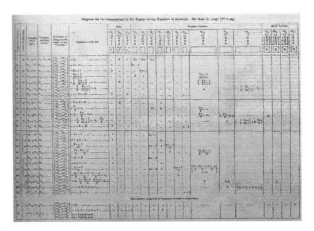

1857: Leon Scott creates the phonoautograph (a machine that records sound waves on pieces of paper).

1857: Thomas Edison invents the phonograph (a machine that can record and play back sound).

1868: Christopher Latham Sholes invents the first workable typewriter.

1890: Herman Hollerith creates the tabulating machine (machine run off electricity and used punch cards to calculate the U.S. census [population count]).

1897: The cathode ray tube (component that displays images on screens by rapidly shooting out a tiny beam left to right) is invented by Karl Ferdinand Braun.

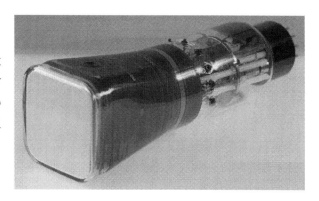

1898: Valdemar Poulsen invents the telegraphone (the first magnetic recorder).

1904: John Ambrose Fleming invents the vacuum tube (device containing no air that can control the flow of electricity).

1911: IBM (International Business Machines) is founded by Charles Ranlett Flint and Thomas J. Watson Sr.

1932: Gustav Tauschek invents drum memory (magnetic data storage device).

1936: Alan Turing designs the Turing machine (a machine that could execute tasks written as programs).

1938: Konrad Zuse invents the Z1 computer (the first programmable computer that utilized Boolean logic and binary).

1940 on: The beginning of the first generation of computers (computers that utilize vacuum tubes).

1942: Clifford E. Berry and John Vincent Atanasoff construct the Atanasoff-Berry Computer (ABC) – the first automatic electronic digital computer.

1943: Grace Hopper helps create the first compiler (a special computer program that is used to convert computer programs written in programming languages to a form that the computer can actually use).

1945: John Mauchly and J. Presper Eckert develop the ENIAC (Electronic Numerical Integrator and Computer), which some consider to be the first digital computer because it is fully operational.

1947: Bell Labs invents the transistor (a device with no moving parts that can alter the flow of electricity in a machine).

1950s: The first monitor is used with a US military computer.

1951: J. Presper Eckert and John Mauchly, along with a team, develop the UNIVAC I (Universal Automatic Computer 1) – the first computer to utilize magnetic tape and buffer memory (area where data is stored for later use). It is also the first computer available for purchase by the public.

1953: The first computer printer is developed.

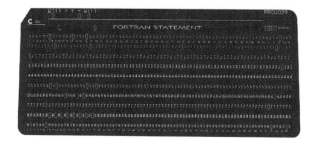

1954: FORTRAN (FORmula TRANslation – a programming language able to perform complex calculations and solve math, physics and engineering problems) is developed by IBM.

1955: An Wang invents magnetic core memory (wires run around a magnetic ring that store data).

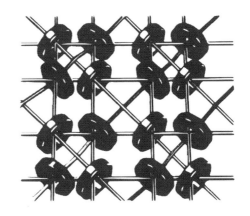

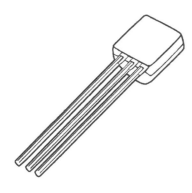

1956 on: The second generation of computers arrive (those using transistors).

1956: The first ever HDD (hard disk drive) is created by IBM.

1958: Jack St. Clair Kilby creates the first chip (a component containing silicon that can control an electrical current).

1959: COBOL (COmmon Business Oriented Language – a programming language developed to bring about one programming language that could work on several different types of computers) is developed by Grace Hopper and a team.

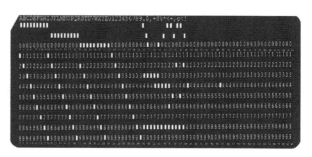

Decimal	Binary	ASCII	Decimal	Binary	ASCII	Decimal	Binary	ASCII
33	00100001	!	65	01000001	A	97	01100001	a
34	00100010	'	66	01000010	B	98	01100010	b
35	00100011	#	67	01000011	C	99	00100011	c
36	00100100	$	68	01000100	D	100	01100100	d
37	00100101	%	69	01000101	E	101	01100101	e
38	00100110	&	70	01000110	F	102	01100110	f
39	00100111	*	71	01000111	G	103	01100111	g
40	00101000	(	72	01001000	H	104	01101000	h
41	00101001	)	73	01001001	I	105	01101001	i
42	00101010	*	74	01001010	J	106	01101010	j
43	00101011	+	75	01001011	K	107	01101011	k
44	00101100	,	76	01001100	L	108	01101100	l
45	00101101	-	77	01001101	M	109	01101101	m
46	00101110	.	78	01001110	N	110	01101110	n
47	00101111	/	79	01001111	O	111	01101111	o
48	00110000	0	80	01010000	P	112	01110000	p
49	00110001	1	81	01010001	Q	113	01110001	q
50	00110010	2	82	01010010	R	114	01110010	r
51	00110011	3	83	01010011	S	115	01110011	s
52	00110100	4	84	01010100	T	116	01110100	t
53	00110101	5	85	01010101	U	117	01110101	u
54	00110110	6	86	01010110	V	118	01110110	v
55	00110111	7	87	01010111	W	119	01110111	w
56	00111000	8	88	01011000	X	120	01111000	x
57	00111001	8	89	01011001	Y	121	01111001	y
58	00111010	,	90	01011010	Z	122	01111010	z
59	00111011	;	91	01011011	[	123	01111011	{
60	00111100	<	92	01011100	\	124	01111100		
61	00111101	=	93	01011101	]	125	01111101	}
61	00111110	>	94	01011110	^	126	01111110	~

1960s: the ASCII (American Standard Code for Information Interchange) is created in order to standardize a system to represent English characters using computers.

1960s: Computers begin utilizing the CLI (Command-Line Interface).

1964 on: Third generation computers come into use (computers that utilize silicon chips).

1964: Doug Engelbart invents the first computer mouse.

1966: James T. Russell conceives of CDs.

1967: The floppy disk is invented by IBM.

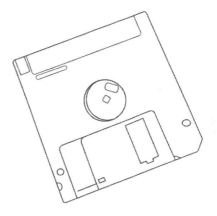

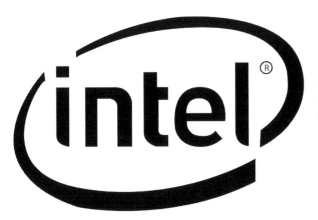

1968: Intel is founded by Gordon Moore and Robert Noyce.

1968: RAM is invented by Robert Dennard.

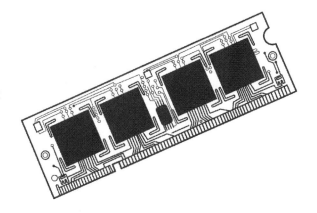

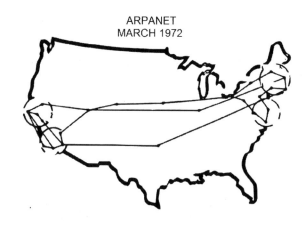

1969: The first instance of a computer-to-computer link is established on the Advanced Research Projects Agency Network (ARPANET).

1970s: The first personal computers arrive on the market.

1971: Intel releases the first CPU (central processing unit) – the Intel 4004.

1972 on: The fourth generation of computers arrives (mice, micro-processors [small component that contains the CPU, memory, etc.] and more).

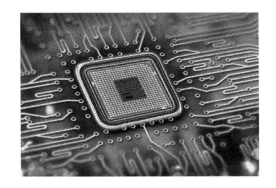

1973: The first GUI (graphical user interface – representation of the various objects in a computer in graphical form) is released by Xerox with the Alto personal computer.

1975: Microsoft is founded by Paul Allen and Bill Gates.

1976: Apple is founded by Steve Jobs and Steve Wozniak.

1980s: The internet is created by a team of researchers.

1981: The first laptop is invented by Adam Osborne.

1981: Two separate inventors create the first routers.

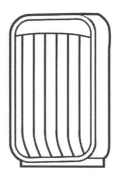 

1989: Tim Berners-Lee invents the World Wide Web.

1996: USB technology is invented by Ajay Bhatt.

1997: Wifi is invented by John O'Sullivan and a team of workers.

1998: Google is founded by Larry Page and Sergey Brin.

2004: Facebook is founded by Mark Zuckerberg.

2010 on: The fifth generation of computers arrive (artificial intelligence).

2014: The Tech Academy is founded with the purpose of making technology understandable to everyone.

And we would be remiss if we didn't include this:

2020: This book was written. A major accomplishment because it provides the only central location of all basic tech and computer data written in a way the average person can understand.

As a note: There are many other major advancements in computers that could be listed here. An entire book could be written about each major technology company. The purpose of this chapter was to provide a recap of what we covered *in this book*.

SUMMARY:

People all over the world have made today's computers possible. The technology you see all around you is not due to one person, but from the contributions of millions. The modern world is the result of teamwork and collaboration.

So, now that you have all of this data, where do you go from here?

CHAPTER 123:
THE FUTURE

"Man is still the most extraordinary computer of all."
-John F. Kennedy (American president, 1917-1963)

Congratulations on making it to the final chapter of this book! Finishing this book is quite a feat and we commend you for your persistence!

We have covered a tremendous amount of information that required us years of research, experience and compilation to put together. You are now more knowledgeable in computers and technology than 99% of Earth's population.

Computers are the most impressive and complex machines developed by humankind, and you understand them.

So, where to go from here?

We would like to leave you with some thoughts and suggestions:

1. Technology will only continue to advance from here. No matter how impressive computers become, they will operate off of the basic principles covered in this book, so data you studied here will still apply. In most cases, technological advances are the multiplication of existing technologies and making them smaller so as to increase the speed of operation.

2. You are now caught up to the present day. We recommend that you keep yourself abreast of technological releases and improvements. An important aspect of this is: clear up new terms that you come across (i.e. Google their definitions). Keep in mind that most existing educational resources are loaded with complex terms, so do your best to locate simple explanations. Continuing to educate yourself will ensure you don't ever fall behind.

3. Thank you. The Tech Academy's purpose is to bridge the gap between society and technology. By reading this book, you have helped us achieve our purpose. We are grateful for your time and attention.

4. Encourage as many other people as you can to read this book. There is no other resource that contains all of this data in one location and explained this simply. With the knowledge you have now, you have increased your ability to control

machines. You are more intelligent and competent. You have removed the mysteries associated with technology and have arrived at a point of cause over computers.

Doesn't everyone deserve the knowledge contained in this book?

THE END

EPILOGUE

The Tech Academy is a computer programming and web development school founded in 2014 and headquartered in Portland, Oregon.

We deliver coding boot camps that bring about graduates who are well-rounded, entry-level software developers.

Boot camp: (noun) An intensive training program, as for improving one's physical fitness or skills in a particular subject area. "Boot" comes from Middle English *bot*, meaning "help." "Camp" comes from Latin *campus*, meaning "level ground" (specifically from the Roman usage of a level ground utilized for games, athletic practice, and military drills).

A coding boot camp, also commonly called a "developer boot camp" or "programming boot camp," is an intensive training program in software development. These boot camps are also referred to as "code schools."

Developer boot camps are a relatively new element of the technology education landscape; the first boot camps began in the San Francisco Bay Area in 2012. The educational roots of coding boot camps go back quite far, from traditional apprentice programs to the career schools that sprung up in the early 20th century.

The rise of developer boot camps was driven by the shortage of technical talent faced by the technology industry.

In response to this shortage, the technology industry has had to look for non-traditional ways to create the technical talent it needs. Rather than a replacement for the traditional college path to a career in software development, coding boot camps are just one more way to arrive at a very desirable place: employed in a well-paying, challenging field with good job security.

Whereas colleges are good options for those who can afford it and who are able to study for two to four years, boot camps can be a resource for students that want to learn coding who have less available funds and time. Both are excellent options.

There are many code schools in the world. Usually, they have these characteristics:

a) The programs usually take about two to six months full-time.

b) The technical skills taught are aimed at getting immediate employment as a junior-level software developer.

c) The training environment is "immersive," meaning that students immerse themselves in the subject, often putting other life concerns on hold as they work through the training.

What sets The Tech Academy apart is our educational approach:

- No background required – While some tech schools require complex entry testing for students, we require no technical knowledge. As long as you can read and write, you can learn to code at The Tech Academy.

- Flexible scheduling – Students choose their study schedule. There are no firm class times, which allows for full-time and part-time training.

- Bottom-up – We start with the basics and fundamentals and build from there. The difficulty level increases as students progress.

- Open enrollment – Students can start anytime. There are no set start dates.

- Job placement – We provide job placement training and assistance to our graduates. Not only is the Job Placement Course on every boot camp, we have support staff that assist graduates in their employment search.

- Self-paced – students move through the content at their own speed. This allows them to take time on new subjects and to move through the topics they know well already with speed.

- Proficiency-based – we care about the outcome and abilities of our graduates. We set them up to perform the expected functions of their position.

The Tech Academy also delivers corporate training (custom group classes), publishes books and offers a wide range of other services.

The Tech Academy is a code school with a logo that contains a bridge. The bridge represents a passage of the gap between technically trained individuals and general society – it is a path that leads to an understanding of technology and competence in coding.

The Mission Statement of The Tech Academy is:

TO GRADUATE ENTRY-LEVEL TECHNOLOGY PROFESSIONALS THAT EXCEL IN THE BASICS OF THEIR FIELD AND THEREAFTER HAVE SUCCESSFUL CAREERS IN THE TECH INDUSTRY, AND WHOSE ACTIONS RAISE INDUSTRY STANDARDS AND SURPASS CLIENT EXPECTATIONS.

Now that you have completed this book, we recommend enrolling in one of our coding boot camps or receiving training from our school in some fashion.

OUR THANKS

"Friendship is the hardest thing in the world to explain.
It's not something you learn in school.
But if you haven't learned the meaning of friendship, you really haven't learned anything."
-Muhammad Ali (American boxer, 1942-2016)

The amount of people to thank for making this book possible are too many to list.

To you, the reader – for taking the time to educate yourself in this pervasive and ever-growing subject.

To our wives – thank you for putting up with us. Your jobs have always been harder than ours and we love you endlessly.

To our children – you provide us with the motivation that gets us out of bed in the morning and keeps us burning the midnight oil.

To our siblings – for your humor and friendship, which has been a light during dark times.

To our friends – without you, The Tech Academy would not exist.

To our parents – you're responsible for our success.

To the rest of our family – you have our eternal gratitude and love.

To all current and past Tech Academy employees – we recognize your contributions and thank you for making us what we are today.

To every Tech Academy student and graduate – your feedback and faith in us has enabled us to survive and grow.

To every person that's contributed to technology, including all mentioned in this book.

To Steve Jobs – for his leadership, insistence and imagination.

To Steve Wozniak – for creating things that make modern computers possible.

To Bill Gates – for all he's done not only in terms of technological contributions, but actions to make the world a better place.

To Mark Zuckerberg – for getting the world in communication.

To Elon Musk – for his drive, inspiration and commitment to advancing our world.

To Jeff Bezos – for his impressive production, creative spirit and inventive mind.

To Larry Page and Sergey Brin – for making it possible for the average person to access the largest body of information ever assembled.

To Tim Berners-Lee – for connecting the world.

And to L. Ron Hubbard, whose study technology made this book possible. There is no single person that contributed to the creation of this book more than he because without his teachings, we wouldn't have had the knowledge, ability or persistence to uncover and simplify all of this data.

If you are interested in study technology, the The Learning Book, published by Heron Books, gives the basics of this technology. This book can be obtained at this web page: heronbooks.com/store/The-Learning-Book-p180263737

For a comprehensive and detailed treatise, The Study Handbook is recommended, also published by Heron Books. The book is available at this web page: heronbooks.com/store/The-Study-Handbook-p143416256

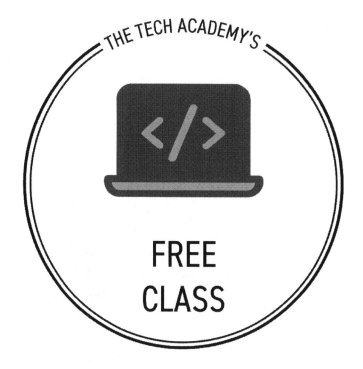

Want to learn the basics of computer programming in a few hours?

Enroll in an online, *free* Intro to Coding Class from The Tech Academy now!

These classes were designed for absolute beginners.

All important terms and concepts are defined at the beginning of each class and no previous knowledge or experience is required.

We have free classes for kids and adults!

Try out coding and enroll in a free online coding class today!

learncodinganywhere.com/freeclass

OTHER READING

Be sure to check out other Tech Academy books, which are all available for purchase on Amazon:

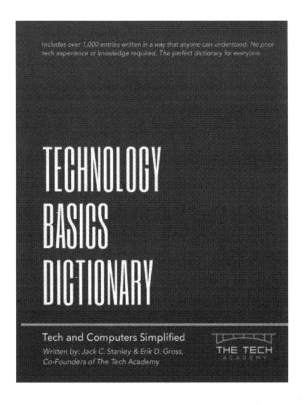

LEARN CODING BASICS
IN HOURS
WITH SMALL BASIC

Programming for Absolute Beginners

Written by: Jack C. Stanley & Erik D. Gross,
Co-Founders of The Tech Academy

LEARN CODING BASICS
IN HOURS
WITH PYTHON

Programming for Absolute Beginners

Written by: Jack C. Stanley & Erik D. Gross,
Co-Founders of The Tech Academy

PROJECT MANAGEMENT

HANDBOOK

Simplified Agile, Scrum and DevOps for Beginners

Written by
Jack C. Stanley & Erik D. Gross
Co-Founders of The Tech Academy

Made in the USA
Middletown, DE
25 March 2024

52029655R00254